SC
PL

Presented to
the Santa Cruz
Public Libraries by

JAMES B. RICHARDSON

MICHAEL BLOOMFIELD

MICHAEL BLOOMFIELD

THE RISE AND FALL OF AN AMERICAN GUITAR HERO

Ed Ward

with additional research and material by Edd Hurt

CHICAGO
REVIEW
PRESS

An A Cappella Book

Produced by Multiprises, LLC

Published by Chicago Review Press Incorporated
814 North Franklin Street
Chicago, Illinois 60610
ISBN 978-1-61373-328-8

Library of Congress Cataloging-in-Publication Data
Names: Ward, Ed, 1948–
Title: Michael Bloomfield : the rise and fall of an American guitar hero / Ed
   Ward.
Description: Chicago, Illinois : Chicago Review Press, [2016] | Includes
   bibliographical references and index.
Identifiers: LCCN 2016019216 (print) | LCCN 2016020777 (ebook) | ISBN
   9781613733288 (hardback) | ISBN 9781613733295 (PDF edition) | ISBN
   9781613733318 (EPUB edition) | ISBN 9781613733301 (Kindle edition)
   Subjects: LCSH: Bloomfield, Michael. | Guitarists—United States—Biography.
   | Blues musicians—United States—Biography.
Classification: LCC ML419.B58 W4 2016 (print) | LCC ML419.B58 (ebook) |
   DDC 787.871643092 [B] —dc23
LC record available at https://lccn.loc.gov/2016019216

Typesetting: Nord Compo

Printed in the United States of America
5 4 3 2 1

To the next kid who thinks he can amaze people when he picks up a guitar and starts to play—and to the memory of Lester Bangs, a friend.

A NOTE TO THE READER

Ed Ward's *Michael Bloomfield: The Rise and Fall of an American Guitar Hero* was first published, briefly, in 1983. This is a completely revised and greatly expanded edition with much new research—for all intents and purposes a new book.

CONTENTS

FOREWORD

by Billy F. Gibbons

Talk about impact . . . ! Talk about influence and inspiration! We're talking Bloomfield: Mike Bloomfield, guitarist and stylist extraordinaire. From distant observer to distinguished performer, Mike B. and his guitar ran the gamut, traversing all there was and would be within his vision, where guitar inventiveness became trademarked in his all-too-brief career.

Yes, we're talking *the* one-and-the-same Bloomfield whose blues bloomed and boomed under the dexterous developments that dealt his hand and landed him in the game where he knew he wanted to be.

Sounding familiar . . . ? Perhaps so with the Bloomfield we came to know seemingly appearing from out of nowhere fast. Yet the overnight sensation was a long time in the making. Starting with that pawnshop six-string, the unraveling of the alluring mystique of sounds abounding all around in his very hometown began to make sense once the pieces to that powerful puzzle, them blues, began to gather. And it was this allure that became the stepping-stone to take his curiosity to the street. Although a stranger now frequenting those strange outposts of that strident sound, he was not alone. Several like-minded individuals were similarly drawn to the task of attempting to emulate the basics of that thing they were after.

So, banding together as newfound souls with a friendly sort of mutual bond was the obvious way in to getting way out, way outside any notion whatsoever of creating something predictable. Rather, some very unpredictable expressions began to emerge between Bloomfield and the aggregation with the likes of Paul Butterfield, Charlie Musselwhite, Nick

Gravenites, Norman Dayron, guitarist Elvin Bishop, Barry Goldberg, and the fashionable Mark Naftalin. These were the guys surging toward forming this nucleus actually expressing something not only believable—they began laying down sound that was solid . . . sounds that were standing up to a stiff legion of loyalists not necessarily impressed with anything less than what the head honchos of the day were laying down with the late-night crowd. Muddy Waters had it, Jimmy Reed had it, Howlin' Wolf more than had it . . . hell, it seemed like everybody on the South Side of Chi-Town either had it or was bound and determined to get it, and here Bloomfield was smack-dab in the midst of gettin' it. And gettin' down pretty hard.

Keep in mind this was mid-'60s stuff. A time when people were waiting to get what they were wanting, waiting to feel what they all wanted to feel, and all of a sudden, all of it managed to find its way to wax. Bloomfield, wringing out his tasty additions for Butterfield and band, hit the mark. Mike's presence heard on those superb entries into the field are what we came to know and admire and ultimately have come to miss. This is where we might best leave it for now. There's certainly a somewhat vague awareness of what came after right up to the end, yet Mike's legacy of tantalizing and tasteful tags on "them blues" luckily lingers on. Yes, we're talkin' Bloomfield.

INTRODUCTION

Like a million other kids in the early 1960s, I bought a guitar, got as good as I could on it, and then bought a better one. I worked hard learning the licks that would impress, the songs that were important. I strove to take all ten fingers and make them crank the fast-picked ragtime melodies and make it all seem easy. I learned to bend strings in emulation of the great blues singers. And when my heroes began tending toward electric instruments, I defended them.

Bob Dylan, for instance. He'd "gone electric" at the Newport Folk Festival, but he'd been writing songs that begged for electric instruments for some time. And Elektra, the folk music record label that was at the cutting edge of things, had just signed some hotshots from Chicago called the Paul Butterfield Blues Band, an integrated band that played blues, members of which had backed Dylan at Newport. If Elektra considered this folk music (and it was true that the pages of *Sing Out!*, the folkies' bible, had been filled with the argument that Chuck Berry was a bluesman, and if that was true, so were the Rolling Stones), then so did I.

The Paul Butterfield Blues Band's debut album came out in the fall of 1965, and I dutifully bought it. I can safely say that this thirty-eight-minute record, titled simply *The Paul Butterfield Blues Band*, changed my life, disordered my perceptions, and totally rearranged the way I thought about popular and folk music.

There was this guitar player on the record, a guy who was doing stuff that was absolutely impossible, who was playing rapid-fire notes and sweet swoops, who howled and screamed, begged and teased, and held the entire record together. This guy had to be the Paul Butterfield the band was named for, because he was all I heard when I played the record. But no, Butterfield was the guy who honked his harmonica like a saxophone.

The guitarist, the album cover said, was someone named Mike Bloomfield.

Well, I tried. I sat there with my very good acoustic guitar, and I listened to those lightning attacks on the fingerboard, and I felt a tiny glow of triumph when I finally figured out, and could play, the Elmore James lick on "Shake Your Money Maker." Several weeks later, when that was still the only lick I'd learned, I began to get disillusioned. Slowly, it dawned on me that the typewriter was more my instrument than the guitar. It was all the fault of that Bloomfield character, but I guess it was all for the best.

Of course, he had just the opposite effect on a lot of people who had more talent on the guitar than I. In the course of researching this book, I have heard from innumerable guitar players, famous and not famous, good and not so good, and they all say, "I started playing because of him," or "I completely changed my style after I heard him play." (The great British guitarist Eric Clapton wasn't at all known over on US shores in those days.)

Before Bloomfield, there was no glory in being a guitarist; after he appeared, mastering electric lead guitar became the test of manhood. Before him, many music fans thought blues was acoustic music played in a fingerpicked style in the manner of Mississippi John Hurt, or the eccentrically accented fingerpicking of Mississippi-born guitarist and singer Skip James, or Fred McDowell, Robert Pete Williams, or Sleepy John Estes, all of whom played blues on acoustic guitars and had been "rediscovered" by the folk movement. After Bloomfield, the circle opened wide to encompass Muddy Waters, B. B. King, Albert King, Otis Rush, and yes, Chuck Berry.

If Michael Bloomfield hadn't come along to fuse the virtuosity of Chicago electric blues with the energy of rock 'n' roll, someone else would have, but we were very lucky indeed to have had such a fine teacher as a pioneer.

This book reveals Michael's story as he told it and as his friends and colleagues remember him. It is the story of what he achieved, what he created, and what it cost him. It is the story of Michael Bloomfield, an American guitar hero.

1

THE DEVIL
AND ROBERT JOHNSON

Two days before he died in February 1981, Michael Bloomfield was interviewed by a pair of San Francisco radio producers, Tom Yates and Kate Hayes, who were gathering information from rock 'n' roll guitarists for a syndicated radio series on the evolution of rock guitar.

"Robert Johnson is a brand-new thing," Yates began his question, which swiftly became a statement that spelled out some of his notions about the origins of rock guitar. "When we first came up with the concept of the show, I ran into my library and I grabbed two Robert Johnson albums and a Charlie Christian record, and tried to find Django Reinhardt, and said, 'This is probably where we'll start.' And what's happened, because we've been talking to people who are all rock- and blues-based, [is] that Robert Johnson comes through like a bell. Amazing people. You expect it from Clapton; I didn't expect it from Ted Nugent."

"Oh, I would," Bloomfield replied, to Yates's obvious surprise. "I would expect it from Teddy, or from [Eddie] Van Halen. Sure, of course. They know. Why wouldn't they know? Ted, he's a Detroiter; he must have come up through Clapton. If he had gotten the first John Mayall record with Clapton playing on it, the *Blues Breakers* record, he does Robert Johnson songs on it. It's in the liner notes. Why wouldn't he know that? I'm not saying that he was a folkie, or even a bluesman. But I'm not surprised."

Hayes gamely continued to question Bloomfield about Johnson: "What was it about Robert Johnson that makes him so vital?" she asked.

"I'll tell you a bunch of things about him, all right?" Bloomfield said. "First, musically: Robert invented some of the guitar licks that are still used today. It was like [bluegrass musician] Earl Scruggs invented a style of banjo out of nowhere. I mean, guys who played before him just didn't sound like that. He was a banjo player who—out of I don't know what, out of his mind, with no antecedents—discovered this style of banjo.

"Robert Johnson had many influences, but he discovered certain guitar licks that were uniquely his, and that are still used today. That sort of boogie-bass guitar [Bloomfield sang the lick from Elmore James's "Dust My Broom"]—that's *his*! No one did it before him. He just thought it up one day. It's not a big thing. But it became a style that's all Elmore James ever played, that's all Homesick James ever played, that's all the original Fleetwood Mac guys ever played, except when Peter [Green] was playing like B. B. King. It was a definite thing.

"Now, Robert was the stuff that myths are made of. This was a guy who hung around all the blues singers who were making popular records at that time, as I did when I was his age, and couldn't play worth a damn. He'd always try to sit in, and they'd say, 'Sure, let him play.' And he couldn't play. He would almost be retarded in his ability to play music, and he was so shy, so painfully shy all his life, that he could barely get the request out to ask could he sit in and play.

"And these musicians were travelers, and they would leave the area where Robert lived, and they would go away. They came back a year later, and Robert again would ask to play, and he still couldn't play. Two years passed—and I've heard this from four bluesmen who knew Robert Johnson intimately in his younger days—and they came back, and Robert could not only play, he could outplay them. He could outplay the guys that he could not even vaguely imitate two years prior.

"So, as it's been told to me—and this sounds so strange, but a lot of southern people believe this—it's been told to me that they say that Robert sold his soul to the devil. He went to a fork in the roads, a crossroads, and he put his guitar down there and he made a deal with the devil, that the devil would give him the ability to be good with women, good with gambling, good with the guitar. He could take him at a young age and let him burn in hell. And the devil said that was a good deal.

"And if you've ever listened to songs like 'Stagger Lee,' or any songs that are about that, it's usually a moral tale about the devil making a deal with someone for powers for his soul. And Robert made that deal, and all these guys who told me this—Johnny Shines, Sunnyland Slim, Muddy Waters, Elmore James—were four men who distinctly told me the same tale of Robert selling his soul to the devil, though I think Muddy had heard it from someone, because he was even younger than Robert Johnson. He learned from Robert when he was a young man. But Johnny was an absolute contemporary of Robert's, the same age, and they hung around together.

"So Robert got amazingly good, and he had a chance to make some records for Columbia Records, and he did, and they were just superb records. Some people say they're the greatest country blues records of all. I don't know if I really agree with that, but you can hear a young man with an amazing amount of young man's energy, the kind of thing that you would find in early Pete Townshend or early Elvis, or in any young man who's really burning up his energy. And you can hear this in Robert's records; it just leaps off [at] you from the turntable.

"There's various discrepancies about what age he was, but everybody agrees that he didn't live past thirty. He recorded about sixty-something sides, and he was killed. Apparently, if you pay credence [to] selling your soul to the devil, the devil collected his dues real early. So that's probably why many musicians know who Robert is. Maybe they just know him from the musical standpoint. Maybe they know that Clapton listened to him, maybe they know Muddy Waters listened to him. But I know him as this entire mythic creature. The thing that interests me most of all is that I've seen this one photograph of Robert Johnson. He was a really handsome man. Very gentle-looking fellow.

"You know, there's a story about how shy he was. He was in a recording studio, and he couldn't face the engineer. There was a band of Mexican musicians, and they came in, and the engineer said they had never heard blues, and they had very seldom seen black performers play. He said, 'Would you let them watch you?' And Robert finished the entire session facing the wall. He couldn't look at them, or allow the musicians or the engineer to watch him play. It was done in a hotel room, and he put the mike in the corner and he sat facing away from them. They could hear him, but he was too shy to let them see him play. And this very shyness that he had, which is the opposite of the way he was when he was in front of a paying crowd in a honky-tonk or a nightclub, or at a fish fry, and even less so around women. So that's what I know about Robert Johnson."

About seventeen minutes into the interview—Yates and Hayes said the session ran overtime, and that they had made plans to return to talk again a few days later—Yates asked Bloomfield what Robert Johnson songs he would recommend to "expose young kids to."

"I would say 'Dust My Broom' or 'Sweet Home Chicago'—the whole Jimmy Reed beat on guitar came from those songs," Bloomfield said. "I would say that for its musicological import. I would say 'Come On in My Kitchen' for its absolute feeling and sensitivity. 'Hellhound on My Trail'—it's not only sensitive, but it's actually tortured. You get this idea, maybe this guy really did think he sold his soul to the devil. You can hear this in so many of his lyrics, this thought that someone's chasing after him: blue ghosts, devils, hellhounds. And then a song called 'Me and the Devil [Blues].' It's fierce. It sounds like someone just terror stricken trying to run away from whatever's getting him."

In the 1930s Robert Johnson lived in a Mississippi so alien to our times that it might as well have been Africa. In twenty-first-century America we do not experience hellhounds as a reality. Fear and anxiety are as much a part of our times as they were of Robert Johnson's, but we don't personify them; we treat them. An intelligent, well-read man from the Jewish upper middle class could not possibly share even a modicum of the experience that haunted Robert Johnson, or so we tell ourselves, and to sell one's soul to the devil, one has to believe that the transaction is possible.

Michael Bloomfield was not Robert Johnson. That is not the point of the story. But his identification with Johnson's fear was real. So was his concern for his soul. Let's just put it this way: Satan is irrelevant to this story; Robert Johnson is not.

2

FATHERS AND SONS

Michael Bloomfield's father, Harold Bloomfield, was already a prosperous man by the time he married Dorothy Klein in 1940. Born in Chicago in 1914, Harold Bloomfield had gone into business with his father, Samuel, and his brother, Daniel, in the 1930s. The previous decade, Samuel had made and lost several fortunes in California, where he tried his hand at several business ventures with his brother-in-law, Simon Wexler. Returning to Chicago during the early years of the Great Depression, Samuel had an epiphany that would lead to the formation of Bloomfield Industries.

"He saw a pie case in a diner," Michael's brother Allen says. "They had zinc-cast uprights, and they attached to the bottom of the counter. The case's rear-hinged door would open so that you could slide in the pies." Seeing an opportunity in the business of merchandising pies and desserts, Samuel bought the patent and rented space in a factory. By 1933 he was manufacturing pie cases in a two-thousand-square-foot facility in Chicago. With capitalization provided by Samuel, Harold Bloomfield was in charge of putting the cases together, and his brother sold them. Later in the decade, they began manufacturing kitchen utensils, salt and pepper shakers, and the classic domed sugar pourer with the little flag over the hole. By the time World War II started, the Bloomfields had moved their operations to a fifty-five-thousand-square-foot building.

During World War II Bloomfield Industries manufactured items for the war effort, including stainless steel partitioned trays and disposable can openers that soldiers used with their K rations. Suitably capitalized by government contracts, Bloomfield Industries possessed surplus equipment after the war ended, and they expanded their operations rapidly. By this point, Bloomfield Industries manufactured over a thousand items, including transportation equipment, serving ware, and cookware. The items were, and continue to be, marked on the bottom with a "B" in a circle and the word "Chicago." After Samuel Bloomfield died in 1954, Harold and Daniel took over the business, and it was Harold's aggressive management that pushed it to the forefront.

Michael Bloomfield's mother, Dorothy Klein, was born in Chicago in 1918, into an artistic family. "My mother's parents were born in Czechoslovakia, and her whole family was interested in music," she said years later, after her son became famous. "Most were violinists. They played Hungarian music, and they were all very talented. My mother was an actress, and my aunt was a very fine pianist." After graduating from Chicago's well-regarded Goodman School of Drama, Dorothy modeled and acted. She was an exceptionally beautiful woman—Allen Bloomfield describes his mother as "a Hedy Lamarr duplicate"—and she took advantage of her looks and her theatrical training by becoming a model for Wrigley chewing gum and Jantzen swimwear. She also acted on radio and with touring theatrical companies.

"She was living a good, safe life, and she was highly sought after because she was so beautiful," Allen Bloomfield says about his mother before she married Harold Bloomfield. "She was an artist, and she thought in an artistic way, and a certain practicality was not always readily accessible to her." On the other hand, Harold Bloomfield was an ambitious businessman whose eye seems always to have been on the main chance. "My father had been very highly disciplined, and had a really incredible drive and work ethic, and he was very virile," Allen says. "Whether he employed one person or he employed seven hundred, you had a measure as to what your value was, as far as capabilities. And he was grounded completely in the reality of measurability."

Allen Bloomfield says that his parents had different ideas about everything from running a household to raising children, and if Michael Bloomfield inherited his father's work ethic—no one ever toiled more diligently at becoming a great musician than he did—it could be that a certain practicality was no more accessible to him than Allen Bloomfield says it was to their mother. The tension between his need for artistic expression and its application in the rough-and-tumble world of the music business would mark Michael Bloomfield's career from start to finish.

———————

Michael Bernard Bloomfield was born on July 28, 1943, at Chicago's Michael Reese Hospital, which had been founded in 1881. It was a leading research and teaching hospital, and one of its facilities, the Simon Wexler Psychiatric Research and Clinic Pavilion, had been named for Bloomfield's uncle, a noted philanthropist and businessman. Michael's brother, Allen David, was born seventeen months later, on December 24, 1944, also at Michael Reese Hospital.

The family lived in various locations in Chicago before settling at 424 West Melrose Street on the North Side, close to Lake Shore Drive, the main thoroughfare of Chicago's affluent Gold Coast area. The kids attended Nettelhorst Elementary School on North Broadway Street. It was a lively neighborhood for the two boys to explore, as Allen Bloomfield remembers. "Going west [on Melrose], your next main street running north and south would be Broadway, and Broadway was sort of a commercial street," he says. "On one corner you had ABC Toyland, a place where they sold sodas and hot dogs and had comic books and just everything you might imagine." Michael and Allen rode their sturdy Schwinn bicycles around the area, and the brothers took different approaches to maintaining them—Allen meticulously polished the bell on his and parked it by using its kickstand, while Michael would simply abandon his on the ground after he finished his ride.

The family was wealthy, but Allen says he and Michael weren't aware of their position in Chicago society. "We didn't think in terms that we lived in a nine-room apartment on the higher floor in relation to somebody living in a two-family house," he remembers. Still, there was plenty for an observant child to notice in a sprawling city composed of neighborhoods demarcated by economic status and ethnicity.

"Even on the block before you got to Broadway there were some small two-family apartment buildings, and in these little apartment buildings you would have the first taste of immigrants," Allen says. "There were gypsies, and there were Hispanic people. I don't remember seeing black families on our block or even on the blocks that surpassed [Broadway] going west. You'd have to go quite a bit west to find that.

But there were people who came in from Virginia or Tennessee, and they kind of filled in the demographics."

Michael developed asthma when he was about one and a half years old, and the family went to Tucson, Arizona, to take advantage of the arid climate. Michael's asthma cleared up, and he and Allen enjoyed a vigorous, mobile childhood that was marked by summers at Colorado dude ranches and winters in Miami, where they would stay long enough for the boys to be enrolled in schools there.

When Michael was twelve, the family moved to Glencoe, a wealthy suburb on the North Shore of Chicago with a large Jewish population. "We moved to Glencoe because I thought that the schooling would be better there," Michael's mother later remembered. "That was the biggest mistake of my life. [Michael] should have been in a highly progressive school. We put him in the wrong schools. Glencoe was a very wealthy area, and their standard was: you had to conform. God forbid you should be a nonconformist. And Mike was a nonconformist."

At New Trier High School in nearby Winnetka, Michael was an outsider—the type of boy that the usual contingent of jocks and cheer-leaders would poke fun at. He was uncoordinated and not interested in sports, unlike his father, who was a robust athlete. Michael was put into accelerated classes at New Trier, but he proved to be an indifferent student. Bloomfield was a born autodidact, who devoured books and had an uncanny, photographic memory, and he was on his own accelerated course from the beginning. Hungry for friendship, he began spending time with fellow nonconformists Roy Ruby and Fred Glaser, New Trier classmates who came from similarly affluent Glencoe families. They would skip school and hang out at Leo's Delicatessen, where they would charge corned beef sandwiches to their parents' accounts.

The Bloomfield family had a black maid and gardener who lived in their house, and Ruby's family had a live-in maid as well. "All of us had bad parents and bad parenting, but we loved the maids," Glaser said. "Our parents were mean, unpleasant, middle-class people who didn't understand us. The maids were cool, hip, sophisticated people who did understand us and liked us. So naturally we were attracted to them, and we were attracted to black culture."

Michael's mother remembered him as a child who was remarkable in a very ordinary sort of way. "He was very bright, very alert, very normal," she told me years later. "He did the normal things at a very early age." But it quickly became apparent that school wasn't for him. Like many a bright child set in a classroom with others who aren't moving as quickly, his first reaction was boredom. The boredom turned into mischief, and the mischief into trouble. Bloomfield liked to play pranks in his neighborhood and at his school, and his combination of sharp wit and rebellious tendencies made him appear obnoxious to some of his friends and teachers. The words "discipline problem" cropped up. Here was a kid who needed an outlet. The radio, and then the guitar, would give him one.

At around the same time the family moved to Glencoe, Michael and Allen received a pair of guitars. Their cousin Charles Bloomfield had one, and the brothers wanted to follow suit in the name of what Michael and Allen always called "relative rivalry." Allen gave up playing after a couple of months, but Michael kept at it, put himself to the task of figuring it out. His first instrument was a cheap three-quarter-size Harmony guitar.

Like any Jewish lad approaching the magic age of thirteen, Michael began to study Hebrew in preparation for his bar mitzvah, the ceremony in which a Jewish boy becomes a man. Of course, this is a time for considerable rejoicing, and most families spare no expense to make this public ceremony and the reception that follows a momentous occasion for the son and the guests.

During the service, the future performer displayed a flair for the dramatic, as Allen Bloomfield remembered later. "It's like his first performance, if you will," Allen said. "He goes beyond the call of duty of just reciting the *Haftorah*, which is the part you have to memorize. . . . Michael added certain dramatics to it for—I don't know, we'll just call it 'theatrical effect.' He would look up at the ceiling, raise his eyes, and sort of have a dialogue with, if you will, or speak directly to, The Absolute. . . . And he looked quite funny, because he had on this sharkskin or silk suit, which was really fancy for a kid of 13, and a tie with a big Windsor knot and everything."

It is traditional that those who are invited give gifts, and although it is officially frowned upon, there is often quite a bit of competition among the relatives to outdo each other's generosity. Michael received the usual envelopes filled with cash, perhaps some stock certificates, and very likely some books on Judaism. But he also received a portable transistor radio, still a novelty in 1956. The radio was ivory colored, with a telescopic antenna and a waffle front. He told Allen, who was a little envious of his brother, to take whatever he wanted. Michael was more than willing to share the bounty, but he kept the radio.

The music available in the Bloomfield household was typical of what was heard in many middle-class, mid-1950s households—light music. "My parents weren't really interested [in music]," Michael told Tom Yates and Kate Hayes. "They listened to things like *South Pacific* or merengue records, cha-cha records, I don't know—stuff like that. So I was just a product of the radio, and all I wanted to do was imitate radio as fast as I could."

Black and white southerners had come to Chicago during the Depression and World War II in search of work, found it, and stayed. To a certain extent, these groups adapted to life in Chicago, but in other ways, they kept bits of their culture with them, just to remind themselves who they were and where they'd come from. Music was a part of what they kept—hillbilly music and blues roared nightly out of neighborhood bars, jukeboxes, and the PA setups of live bands. It was on the radio, too. All over it.

"There was really great radio in Chicago at that time," Michael told me. "When I was really young, I couldn't tell the difference between black music, rockabilly, rock 'n' roll . . . I mean, they could be playing 'Shrimp Boats Are A-Comin',' or some Ersel Hickey record or Muddy Waters, and I dug 'em all. I really couldn't tell the difference between 'em."

And even in Chicago, some of the big clear-channel stations would boom in through the tiny speaker on Michael's radio. "There was John R. [Richbourg] from Nashville," he remembered. "There was XERB from Mexico. . . . In Chicago, there was the Sam Evans show, *Jam with Sam*. There was Richard Sands's show, *Open the Door, Richard*. There was Skeets Van—all these black disc jockeys, except I didn't know they were black at the time. God, all the blues you'd ever want to hear in your life, all the R&B you'd ever want to hear in your life, all the rockabilly you could get out of Nashville and Memphis." Michael estimated that there were seven blues shows just on local radio, three during the day and four at night. And that was just blues.

Not that he was entirely unfamiliar with blues. "In Chicago, when I was a little kid, driving around with my folks, I'd go through certain parts of town, man, go to the black parts of town, and I'd hear music coming out of stores, and out of record stores, and jukeboxes," he told radio show host Dan McClosky in 1971. "I never knew what it was, but I just knew it knocked me out."

In fact, Chicago was saturated with blues at the time, thanks to the presence of the country's major blues record company, Chess Records, which recorded some of the most important blues records in its studios at 2520 South Michigan Avenue. During the early 1950s Chess had made national hits out of some of its snarling, electric urban blues records, and by the time Michael Bloomfield was curling up under the covers with his new transistor radio, such classics as Little Walter's "My Babe," Muddy Waters's "Forty Days and Forty Nights," Howlin' Wolf's "Smokestack Lightnin'" and "I Asked for Water (She Gave Me Gasoline)" were current hits on Chess. And that's without even considering the number of hits Jimmy Reed, another Chicagoan, was cutting for Vee-Jay, or the very definite contributions being made by the Chicago doo-wop of the Moonglows or the strange melding of country and western and blues that produced Chess's best-remembered artist, Chuck Berry. There were other blues labels, some very short lived, too. Eli Toscano's Cobra Records, to name one, served as a sort of farm team for Chess, thanks to Willie Dixon's temporary disagreement with Leonard and Phil Chess. Working at Cobra, Dixon produced some of the first recordings by Otis Rush, Buddy Guy, and Magic Sam.

Of course, these were just the names that were making waves across the country. In those days, local radio played scores of regional hits, and many a Chicago bluesman was a hero in his hometown and as far away from it as the radio signal reached but was completely unknown elsewhere.

Nor was the excitement limited to the black side of town or exclusively to the blues. Country music was undergoing a shake-up unlike anything that had happened to it in years. George Jones, the Louvin Brothers, Ray Price, and Conway Twitty were moving country music in new and exciting directions. The shock waves from Memphis, where Elvis Presley had been fusing blues and country music since 1955, were felt in every hillbilly band in the land.

The young musicians felt it was their special duty to rock the music they played just a bit more, and with southern radio beaming up the latest by Jerry Lee Lewis, Carl Perkins, and the rest, rockabilly began to find a home in Chicago. Even that blues bastion, Chess, started recording and leasing rockabilly songs, on its Chess, Checker, and Argo labels, by such unknowns as Mel Robbins, Bobby Sisco, Rusty York, and Russell Bridges, who was later known as Leon Russell. Chess even scored one monster hit in this area, Dale Hawkins's "Susie Q," a sinuous one-chord jam based on a lick that Howlin' Wolf played. The company also released records by Bobby Charles, a Cajun they'd signed before they knew he was white. Charles had scored a big hit with "See You Later, Alligator."

As for Michael Bloomfield, he was interested in a very specific aspect of this whole thing: the fact that the people who played all this stuff were just exactly what he didn't think he was, namely, tough. Michael Bloomfield might have been a man as far as his religion was concerned, but according to the kids who went to his suburban school, he was a wimp, a zero, a nobody, a schlub.

"All I knew is if the music implied hardness, toughness, or badass on any level, then I liked it," he told me. And to Dan McClosky he said that "it had to do not only with the music but with the social-aesthetic thing of that time, the greaser image." He added, "Man, I had every Elvis Presley magazine, this fat little Jew with his hair combed like Elvis Presley, waddling around. You laugh, man, but it was very serious to me. The aesthetic thing of it was very important to me. I saw myself in my mind as this long, lanky hillbilly, and the radio just was the reinforcement of that whole lifestyle."

Then there was another momentous discovery. Michael's grandfather, Max Klein, owned a pawnshop, Uncle Max's, on Clark Street on the Near North Side, and Michael started helping out there when he was thirteen. "My granddad was a pawnbroker and had been one for forty or fifty years, and guitars hung in the window," he told Tom Yates and Kate Hayes. "And I just put it together, and realized that the one thing that sort of tied all these things together, there seemed to be the guitar involved. When I would see Elvis pictures, he had a guitar, and when I would see posters in Chicago of the various blues singers I would be hearing on the radio, I would see them with guitars, and I worked in a store with guitars, so one day I brought [an acoustic] guitar home with me, and that's how I started playing guitar." The tiny three-quarter-size Harmony was abandoned.

Not only did Michael not share his father's athleticism, but also he showed no desire to follow in Harold's footsteps as a businessman, so he took up the guitar in earnest. "Just being a social misfit was a help, because the guitar, I took it to be my own, you know, took it to be a thing I could do," he told Dan McClosky. "I was left handed, but it was real hard for me to learn because I learned right handed. It was the only thing that I focused on, that I could do with some success. I was the only person that knew that I was getting anywhere at it, anyway." Paradoxically, his left-handedness turned out to be a real boon, since the left hand is the fingering hand, and he quickly found that he could move that hand very fast up and down the fretboard.

This new development divided the Bloomfield family. Harold saw his eldest son drifting into what he considered one of the most useless pursuits possible for somebody who had all the advantages: music. Dorothy, an ex-performer, was a bit more sympathetic. Her hairdresser, Tony Tenaglia, was a guitarist who gave lessons in his spare time under the name Tony Carmen. "He was a real nice guy," Michael remembered. "The lessons I took had nothing to do with what I wanted to learn, but he did teach me chords, how they worked, and how to play them in different keys." The lessons lasted a year. Harold was becoming more upset, making heaven-knows-what connections in his mind and wondering just what it was that his son was learning from this *hairdresser*. According to Michael, he derided Michael's instrument, calling it a "fruit box" and smashing more than one of them.

However, Allen Bloomfield disputes Michael's story. "I think that was just a fabrication," he says. "I never heard him call them 'fruit boxes.' Our father was not the type of guy who would smash a guitar. It was never, ever going to be something on that level. He'd hit you in the face. He'd correct you instantly. There was no lag time in that. He'd never take it out on a guitar. He would go right for you."

Harold Bloomfield seems to have been in every way an intimidating figure. There is a remarkable photograph of the family taken in 1956, when Michael was twelve or thirteen years old. Michael's mother beams at the camera, while Allen stands behind Michael, who is seated between his mother and father. Allen smiles shyly, while Michael gazes at the camera in a self-confident manner, his eyes full of mocking intelligence. His father looks sideways at Michael with a curious mixture of disapproval and pride.

"He was a quiet guy in his demeanor," Allen Bloomfield says about his father. "He was not a loud guy. If he said something, he meant what he said, and you could be sure that if there was any sense of threat to it, he would fulfill it. He wasn't the type of guy who shot his mouth off for the sake of doing it."

As Michael told Dan McClosky, "[My father] wanted me to be everything that I wasn't. He wanted me to be a jock, he wanted me to be a good student, he wanted me to be this and that. He just couldn't understand—at three o'clock in the morning he'd hear me listening to *Jam with Sam*, this really old-fashioned soul station. The AM radio, I swear to God, was a freaky thing with me. To hear Sun records, to hear Elvis records, or maybe get John R. from Nashville, playing this music that I just loved, it was like a whole world opened to me."

Harold didn't realize it, but his son Michael was already lost to him, and he was never coming back.

3

GETTING GOOD

"I started playing the guitar when I was thirteen years old, and I was very bad for two or three years, and when I was about fifteen and a half, I got great." It was with this characteristically immodest statement that Michael Bloomfield started telling me his life's story when I interviewed him in 1974. It's the sort of statement that one takes with the proverbial grain of salt, except, in this case, he just happened to be telling the truth.

Michael never denied that Tony Carmen gave him a solid basis for learning on his own. Inspired by what he learned in Carmen's guitar lessons, he plowed through fake books, which were large, usually illegal volumes of transcriptions of standard songs that provided basic chords and melody lines for bands to use when they needed to play a request. He worked and worked on his fake books, late into the night. "He practiced very quietly and he never used an amp in the house," his mother told me. "Everything was done in his room, quietly. Every day he'd work. He'd practice his riffs and runs, keep his fingers limber. When he was in his room alone, that was the part of his life that was his. It had nothing to do with us."

In 1957 Bloomfield and his friend Roy Ruby went with Bloomfield's maid, Mary Williams, to see Josh White, a folk-blues singer who had started recording in Chicago in the late 1920s, and a major draw. Williams knew White, and she made arrangements to take the boys to see him perform at the Gate of Horn, a folk venue on the Near North Side. Located in the basement of the Rice Hotel at 755 North

Dearborn Street, the Gate of Horn was the brainchild of Chicago-born club owner Albert Grossman.

When Bloomfield was beginning to explore the guitar, he also met Horace Cathcart, a bassist from Lake Forest, Illinois, at a private party at a house on the city's North Shore. Eager to learn bass, Bloomfield began playing with Cathcart at parties and folk clubs along the North Shore. About a year later, Bloomfield put together a band called Mr. Lonely and the Twisters, and the group played dances at New Trier High School.

By the time Michael was fifteen, he was performing publicly with, as he told me, "crazy bands with clarinets, polka bands," and the like. He would play anywhere people would let him, and he would try to see as many other guitar players as he could. He was also picking up tricks from radio and records. The first blues tune Bloomfield mastered was Texas guitarist T-Bone Walker's version of Bernice Carter's "Glamour Girl." He and Roy Ruby also marveled at the weird, spidery guitar licks Chuck Berry played on Berry's 1957 instrumental "Deep Feeling." As a budding teenage guitar hero, Bloomfield was entranced by the work of Scotty Moore, who played the simple, indelible solos on early Elvis Presley records. He was also listening closely to the work of Cliff Gallup, the guitarist on many of Gene Vincent's rock 'n' roll numbers. As he told Tom Yates and Kate Hayes, the guitar solo on Vincent's 1957 song "Blues Stay Away from Me" was a major influence on him, and Bloomfield also thrilled to Gallup's work on "Who Slapped John," recorded the year before. Already, Bloomfield was a musical omnivore who had developed his lifelong habit of close listening to records: "I liked Bo Diddley records even though there was no solo guitar. His guitar was so strange sounding," he told Yates and Hayes.

Michael remained a discipline problem at New Trier, and his obvious intelligence still wasn't being directed into his studies. All he wanted to do was master the guitar and perform. In 1959, when he was a sophomore, Bloomfield and his classmate Roy Jespersen put together a group they called the Hurricanes, after Johnny and the Hurricanes, an Ohio rock 'n' roll group who had hit the charts that year with the instrumental tunes "Red River Rock" and "Beatnik Fly." Jespersen played drums, while Roy Ruby played rhythm guitar. Bloomfield played a Gibson archtop electric guitar.

The group played dances around the North Shore, with Michael's father driving them to gigs. As Jespersen remembered it, Harold Bloomfield gave the boys some sage advice one evening: get paid up front. The quartet, which also included a friend of theirs named Craig Sherman on upright bass, got a chance to play a talent show at New Trier in 1959. For almost anyone else, playing a high school talent show would seem an innocuous pastime, but the budding rocker had a trick up his sleeve.

For their turn in the talent show, the Hurricanes had worked up a Chet Atkins–style instrumental. They had been told in no uncertain terms by the school's dean that the band was to take no encore, and they were certainly not welcome to play any rock 'n'roll.

The group finished their first number, and sure enough, the band of rock 'n' roll rebels launched into their encore, a rendition of "Hurricane," a raucous number Bloomfield had come up with. As he later described it to Dan McClosky, "Hurricane" was an "E chord—a simple version of [Link Wray's] 'Rumble.'" It was too much for the school's authorities, who had already observed how uncannily the awkward boy moved through the school employing brazen stratagems designed to drive the teachers crazy, such as disrupting classes by citing works he had read outside the curriculum. New Trier High School expelled Michael Bloomfield, which was no small accomplishment, since the school did try to do its best to accommodate a respectable number of suburban weirdos and misfits.

His parents dispatched him to Cornwall Academy, a prep school in Great Barrington, Massachusetts. "It was terrible on him," his mother remembered. "That was the worst thing my husband could have done, because Michael was a free soul."

But one result of his banishment was to introduce Michael to drugs and radical intellectual ideas even faster than would have happened back in Chicago. Roy Ruby had also been sent away to a prep school, the Windsor Mountain School, in Lenox, Massachusetts, not far from Great Barrington, and the two exiles played music together, hung out, and broadened their intellectual and social horizons.

In the summer of 1959, Bloomfield sat in with guitarist Luther "Guitar Junior" Johnson at a Chicago club called the Place, at Sixty-Third Street and St. Lawrence Avenue, in a totally black area of town. A native of Itta Bena, Mississippi, Johnson had moved to Chicago in 1955. This was the first time Bloomfield played in a South Side club. By some stroke of luck, these barely postpubescent Jewish kids from Glencoe, way up north, were not only allowed in but received the privilege of sitting at a front table. Astonishingly, it was an audition night, and Michael got a taste of the electric blues, Chicago style.

"Do you remember what it sounded like, coming down the street, hearing the music before you got in the club?" Michael asked Roy Ruby during their 1971 interview with Dan McClosky. "The excitement you would feel hearing that blues coming out the doorway, halfway down the block?"

"I was afraid," Ruby replied. "I was in a strange place and you presumably knew where we were, vaguely, and you had heard about this place." Welcome to blues culture: the band included a mean-looking bassist who played with a thumb pick and a fat female saxophonist who wore a red dress. She decided that this kid was worth having fun with, and she walked over to the front table and engaged Ruby in a surrealistic question-and-answer session:

"She said, 'You got it?' 'Got what? What do you mean?' 'You got it? What you got? You've got it, don't you?' Now everyone is laughing; the whole place is breaking up; people are falling all over [themselves]. There are two fourteen-year-old white kids sitting in the middle of this place. I mean, this is before the blues movement started, and these people were friendly. They didn't know about white people. They were just friendly. Everyone's cracking up. She said, 'You've got it, don't you?' I said, 'What do you mean? What do I have?' This goes on about twenty-five minutes. I'm completely embarrassed, crawling under the table, don't know what is going on. It's like being in Africa or something. And they're like, you know, 'What's the password?' When I finally gave up and was about to slink out the door, finally she blasts out the answer. She turns around, takes the saxophone from her mouth, spreads her arms wide, spreads her legs, leans backward, looks at the ceiling and screams, 'You've got your ass, don't you?'"

Years later, the story still had the power to reduce Ruby and Bloomfield to giggling idiots.

That was a historic evening. Not only did they discover how easygoing black clubs could be, but they were gratified to discover that the Place's patrons enjoyed the way Michael was playing the blues.

"I'd come home from boarding school, and Michael has now graduated from playing with little bands around New Trier," Ruby told Dan

McClosky. "We drove around Chicago in the back of a truck playing acoustic instruments. We stopped once at an empty storefront in
downtown Chicago. We got out of the truck, loaded our instruments
into the storefront, plugged them in, and began playing the one song
that we knew how to play. We played this one song for about a year,
'Hurricane.' We played it loud until the police came. Somebody came
and threw us out of there."

Michael lasted less than a year at Cornwall. Fred Glaser remembered
that the duo came home in 1960 with quantities of marijuana in their
pockets. Michael tried to reenroll in New Trier, but he wasn't allowed
to graduate. He ended up going to Central YMCA High School in the
Loop, where Nick Gravenites, who was five years older than Michael,
had already done a stint. "[It] was where they all go after they've been
thrown out of the public schools . . . full of junior hoodlums and hood-
lumettes," Gravenites told me. At Central, Michael reconnected with
another troublemaker who had gotten thrown out of high school. Barry
Goldberg knew about Michael, who had gained a reputation as one of
the hottest guitarists on the North Side. They had run into each other
while leading rival teenage rock 'n' roll groups on the North Side, and
Goldberg had played piano in the house band at a club called Teen-
land, where he built up his chops by backing up such visiting artists
as Johnny Tillotson and Ral Donner.

Most of Michael's playing would be done on the North Side, in
rock 'n' roll bands playing Top 40 hits and wearing uniforms while
the all-white crowd jitterbugged on the floor. But his hanging out—
every moment he could spare away from paying gigs—was done on the
South Side. One of the first places they went was Pepper's, the bar that
was Muddy Waters's domain. Because they were underage, they were
forced to stand on the sidewalk while Muddy played inside, though
he did come out to shake their hands in between sets. Muddy was the
unquestioned godfather of the Chicago blues scene, the source of
the Chicago sound, and the man who had gone from Stovall's planta-
tion in Mississippi to become the king of the South Side.

"I would go down the street, man, and from two blocks away I'd
hear that harmonica come out of the club, I'd hear that harp," Michael
told Dan McClosky. "And I'd hear Muddy's slide. I'd be trembling. I'd
be like a dog in heat. I didn't know what to do. I'd get near that place,
man, and I'd be all aquiver. . . . I heard Elmore James," he told Dan

McClosky. "I heard Sonny Boy, Little Walter, Wolf, Muddy, Albert King, way before they were known anywhere but the ghetto. Lowell Fulson, and many of the smaller, more obscure cats: [J. B.] Hutto, Jimmy Rogers, Eddie Taylor, this guy named Little Mack [Simmons]. Endless guys. By the time I was around seventeen, I was interested in it from a musicological standpoint. . . . I would go down there thinking I was really some hot stuff, you know, 'cause I had some fast fingers and I had plenty of licks, but I didn't have no soul or nothing. All I had was that speed and some brash Jewboy confidence. I would go down there, and I wouldn't know what the hell made my music different. Why couldn't I really sound like them other cats sounded?" He later brushed off the experience by saying, "Well, you got to fuck up there." But he'd had his taste and he wanted more.

4

BLUES FOLK

Growing up on the South Side of Chicago, Nick Gravenites was a roly-poly Greek kid running around the family business, Candyland, a store that sold cigars and magazines along with the ice cream, candy, and flavored syrups that were made right in the back of the shop. Gravenites was born in 1938 to Greek immigrant parents who lived in Brighton Park, a southwest Chicago neighborhood that he later described in his column Bad Talkin' Bluesman as a "white ghetto."

Located at Thirty-Fifth Street and Archer Avenue, Candyland was a paradise of gleaming tile and mirrored walls, complete with a Rock-Ola jukebox. Nick Gravenites's father, George, had turned it into a thriving concern, but he died when Nick was eleven years old. Nick went to work at the busy shop, and the young boy became aware of the gulf between the habits and aspirations of his parents and the glittering possibilities of American life in a huge city.

His early life paralleled Michael Bloomfield's in many ways. When Gravenites turned thirteen, he became a discipline problem for his parents and teachers. Hanging out in the neighborhood streets, the stocky youngster began smoking cigarettes, participated in muggings, and stole from local warehouses. In 1951 he went to St. John's Military Academy in Wisconsin, lasted three and a half years, and got himself expelled shortly before he was set to graduate. Gravenites wound up at the Central YMCA High School, the same educational institution that Michael Bloomfield and Barry Goldberg would attend a few years later. Impressed by his writing skill, an English teacher at Central had taken a special interest in Nick, and almost before Nick knew what had happened, he found he'd applied to—and been accepted by—the University of Chicago.

"The university was sort of a pocket of sanity in the midst of Chicago stick-'em-up," Gravenites told me. "It was the only area besides the Near North Side where there was any interracial housing. It had a sort of a radical reputation, and it was sort of like an island." It also had one of the first big campus folk scenes. Nick entered the University of Chicago in 1956, and he was immediately drawn to this bohemian, rebellious scene. It was huge and it was diverse. Some of the folkies were busy investigating the Appalachian folk tradition, playing banjos and reading about folklorists' field trips. Others naturally went for the more commercial aspects like the Kingston Trio–style singers. Still others went for blues. The University of Chicago Folklore Society encouraged students to take an interest in all of it, and Gravenites was eager to learn.

"Folk music at that time, and particularly at the University of Chicago, was really a big deal," Gravenites told me years later. "There were hundreds of people that came to these hootenannies. It was a huge organization, and everybody was listening to folk records at that time." Folk fans in 1956 were listening to Harry Belafonte and to the Weavers, but they were also discovering the music of such blues performers as Leadbelly, Lightnin' Hopkins, Josh White, and Big Bill Broonzy.

"When they held get-togethers, they'd have to hire the big hall to fit 'em all in," Gravenites said about the Folklore Society's hootenannies and wingdings. "During orientation week, thousands of people would show up to their activities. And there was a lot of interchange between Chicago and Ann Arbor and Madison, Wisconsin, too.

"We were some of the first people to start the folk revival, and we were the first to start playing electric music, electric blues, which was heresy to the folkies on the East Coast, something they still haven't forgiven us for."

Along the fringes of the folk scene were a bunch of people not too different from Gravenites's old self. His thuggish, hoodlum impulses hadn't been completely tamed by college life, and Gravenites roamed around Chicago, guitar case in hand. He met banjo players, dulcimer experts, and pool sharks. Along the way, he picked up basic guitar skills from a fellow University of Chicago student named Ed Gaines. Shooting pool at the University Club, Gravenites got to know the bootblack who worked at the club's barbershop and held down a second job as a bouncer at a place called Frader's Jukebox Lounge, which was located at 834 East Forty-Third Street on the South Side. Frader's would become one of Gravenites's regular hangouts, but he saw his first electric blues show at the 708 Club, at 708 East Forty-Seventh Street. One day in 1958 a friend of his, John Reiland, took Gravenites down to the club, and it was a revelation.

As Gravenites later said about the 708 Club, "Whites didn't know about it, but blacks did." What he and his friends saw at the 708 Club was nothing less than a battle of the bands between two great blues performers, Junior Parker and Otis Rush. Parker's band had a horn section, while Rush played the kind of biting lead guitar that the young Michael Bloomfield was no doubt studying at the same time.

"It was the loudest music I had ever heard in my life," Gravenites wrote three decades later in one of a brilliant series of columns for *Blues Revue* magazine. "After two sets, I was glad to get out of there." Suitably impressed, Gravenites began catching the blues revues at Frader's, which boasted its own live broadcasts and a sound truck that would blast out advertisements for the club as it rolled through the local streets. A typical evening would start out with a dancer performing in a skimpy outfit, and an array of singers would receive the expert backing of the house band, a drummer, and a Hammond organ player.

"I'd been basically a folk player," Gravenites told me. "But I started hanging out in this club because, well, I drank heavily, smoked reefers, dropped bennies, wore shades at midnight. I was armed most of the time, and I was a little bit nuts, a beatnik hoodlum. That's what I figured I had to be in order to do this thing. I think that's what the blues scene was for a lot of us white guys, a lesson in race, in color, in externals; a lesson in going through prejudice and ignorance all the way through to the other side.

"It wasn't a race relations type of thing; we were just funky people, that's all. It was the music that got me. I'd go to Frader's and smoke reefers in the back with the boys, drink, get fucked up, party and run around, and eventually I got to sit in, as a joke, like a comedy act. It was an all-black audience. So I'd get up there and do a couple of Lightnin' Hopkins tunes, and people would laugh, like, 'Look at this—a white boy singin' blues!' To them, it was welcome comedic relief."

As Gravenites remembers, "Back in the old days, we used to read articles that asked, 'Can whites play the blues?' The folk music magazines pretty much discounted all white blues, just as a matter of policy." So when Gravenites described hanging out in black blues clubs as something that went beyond race relations, he was pointing to a split between the way white fans of folk and blues perceived the music and the way its black practitioners lived it. In Gravenites's philosophy, blues music was both a way of life and a musical aesthetic that blacks and whites had to work to master. Visiting a place like Frader's was about being alert, staying cool, and developing a realistic, tolerant view of the less salutary aspects of human nature that were on display in the blues clubs.

"I was under the initial impression that the ghetto was dangerous to me and that blacks were trouble for me, but after my initiation into the blues culture I realized that I was the dangerous one, I was potential trouble, because I didn't understand nothin' about nothin', living in a white man's fantasy world," Gravenites wrote in a 1995 *Blues Revue* column. "I didn't understand about 'woofin',' the boasting, the name-calling, the bluster and bluff, the verbal give-and-take of the black culture I was a guest in. Sure, there was a lot of violence in the bars, but a lot of it was hollerin' and screaming, brandishing weapons, shootin' guns in the floor and in the ceiling, getting a brick from the street, but rarely did anyone get killed."

Eventually a small coterie from the University of Chicago began making the scene in these clubs. They were mostly folkies who, like Michael, woke up one day to the fact that the greatest blues being made at the time were being played just a few blocks from the university. There was Elvin Bishop, a National Merit Scholar from Oklahoma, who was beginning to play serious electric guitar, and Norman Dayron, a sociology teacher who had started at the University of Chicago in the fall of 1958. Born in the Bronx in 1940, Dayron had a strong interest in hi-fi, and he lugged tape recorders into the clubs and made some historic recordings.

Meanwhile, Paul Butterfield was another Chicago guy who had been investigating clubs on his own. A South Side kid who grew up near the university, Butterfield was a self-possessed young man with impeccable manners and a sure feel for the dynamics of complex social situations. He immediately ingratiated himself to the blues performers and audiences on the South Side.

"He wasn't too good when I first noticed him," Muddy Waters told me, "but he got good."

Gravenites agreed. "He was another part of the comic relief in these blues revues, except that he was really good," he said. "The black audiences loved this guy, and not even in an audience-and-performer way. It was an emotional thing. He was a nice kid, and he'd play shuffleboard and pinball with the regulars, and then when it got to be his turn, he'd get up there with his harp and really blow."

These university blues fans discovered that bands held residencies at the blues clubs. Muddy Waters held down Pepper's at 503 East Forty-Third Street, while Magic Sam could be found at the 620 Club at 620 East Sixty-Third Street. Earl Hooker and Junior Wells helped cement their reputations at Theresa's Lounge at 4801 South Indiana Avenue, and Howlin' Wolf ruled Silvio's, owned by Silvio Corazza, at 3200 West Lake Street. There was no cover, just a security guard to get past at the door.

Of course, the residency rule wasn't hard and fast. There were open clubs and there were often jams at clubs. And there was the time-honored tradition of "headhunting": if a group had a good gig, another band would come along and try to take it from them. "Muddy Waters had established the precedent of headhunting," Michael told me. "His band was called the Headhunters, and they would go out and find other bands and try and just ruin 'em, make 'em look so bad they'd never get hired there anymore."

But the music that came out of all this could be exciting, and Michael, as much as the university crowd, was going to school in these clubs every chance he could get. Norman Dayron says that, unlike the crowd he hung with, which included Gravenites and Butterfield, Michael never bothered to carry a gun or to watch out for himself in any way. He was in it for the experience and was relaxed enough that nobody ever paid him any mind.

Nothing, it seemed, would stop Michael from investigating the blues. "For a while, it was sort of shocking," Bloomfield told Dan McClosky. "And after a while, that's just how it was and I didn't even think about it no more. It was just how people were, you know. You played at a club where there were a lot of pimps and bad guys. Like, a bad guy was a guy who had a gun and would use it. You would call that cat a bad guy, because he would shoot you if you had trouble. You just got used to it. Everybody robbed from everybody else. Everybody was guilty, everybody was innocent. They were the poor innocent guilty children of messed-up ghetto society. I remember Wolf used to introduce me. He used to say, 'I got some white friends from the suboibs down here tonight,' and he'd introduce me. I'd be up there playing, and some dude would pull a gun on another dude, and another dude would pull a knife on another dude, and the whole band would hide."

During his 1971 interview with Dan McClosky, Bloomfield told a story about South Side club life that gave McClosky pause. "Oh, man, I remember a time I was standing at a bar and a guy walked in, and he took a woman's head and slammed it on the bar top, and he said, 'Bartender, get this bitch a beer,'" Bloomfield said. "That freaked everybody out."

McClosky asked, "How did she recover from it?"

"Her head—her severed head—was put on the bar," Bloomfield clarified. "She wasn't there; it was her head. See, you don't understand the story. This guy cut off his old lady's head in some horrible fight, and took her head, and slammed it down on top of the bar. What a scene that was. I was appalled."

It's a good story, but Bloomfield had a habit of embellishing the truth to keep himself and everyone around him interested. When he met his wife, Susan Smith, he told her the story of how he had once been a Mouseketeer. She later said that Michael "lied all the time, but it wasn't lying . . . he liked to tell people what they wanted to hear. He would tell elaborate stories, and people would believe him. But I've never thought of him as a dishonest person." Maybe he did see a man slam down a paper bag with his wife's head in it and demand she be served a drink. But Charlie Musselwhite said he didn't believe it. "That never happened," he told writers Jan Mark Wolkin and Bill Keenom in 2000. "That's a folk tale in Chicago. I've heard that over and over from different people—different versions of it, you know."

For the most part, however, Michael kept to himself. The university clique had their own social thing going on, which included weekly twist parties, as they were called. These started out as Wednesday-night record parties in the student lounge, which was called the New Dorm, and moved to Ida Noyes Hall, the student union. When Paul Butterfield and Elvin Bishop began taking them over, they became dance parties featuring Butterfield, Bishop, and such South Side blues players as Little

Walter, who sat in a few times with them in a group called the South-side Olympic Blues Team. They played to a racially mixed audience that included students and people from the surrounding neighborhood.

Michael's scene was different. "I was doing three types of gigs," he told me. "I was playing with fraternity bands from Northwestern, who were playing all these roadhouses and liquor joints in nowhere places like Highwood, an army base town, or DeKalb, Illinois—all these shit bars with us playing Top 40. Then, anytime I could get a gig with a black band, like at the Pride and Joy, I took that. I would play with the lowliest black guy just for the experience. Then I would do folk gigs by myself whenever I could, and then Sundays, I would play Jewtown, an open market in Maxwell Street, where anybody who could play music would come and play for whatever money people would put in the hat. I was making enough to stay alive, but no more than that.

"Then, when I was eighteen years old, I gave up the electric guitar. I thought there was no future in rock 'n' roll. For three years, I played nothing but acoustic folk music. Not like the Weavers or Pete Seeger, but more like fingerpicking sessions with guys like Danny Kalb or Mitch Greenhill. I played with bluegrass bands and learned all those licks."

During his folkie period, Bloomfield studied all manner of acoustic music, and the radio, again, provided him with part of his education. "Because of the atmospheric conditions around Chicago, he could pick up bluegrass stations like WWVA from Wheeling, West Virginia, where you could hear the Stanley Brothers or the Blue Sky Boys or the Delmore Brothers, as well as some of the more commercial things," Norman Dayron recalled. "But I think you heard more of the pure stuff than the commercial stuff. You could hear Bill Monroe. You could hear Ralph and Carter Stanley."

He collected records by Doc Watson, Merle Travis, and Chet Atkins, and listened hard to blues players such as Skip James, Robert Wilkins, and Blind Blake. There were a lot of great American guitarists to check out, and more being discovered (or rediscovered) every day, or so it seemed.

As part of the folkie scene, Michael took to hanging around the Fret Shop, the local folklore emporium. Located near the University of Chicago on Fifty-Seventh Street, it was a place where you could buy guitars, strings, and songbooks, and generally hang around picking and shooting the shit with the other folkniks of the period. Nick Gravenites met Michael there in 1960, and he remembered how impressed he was by Michael's playing. "[He was] sittin' there playing the guitar and his fingers just flying all over the fuckin' fret-board, and I was jealous," Gravenites told me. "He was younger than me, he was a smart-ass Jewish punk from the North Side, and . . . it wasn't that he was particularly offensive, it's just that he was so talented, it pissed you off."

Dayron also first met Bloomfield at the Fret Shop—in the fall of 1960—and he had an experience similar to Gravenites's. "I'm standing in the shop, and I hear this fantastic three-finger guitar playing—very fast, very clean," he said. "I thought it was a record or something. I thought [owner] Pete [Leibundguth] was playing this very hip thing, so I turned around to see where this music was coming from, and I see this guy sitting on a metal chair, bent over one of his guitars that was in the store. . . . It was almost like he had this perfect tension between his fingers and the strings, and it was just tremendously alive music."

During his folk period, Bloomfield continued to work at his Uncle Max's pawnshop on Clark Street, and he was a conduit for guitars to the folkies. It was there, after he'd forsworn electric music, that a couple of girls came looking for a guitar in the spring of 1961. "It was a crummy kind of neighborhood," Susan Smith told me. "But my friend decided she wanted a guitar, and that's where you went to get a guitar. We went to his grandfather's pawnshop, and I don't think I ever would have met him otherwise." There was something about Susan that attracted Michael immediately, although it certainly wasn't mutual.

"The first date I canceled," she said with a smile. "He was very aggressive. I'd never met anybody like him. He told me all kinds of crazy stories. And we lived so far apart. He was in Glencoe and I was at 8600 South, and I don't know how many miles that was, but it was a lot. But we did finally have our first date, because we went to a movie that Frank Hamilton, whom I was taking banjo lessons from at the time, was in, and then we went to the Fickle Pickle coffeehouse, where he wanted to sit in with some guitar player. I had no idea who it was. He was lugging around his amplifier and some big black Gibson guitar. It was just part of him."

The couple had plenty in common besides folk music. They both hated their home environments and felt stifled by their parents. They spent as much time as they could together, exploring Chicago, with Michael blowing Susan's mind with his knowledge of the city. She introduced him to the Folklore Society at the university and the more organized aspects of the folk scene. She couldn't have cared less that he was a musician, and even disasters like having to jump-start his car every time they wanted to drive somewhere seemed insignificant when compared with the fact that they had found each other, were in love, and were in the middle of a city whose every block seemed to hum with music and energy of one sort or another.

Bloomfield briefly attended Roosevelt University in 1961, and in early 1962 he played the University of Chicago Folk Festival, where he performed with blues singer Reverend Gary Davis. During the spring, he played electric guitar at the twist parties at Ida Noyes Hall. Then, that summer, Bloomfield and Fred Glaser took a Greyhound bus to Denver, Colorado. They needed to get out of town for a while—Glaser was trying to avoid marrying his girlfriend, whom he had gotten pregnant, and Bloomfield was ready for a vacation. They hung out in Five Points, a black neighborhood in Denver, and hitchhiked the forty miles north to Boulder.

Bloomfield played at the Sink in Boulder, and he recorded four blues guitar pieces in the kitchen of the coffeehouse across the street, the Attic. He was giving Judy Roderick, a Michigan-born folk and blues singer who was singing in Boulder and Denver clubs, some pointers on blues guitar styles.

After returning with Bloomfield to Chicago in the fall, Glaser acceded to the inevitable and got married. Soon after, Bloomfield and Susan Smith followed suit. Fred and Bobbie Glaser came along for the ride as best man and maid of honor when Bloomfield and Susan Smith went across the state line to New Buffalo, Michigan, to make it official on September 4, 1962.

The newlyweds kept their marriage secret for a couple of weeks, and they didn't live together. When Michael's and Susan's families finally found out about it, they were opposed to the marriage—Susan wasn't Jewish, for one thing—but it was Michael's mother who rallied first. "I thought he was too young to get married, but once they did it, I threw a big cocktail party," Dorothy told me. "My husband was opposed to it, but I threw the party, and I accepted Susan, and she's been my friend ever since."

Susan found employment with an insurance company, and Michael continued to play for whatever money he could make. They got a place to live in the Carl Sandburg Village apartments at 1360 Sandburg Terrace, and Bloomfield got deeper into his experiential blues research, with more and more of a scholarly tone coming into it. Susan fed Michael's interest in acoustic folk music, and part of his fanaticism for the first generation of Chicago bluesmen is traceable to her influence.

Then he realized something: he could continue to research the blues, help the players themselves, and make money doing it! He approached Herman Fleishman, the owner of the Fickle Pickle club, located on Rush Street, and before long, he was the manager, booker, and hamburger chef.

5

THE FICKLE PICKLE, BIG JOE, AND BIG JOHN'S

Charlie Musselwhite, a harmonica player who had come to Chicago from Memphis in 1962 looking for a factory job and stayed to play the blues, described the Fickle Pickle to me as "a coffee place, where you could get cider, coffee, and stuff like that. This was before sprouts, although they would've had 'em if they'd known about 'em, and they'd let you smoke in there." It was a basement club that seated about one hundred patrons, where beatnik comics and folkies mingled with blues fanatics.

It was the perfect place for Michael Bloomfield to indulge what he admitted was becoming an increasingly musicological interest in the blues. He had begun to read what books there were at the time on the history of the blues, and probably pored over Samuel Charters's 1959 book *The Country Blues* and Paul Oliver's 1960 volume *Blues Fell This Morning*, two pioneering studies of the subject. He discovered that the musicians he'd seen on the South Side, like Muddy Waters and Howlin' Wolf, represented the second wave of black immigrants from the South, and that the Chicago blues scene had actually started in the 1930s, when people like Memphis Minnie, Tampa Red, and Big Bill Broonzy found out there was money to be made, people to play for, and even records to be cut, largely for RCA Victor's Chicago-based Bluebird label. Lonnie Johnson had played his first Chicago date in 1930, and Big Maceo Merriweather, Johnny Shines, Washboard Sam, and John Lee "Sonny Boy" Williamson had performed in South Side Chicago clubs in the 1930s and '40s. This revelation drove the musicologist in Michael crazy, and he spent a great deal of time seeking out the survivors of that long-ago time.

"Some of these old guys had died, but a lot of them were still working, and they were getting the dregs of the gigs because nobody wanted to see them," he told me. "The people who had gone to see them were getting too old to go to bars anymore, and they were all on welfare and couldn't get around and whatnot. The younger crowd all wanted to see people like Magic Sam and Otis Rush and the even younger, more R&B-influenced guys like Ricky Allen, Lee 'Shot' Williams, Eddie King, and Bobby King."

Norman Dayron described to me a visit to a Chicago blues club that occurred in 1962 or 1963. "One time we went to a bar called the Pride and Joy on West Ogden Avenue, the roughest bar that exists in the world," Dayron said. "The minute we came in, a shotgun came out, and the bartender started giving us this spiel about how he'd pulled the shotgun not because of us, but because this guy was coming down with a shotgun to blow his wife's lover away, and he was going to blow this guy away the minute he walked through the door. And that's just what happened! But Michael was there to play."

And it's understandable, from Michael's point of view, because he remembered that day as being a jam. "The band consisted of Chuck Berry, me, Little Walter, Sam Lay, Sunnyland Slim on organ, and some putz on bass," he told me. "I think Charlie Musselwhite played on that gig, too, and our theme was 'Canadian Sunset.'"

Bloomfield's research also led him to the Jazz Record Mart at 7 West Grand Avenue in Chicago, a place most blues fans found sooner or later. It was run by an eccentric named Bob Koester who operated a record label, Delmark, which recorded many of the old and new blues crowd, as well as the earliest efforts by the important Chicago avant-garde jazz scene. The Jazz Record Mart was a haven for rare records, occasional concerts, and often the artists themselves, who lived in the basement when they couldn't find other accommodations. Nobody actually seems to have gotten along with Koester, but everybody admitted that it was his love for the blues that rescued from premature obscurity such important performers as Sleepy John Estes.

Koester, who had come to Chicago after starting Delmark in St. Louis in the 1950s, had been booking blues concerts at a bar called the Blind Pig. By the time Bloomfield and the other University of Chicago blues enthusiasts met Koester, Musselwhite was sleeping on a cot in the basement of the Jazz Record Mart. Another guest at Koester's was guitarist and singer Big Joe Williams, who would exert a tremendous influence on Bloomfield and his friends.

The nineteen-year-old Musselwhite had an easygoing personality, but his relationship with Koester was often tense. As Bloomfield told Dan McClosky about Musselwhite, "People just naturally loved him. They loved him 'cause he was just country—country to the toes." Williams had a more irascible personality, though. Born in Crawford, Mississippi, in 1903, Williams had worked in medicine shows in the South after World War I and had recorded for the Paramount and Okeh labels in the 1930s. Known for his songwriting ability and his nine-string guitar, Williams had more recently played Chicago's Gate of Horn and Limelight Cafe.

By all accounts, Williams often clashed with Koester, who took umbrage at the blues singer's drinking and erratic behavior. Talking to Dan McClosky in 1971, Bloomfield described one incident involving the two men: "We bought [Williams] beer, and Koester got on the phone and called the police, and said, 'There's a large, irate Negro here, and he has to be removed,' and Joe hit him with the telephone."

In early 1963 Koester recorded Bloomfield with Williams, guitarist Sleepy John Estes, mandolinist Yank Rachell, and harmonica player Hammie Nixon. The music on the resulting album, *Mandolin Blues*, is rough-and-ready acoustic blues, with Nixon's harmonica squeaking above Rachell's acid mandolin licks and Bloomfield's rhythm guitar.

Seeing the success Koester was having with his blues concerts at the Blind Pig, Bloomfield instituted a regular Tuesday-night blues gig at the Fickle Pickle. "We presented just about every blues singer that was alive in Chicago at that time," he said proudly. And the shows attracted blues fanatics from everywhere. Michael remembered meeting Texas guitarist Johnny Winter at the Fickle Pickle in 1963.

Unlike Koester, Bloomfield had just the kind of outgoing, enthusiastic personality the Fickle Pickle needed to draw customers. Bloomfield began booking Tuesday-night shows in June 1963 with the help of Pete Welding, a Chicago writer he had gotten to know, and a young

Florida-born blues fan named George Mitchell. Mitchell had come to Chicago earlier that year and had gone to work for Koester at the record shop. He was already an old hand at discovering blues musicians, having traveled to Memphis, Mississippi, and Atlanta as a teenager in 1961 and 1962 to record the likes of Will Shade, Furry Lewis, and fife player Othar Turner.

Mitchell and Bloomfield became fast friends, and the two began bringing in local talent. "We found people who hadn't played in ages anywhere, like Washboard Sam, Jazz Gillum, Lazy Lester, and Sunnyland Slim," Mitchell remembers. "Sunnyland was the main one who took me around findin' the people."

No one was making a lot of money booking blues acts into the Fickle Pickle, as Mitchell remembers. "We had to pay [owner Herman Fleishman's] waitress, and the only money we got was at the door. And it was cheap," he says. The cover charge was one dollar, and Mitchell and Bloomfield made between twenty and forty dollars a week. The coffeehouse didn't have a liquor license, but Fleishman also owned a nearby package store called Larry's Lounge; and once Michael began booking Fickle Pickle shows, he would make a habit of emptying the cash drawer after each set and taking the money down the street to Larry's, where he could buy beer and whiskey for his friends.

To draw people into the Fickle Pickle, Bloomfield resorted to some innovative show-business tactics. "It was hilarious. He had on dark glasses, and had a tin can and a cane, like he was blind," remembers Mitchell. "He'd be sittin' on the sidewalk with his tin cup, making his pitch."

As the club became better known, Big Joe Williams began to play there on Monday nights. Bloomfield and Mitchell also relied on Williams and his seemingly endless connections to guide them to old-time Chicago blues players. He took them around Chicago to meet such blues performers as Kokomo Arnold, Jazz Gillum, and Tommy McLennan, who lay dying from tuberculosis in Cook County Hospital.

Many of the old bluesmen were acoustic players, and not only were they attractive to the Pickle's crowd, but the folkies on the University of Chicago campus liked them, too. "We became friends with those old guys," Susan told me. "We'd take them to the university for concerts, and once we took Big Joe Williams to Grinnell, Iowa, for a concert. We both felt that this was a very important thing for us to be doing, that we were really helping out and doing something historically valid, even apart from the fact that we really liked them.

"They never actually came to live in our apartment, but it was crazy because they were alien. They lived in these crazy places on Maxwell Street where you'd never want to go. I learned so much. I remember this one old guy, I can't remember his name, but we all had ice creams, and this guy spilled ice cream on his pants and he was so upset. I thought that was pretty odd, but when I mentioned it to Michael later, he said, 'Well, that's probably the only pair of pants he had.' That had just never occurred to me."

———————

While Bloomfield was cultivating the company of Chicago bluesmen, he continued to play folk music. Norman Dayron recorded Bloomfield playing solo acoustic guitar in Chicago in early 1964, and the performances he captured suggest that Bloomfield had been absorbing ragtime-style guitar. Bloomfield's rendition of his original composition "Bullet Rag" displays prodigious technique. Meanwhile, the traditional folk tune "J.P. Morgan" gives Bloomfield a chance to show off his sense of humor and sardonic, if amateurish, vocal style. As he would be in his later career, Bloomfield was a song collector as much as he was a guitarist—his technique was tempered by a feel for what the lyrics of songs could convey, and he was listening to the Nashville recordings of George Jones, Faron Young, and Ray Price during the early 1960s. He would later include Jack Clement's well-known country tune "Just Someone I Used to Know" in his live sets.

Of all the musicians who were around the scene, it was Big Joe Williams who wound up being Michael Bloomfield's good friend. Essentially a country blues musician, Williams had adapted to the times and played his tunes on an amplified nine-string Silvertone guitar. When Bloomfield and his crowd met him, Williams had been traveling for at least forty of his sixty years, selling himself on the basis of having written the blues classic "Baby Please Don't Go." He'd covered the South and Midwest, the Eastern Seaboard, anywhere his talents could earn him a warm bed and, perhaps even more important, a jug of whiskey. If there was a bluesman alive whom Williams didn't know, and know how to reach, that bluesman probably wasn't such a big deal.

Publicizing them like crazy, Michael tossed plenty of Fickle Pickle gigs Williams's way, and a sort of friendship grew up between this odd couple of the blues. Big Joe began to trust Michael enough to want to introduce him to his world, and Michael, in turn, introduced his friends to Joe's world. One incident involving Michael's friend Roy Ruby is a good illustration of how this crowd maintained their tenuous relationships. (This story, and another one that was even more dramatic, would later show up in Bloomfield's 1980 book, *Me and Big Joe*.)

Ruby had come back to Chicago from boarding school, and Michael asked him to help out with Williams, who had a gig that he wanted to go to. Bloomfield, Ruby, and Charlie Musselwhite traveled with Williams to a roadhouse near Gary, Indiana. The trio of young white blues performers played on the show as comic relief. As Ruby remembered it, the place was located among steel mills and coal fields, and it consisted of a barbecue pit in front and a large room in back, where the band played. The bill was a good one: J. B. Lenoir's big band, Lightnin' Hopkins, Sunnyland Slim, and saxophonist A. C. Reed. Ruby drove his mother's car.

"[Williams] is about sixty years old at this time, and all his life he loves to fight," Ruby told Dan McClosky. "He has scars, thirty wives, a lump on his head like an egg, and Big Joe was a powerful, incredibly strong man. At the age of sixty he looked like he could put a fist through a brick wall. And this man, he would get angry and sullen. When I used to know him and he'd get like that, he'd usually direct it against Koester.

"I thought he was a folk singer, and I'm going out there with Charlie. Charlie lives with him, Michael knows him. Everyone knows, and they're sort of giggling behind my back. I don't know what I'm getting into. So we're out there, and my God, man, Lightnin' Hopkins and Big Joe sat at a table by themselves the whole night. It's a gigantic room, like an auditorium almost, with a cement floor, and metal chairs, and metal tables with Formica tops on them. It was amazing to think, this is like the blues circuit—this is where Jimmy Reed plays, people like that."

Big Joe and Lightnin' drank two or three bottles of whiskey. As Ruby remembered it, Williams became sullen and angry, and on the way home he made a series of barely decipherable utterances. "All the way back, [Joe's] giving me these cursory directions: 'Left!' And I was embarrassed to ask him what he meant, because I felt I was denigrating the Negro dialect by asking him, over and over, what he was saying. Every time I'd ask him, he'd get more and more angry. Sometimes I'd disagree with him. I'd say, 'I think we went this way when we came.'"

The trio finally reached their destination. "[It was] like the most incredible slum of Chicago transplanted somewhere out in the country, for some reason," Ruby said. "You're out in the country and you get to this place, and you begin walking through, and it's a huge area, like a city block of houses built up in these weird ways." They walked up a flight of stairs to a small apartment, which contained some of Big Joe's kinfolk—his brother-in-law or sister-in-law, Ruby wasn't sure. Everyone gathered around Big Joe, asked him where he'd been, and someone gave Ruby a beer.

"Finally things cool down, and Joe says, 'Let's go,'" Ruby said. "And he's still pretty drunk, but he's sort of mellowed. He was pissed at me for being scared, you see. He could feel that I was scared. He was protecting me, and he was going to do me the favor of taking me to see his family. I remember, he was real excited to bring us out there. We were his protégés, and he introduced us to everybody."

It was a strange relationship that these young white kids had with the older man. He never really said what he expected from them, and they tried to give him what they thought he wanted. What was in it for them, of course, was the blues experience, the experience of relating to people from another reality. Big Joe was handy, and he wasn't averse to it.

Michael finally had his fill of the relationship after a frightening 1964 weekend trip to East St. Louis. This time, George Mitchell and another Chicago friend of theirs were along for the ride.

As Bloomfield told the story to Dan McClosky, they had traveled to East St. Louis over the Fourth of July weekend, and it was hot. Bloomfield followed Williams around all day, and Bloomfield got drunk. The next morning, Big Joe made breakfast for his young student of the blues.

"I was laying there, with my first real hangover," Bloomfield said. "He was standing over me raving drunk at seven in the morning, with a barbecued pig nose, dripping hot sauce on my naked chest, burning me, and he was glowering at me, offering it to me for breakfast." The day got worse. Bloomfield followed Williams up a flight of stairs, where a very obese teenage girl sat at the top, unable to fit inside her apartment. "She was dipping spare ribs in an old mayonnaise jar, in mayonnaise that looked like Unguentine," Bloomfield said. "It had been curdled in the sun. I see this woman up there and she's doing this, and I say, 'Joe, I gotta leave.'"

Williams didn't want to leave. He was there trying to find a fiddle player named Jimmy Brown, who had recently cut a record with Williams titled *Back to the Country*. Michael and Big Joe began to disagree. "I had to leave," Bloomfield said. "I was slummed out. Joe wasn't about to leave, and we had a huge fight. I said, 'Man, I'm leaving you here in East St. Louis. I'm going back to Chicago.' Joe wouldn't let me leave, and he grabbed me by the arm, and I snatched my arm back, and I said, 'I'm leaving.' And he went downstairs carrying this tape recorder and his amplifier and his guitar, a real heavy amplifier and tape recorder, and he got in the car. And I said, 'We're going back to Chicago.' He said, 'No! We gonna visit my people! My people live here!' I said, 'OK, listen, get out of the car, because I'm going back to Chicago. You get out the car, man, you just get out of the car.'"

Big Joe refused to get out of the car, and they scuffled. Big Joe stabbed Michael's hand with his penknife, and Michael kicked Big Joe hard in the stomach. "And then we looked at each other and we both felt real bad," Bloomfield said. "It was like hitting my father or something, and he was real bad for getting so drunk and hurting me. He got out of the car, and the last thing I saw as we drove away was this old man walking down this dusty road with his guitar and his amplifier, just walking down the dusty road back toward East St. Louis."

Back in Chicago, the two men saw each other about three weeks later, as Bloomfield remembered. "And you know what he said to me, real embarrassed? You know, he used to get this real boyish, bashful look on his face. He said, 'We sure had us a time in St. Louis, didn't we, man?' I said, 'Yeah, man, we sure had us a time.'"

Maybe it was this experience that showed Michael once and for all that, good as he might be at playing the blues, he was still not part of its milieu, and by virtue of his upbringing never could be. As he told Dan McClosky, the trip had been a put-on from the beginning. The blues fans had asked Williams to help them find a couple of old-time artists, Walter Davis and Mary Johnson, and Williams had agreed, even though he had no idea where they were. All Big Joe wanted to do was visit his kin. Bloomfield said the experience was a classic example of "a gypsy good time," which means not getting what you came for—in this case, being literally taken for a ride. Maybe Bloomfield decided to stay in his place and work for the blues in any way he could as a white Jewish kid from the North Side. Whatever went on in his mind, the loathing in his voice as he described that pig's nose spoke volumes, and went far beyond simply not wanting to eat a pig snout.

———————

The Fickle Pickle was a nice place, but Big Joe Williams—and most of the young white musicians who worked with him—did better in a barroom milieu. In the early 1960s Old Town wasn't quite the honky-tonk it is today. "It was for real," Charlie Musselwhite told me. "Real artists lived there. It was a poor, run-down neighborhood. Now it's all touristy, but then, the tourists didn't know it existed."

On Wells Street in Old Town, there were two bars. One was the Blind Pig, the scene of Bob Koester's occasional blues shows. The rest of the time, a duet called Nick and Paul played there. "Nick" was Nick Gravenites on acoustic and electric guitar, and "Paul" was Paul Butter-field on harmonica. The other bar, Big John's, was just a neighborhood hangout that wasn't doing too well.

Michael, ever the hustler, decided that a little friendly competition might do everyone good, so, as Norman Dayron described it to me, he went to the bar's owner and said, "Listen, man, my name is Michael Bloomfield, and I'm a musician, and I can make this place work for you with music. I don't want no money or nothing. Just give me what you get at the door, and you can have the bar."

Bowled over, as so many people were when Michael came at them full bore, the owner agreed to book a group consisting of Michael, Big Joe Williams, and Charlie Musselwhite for a weekend. At his first show at Big John's, Michael played piano, an instrument he had begun fooling around with during his days at the Fickle Pickle. For the rest of his Big John's shows, he would switch back to guitar.

Big John's clicked almost from the beginning. Located at 1638 North Wells Street, the club held about 120 people, and it boasted a tiny stage, tables with red-checkered tablecloths, and two pool tables in the back. Norman Mayell, the drummer in Bloomfield's band at Big John's, remembered it as a place where "people used to sell Panama Red [marijuana] in little matchboxes for $5." Mayell had gone into Big John's one day, and he ran into Bloomfield and Big Joe Williams.

"I started talking to Michael about the blues, and he said, 'I got to start a band. If I get a band, I could play here,'" Mayell recalled. "I said, 'Well, I play the drums.' And he said, 'Well, get some. We'll get a band together quick.' It was just that casual." Mayell rented a set of Slingerland drums, and the group began their life as a quartet. Musselwhite joined them a few weeks later.

Big Joe, true to his wandering instincts, left after a short time to return to Mississippi, but Michael just brought in a bassist, and the band of young, white blues players kept playing. "The place just got more and more popular," said Musselwhite. "They had to tear down some walls just to get all the people in." Norman Dayron, who was still working toward his degree at the University of Chicago, recalls that Big John's changed from a neighborhood bar to "the preeminent rock 'n' roll hangout."

One thing was certain: the group that became the Big John's house band was in no way designed to take the spotlight off Bloomfield and Musselwhite. The band, which they called simply the Group, included not only Mayell, who would later join the Sopwith Camel, but also guitarist Michael Johnson, keyboardist Brian Friedman, and Sid Warner, a Texas-born musician who had played guitar with rhythm-and-blues saxophonist Big Jay McNeely in Los Angeles in the 1950s. Warner was an experienced musician who had played one of the earliest versions of the Telecaster guitar during his Los Angeles days, and he operated a jewelry shop in Old Town at the corner of North Sedgwick Street and North Avenue, near Bloomfield and Susan's apartment. Roy Ruby occasionally sat in on bass.

Meanwhile, Gravenites had returned to Chicago in early 1964 after spending five years shuttling between Chicago and San Francisco, with sojourns in Boston and New Jersey. He'd gone west in 1959, and he threw himself into the Bay Area coffeehouse scene. During the same period, Butterfield was spending a lot of time traveling to California with his girlfriend, whose family lived in Los Angeles, and he visited Gravenites on one of his California trips. They met up with a producer from Cambridge, Massachusetts, named Paul Rothchild at a Berkeley club, the Cabale Creamery, where they were playing a set. "He made an offer to Paul [Butterfield] to cut a record with him. Paul thought it was an interesting idea, but he explained that he didn't have a band together and wasn't ready in any way to record," Gravenites wrote in a

Blues Revue column. "Rothchild told him that whenever he was ready, he would record him."

Michael was also playing other types of gigs at this time, keeping up with rock 'n' roll, playing occasionally with Barry Goldberg in topless clubs, and even doing a little session work for Chess. This work with Chess was in part thanks to Norman Dayron, who, in order to get closer to the blues, had taken a janitor's gig at the studio. He parlayed this job into a loose sort of staff position.

While Bloomfield was booking shows at the Fickle Pickle and playing at Big John's during 1963 and 1964, he had gotten to know the Fickle Pickle's manager, Joel Harlib, a photographer who sold his work to Chicago advertising agencies. By all accounts he was a slick hustler who seemed to know every waitress, musician, and bouncer up and down Rush Street. He set up what appears to have been Bloomfield's first unaccompanied solo performance, at a Chicago club called Mother Blues, sometime in the summer of 1963. Bloomfield and Harlib got along famously, and they treated every day as an adventure: if they weren't trying to track down Howlin' Wolf's guitarist, Hubert Sumlin, they'd be out trying to score some marijuana. Harlib wasn't exactly Bloomfield's manager, since no one could really manage the eternally wired guitarist, but he believed in him.

It's unclear exactly what was on the audition tape that Harlib took to Columbia Records executive John Hammond in New York City in March 1964. Norman Dayron says it was a recording of Bloomfield playing guitar with a vocalist named Dean DeWolf, who had been performing at the Fickle Pickle with Horace Cathcart and other musicians. It could be that the tape that Hammond heard contained some of Dayron's recordings of Bloomfield as a solo guitarist, as well as a song performed by one of the Fickle Pickle singers. At any rate, Harlib had the courage to make a cold call on Hammond.

"Somebody brought me a record by a terrible vocalist, and I said, 'Who in God's name is the guitar in the background?'" Hammond told me. He had been the first to record Billie Holiday and Bob Dylan, as well as Charlie Christian and Count Basie, so he had helped to develop the careers of some of America's greatest singers and musicians. "And this person said, 'Oh, it's nobody you'd be interested in, just some sixteen-year-old kid named Mike Bloomfield.' And I took the plane to Chicago that night.

"I went to see him way the hell out to North Chicago, Winnetka, somewhere. I heard him that night with a not too terribly good group, and then, a couple of days later, I got him into a studio, and it was utter chaos. He had absolutely no idea how to run a session. And since rock is not my field, I was not the greatest help I could have been, but I got Epic to sign Mike right away."

It is one of life's little ironies that while Hammond was in Chicago, he took the opportunity to visit with an old jazz-hound friend, Rabbi Edgar Siskin. Siskin asked Hammond what he was up to, and when Hammond mentioned Michael Bloomfield, Siskin told him that he had presided at Michael's bar mitzvah, and that he'd never realized Michael's involvement with music was anything but a goof, that he'd settle down with the family business some day. Hammond, who had rebelled from a very wealthy family himself, felt a strong empathy with the kid who wouldn't sell restaurant supplies.

Although Hammond arranged for Bloomfield to come to New York's Columbia studio to record in early 1964, he still viewed it as a demo session. On the demo, you can hear Bloomfield tearing his way through a ragtime guitar instrumental, "Hammond's Rag," and he rips through "I'm a Country Boy" so fluidly and audaciously that bassist Bill Lee seems slightly flummoxed. At the end of "Hammond's Rag," the producer comes on the microphone. "I think we've exploited you enough," Hammond says. "I just want you to know I'm signing you." Bloomfield exclaims, "Oh," sounding like a boy who has just gotten exactly the book that he wanted for his birthday. However, Hammond suffered a heart attack in April after signing Bloomfield to Epic, and it wasn't until December 1964 that Hammond was able to return to Chicago to cut another demo session with Bloomfield and the Group.

Michael always maintained that if the Group's album had come out quickly enough, it would have beaten the Rolling Stones. Hammond was dry on the subject, and probably more realistic. "He could not have competed with the Rolling Stones," he told me. "He was no Mick Jagger, but he was a hell of a guitar player."

If Michael felt any disappointment or hurt because of his failure to head straight to the big time, he swallowed it. He did, after all, have a contract with Epic Records, which was nothing to sneer at, and a deal whereby they would help him place any songs he wrote. So he bided his time and worked at Big John's, and he noticed that Paul Butterfield, a musician he didn't particularly care for, was coming to sit in more and more. Despite their personal antipathy, they sounded good playing music together.

Crowds came as never before. Michael took stock of the situation and realized that he had built Big John's up from nothing, turned it into a scene, and focused so much attention on it that he was attracting the likes of John Hammond to Chicago. After playing at Big John's for about a year, he and Musselwhite asked the club's owner for a raise. They didn't get it, and they moved to a North Side club called Magoo's, which offered the band more money and a chance to play five nights a week.

Replacing them as the house band at Big John's was the Paul Butterfield Band, featuring Elvin Bishop along with drummer Sam Lay and bassist Jerome Arnold, who had cut their teeth playing with such Chicago blues giants as Howlin' Wolf. They would play at Big John's for the next eight months, serving as competitors for Bloomfield's Magoo's band. By the end of their stay, Big John's was attracting music fans from all over the Chicago area, thanks to the publicity from local radio personality Ray Nordstrand, who told his listeners who was going to appear there the following week during his late-night Saturday show on WFMT-FM, *Midnight Special.*

As Gravenites said about the scene at Big John's, "That was the beginning of the white blues explosion right there—'64 in Chicago. Paul [Butterfield] started playing there a couple nights a week, on the weekends, and I think he played there for eight or nine months straight. . . . And the joint would fill up every night." At Big John's, Bloomfield had taught white blues fans how to appreciate the contributions of such men as Big Joe Williams and Sunnyland Slim. Later on, when Paul Butterfield's band took over at Big John's, listeners got to hear how effectively white players like Butterfield and Bishop could interact with black musicians like Jerome Arnold and Sam Lay.

Bloomfield's six-piece group celebrated the new year at Magoo's by playing "Auld Lang Syne" as a blues shuffle, with vocalist Tracy Nelson from Madison, Wisconsin, sitting in. Nelson was dating Musselwhite at the time. It sounds like fun, but Bloomfield's future wasn't in the clubs, and times were tough. "It was dismal," remembered Gravenites, who often played in the Magoo's band. "We didn't make any money, nobody would show up, and we went from club to club." Playing at

Magoo's turned out to be a bad experience for the Group, as Mussel-white recalled. "The people that hung out there—I don't know how to explain them," he said. "Sort of a criminal type, you know, a lot of guys that were going in and out of the joint. . . . Mike, more than anybody, hated playing there. I think he hated the audiences. Because you're play-ing to these people, and they're thinking that they're hip and they're in, and you know they don't have a clue." In fact, Magoo's was operated by a pair of brothers named John and Terry McGovern, who ran any number of dubious enterprises out of the club. Sid Warner described Magoo's to David Dann as a "gangster hangout," and the McGoverns, who owned a series of small bars and clubs around Chicago, treated the band like low-level employees who could be moved from one location to another at short notice.

The Group didn't stay long enough for that to happen. Bloom-field and Musselwhite figured out that Warner was getting double-paid by the bar's owners, and they went by the club one night to check out the situation. There was Warner onstage, playing guitar and leading the band. They got back in their car, drove away, and never looked back.

6

THE BUTTERFIELD BAND

In January 1965 Paul Rothchild was relaxing at a party in Cambridge, Massachusetts, when he got a phone call from a friend of his named Fritz Richmond, who played bass in the house band at a Cambridge folk venue, Club 47. Rothchild was a former New England record salesman and label owner who had attracted the attention of New Jersey folk music company Prestige Records by recording and selling an album by a Harvard Square bluegrass group, Bill Keith and Jim Rooney and the Charles River Valley Boys. Rothchild took over Prestige's folk department, and by 1964 he had moved to Elektra Records, a pioneering folk label that issued records by Oscar Brand, Jean Ritchie, and Theodore Bikel. Rothchild got around—he had signed folkies Tom Rush, Geoff Muldaur, and Mitch Greenhill to Prestige, and he was on the board of directors for Club 47.

Around the same time, Joe Boyd was sitting at the Kettle of Fish club in New York, where recently rediscovered blues singer Son House was getting ready to go onstage. From Boston, Boyd was a blues and folk fan who had gone to work for concert promoter George Wein in 1964 after graduating from Harvard University, where he had presented a show by Lonnie Johnson, the great 1930s blues guitarist he'd found working as the doorman of a Philadelphia hotel. Like Roy Ruby and Michael Bloomfield, Boyd had seen the blues lifestyle up close: traveling with Sleepy John Estes and Hammie Nixon from Ithaca, New York, to Cambridge, Boyd had been obliged to supply them with quantities of bourbon whiskey, and the results had been predictable.

Hanging out in the Boston and Cambridge folk scene, Boyd had gotten to know Rothchild. As he sat in the Kettle of Fish, Boyd talked to Prestige Records producer Samuel Charters, who had written *The Country Blues*, a book Boyd had devoured with the appetite of a true believer. Boyd was spending a last night in New York before heading off to Chicago, where he planned to meet Muddy Waters to discuss the singer's participation in the Blues and Gospel Caravan, a package tour Wein had put together. He told Charters he was going to Chicago, and Charters said, "Well, there's a band there you have to hear. There's a band with white kids and black guys, led by a harmonica player named Paul Butterfield. You should make a point to hear them."

Boyd called Rothchild the next morning, and they agreed to meet in Chicago that evening. By the time Boyd arrived in Chicago, Rothchild had already caught a set by the Butterfield Band at Big John's. What he heard bowled him over. As he said later, "It was the same rush I'd had the first time I heard bluegrass." Rothchild sat in a booth with Butterfield and Elvin Bishop, talking to them about recording for Elektra. "[Butterfield] was going for it," Rothchild said. "He was totally, magnificently jive. Beautiful. I loved him. Chicago street hustler."

Meanwhile, Boyd had already heard of Bloomfield. In fact, he had briefly met the guitarist during a 1962 swing through Chicago with his brother, Warwick, and his Cambridge friend Geoff Muldaur. Hanging out at Koester's Jazz Record Mart, Boyd had run into Bloomfield, but he had other things on his mind that day.

"I was generally unimpressed with white blues players," Boyd says. "[Bloomfield] was OK, but I was in the middle of taping Bob Koester's 78 collection, including Tampa Red, Big Joe Williams, and Sleepy John Estes. What twenty-year-old kid noodling on a guitar could compete with that?" Back in Chicago a couple of years later, Boyd heard Bloomfield sit in on guitar with Muddy Waters one night at Pepper's.

Again, Boyd wasn't bowled over by Bloomfield's playing. "He sounded like a white guy sitting in with a proper South Side blues band," he says. "Good, but not flattered by comparisons with the company, and not as in-the-pocket rhythmically as a real blues player." Despite his reservations about Bloomfield's style, Boyd had liked Bloomfield's intensity, and he perceived a heroic quality in the way the guitarist carried himself onstage. Boyd suggested that Rothchild take a listen to Bloomfield, who was playing at a rowdy blues joint in Evanston,

Illinois, the next evening. Boyd, Rothchild, and Butterfield found their way to the club, where Butterfield joined Bloomfield onstage to jam on a Freddie King instrumental.

"Paul and I exchanged looks," Boyd wrote later. "This was the magic dialectic, Butterfield and Bloomfield. It sounded like a firm of accountants, but we were convinced it was the key to fame and fortune for the band and for us." After the set, Bloomfield sat down with Boyd and Rothchild, and the deal was made. Returning to New York to draw up the contracts, Rothchild arranged for Albert Grossman, who was then managing Bob Dylan, Peter, Paul and Mary, and other currently popular folk acts, to go to Chicago to catch one of the group's sets. The young hotshot guitarist would become a member of the Paul Butterfield Blues Band—and finally get his shot at the fame he deserved.

Bloomfield had already received some attention from the press. Pete Welding, who had helped Bloomfield and George Mitchell book acts for the Fickle Pickle, was a Philadelphia-born writer and blues scholar who moved to Chicago and founded his own blues label, Testament Records, in emulation of Bob Koester's Delmark. Welding reviewed several of the Group's Big John's performances in the December 1964 issue of *DownBeat* magazine. They were "rapidly evolving into one of the finest, fiercest-swinging rhythm-and-blues combinations in Chicago," Welding wrote.

Bloomfield wrote some music journalism of his own during this period. He interviewed Muddy Waters for *Rhythm and Blues* magazine in July 1964, and he and Welding talked to John Lee Hooker for the magazine later that year. Bloomfield mentioned Welding's forthcoming Testament release, *Rough and Ready*, in one of the columns he wrote for *Hootenanny* magazine that year. He and Joel Harlib were the magazine's "Our Men in Chicago," and they diligently covered the minutiae of the scene: "Ed Gordon of It's Here on North Sheridan Road is presenting Dean DeWolf, Ed McCurdy, Josh White Jr. and Mike Settle," they wrote.

Bloomfield always maintained that he had been scared of Butterfield during their early days together in Chicago, and it's not clear exactly why. For sure, they had very different personalities. In many ways, the adult Bloomfield remained what he had been at New Trier High School: a big, friendly, open-faced kid who was ready to talk about music or books—or, for that matter, the secrets of pawnbroking he had picked up while working for his grandfather—with anyone at any time. By contrast, Butterfield possessed what Norman Dayron characterized as a "hard Irish kind of cool," and he carried himself with a quiet assurance that could be off-putting to some people. Seven months older than Bloomfield, he had grown up in a middle-class family in Hyde Park. His father was a respected lawyer who was known for doing pro bono work on the South Side of Chicago, and his mother was a painter who taught art at the University of Chicago.

"The Paul Butterfield I knew was a sweet guy, a nice kid who liked to jive," Gravenites wrote in a *Blues Revue* column. "Paul was raised in a inter-racial neighborhood, had many black schoolmates and friends, and enjoyed rewarding relationships with many southside black and interracial families. There was no 'thug' in him, no gangster vibes, no savagery, no violence, no hatred that I could see." No doubt Butterfield affected an air of toughness and invulnerability when he sat in at South Side clubs, but that was part of the routine. It was a matter of manning up and making sure you didn't violate the social codes of the people around you.

At any rate, the Bloomfield and Butterfield partnership worked out fine onstage and in the recording studio, where it counted. "For a while [Paul] thought I was a turkey, and then, when he realized I was not a turkey, he gave me utter freedom to do what I wanted to do," Bloomfield said. "And it worked fine. The thing became a real good act, and I added a lot to the band. The band added a huge amount to me—it made me a pro, because Paul was a professional."

Getting ready to move to New York in early 1965 to begin recording with the Butterfield Band, Bloomfield and Susan put all of their things in storage in Chicago. She felt they'd be gone a while, and she was definitely looking for a change. "I was a bored kid," she told me. "I didn't like my life at home, and it was wonderful to go places and meet people. For me, even going to a supermarket in New York and seeing the way it was different from the ones in Chicago was a big treat." Susan and Michael rented a basement apartment in the heart of Greenwich Village, and the band started working on their debut album.

The first recordings the Paul Butterfield Band did weren't released at the time. "We recorded for a couple of days, and we didn't put that out," Butterfield recalled. "We decided we wanted to do something more with it. And Michael played keyboards." They cut a whole album's worth of material in early spring 1965, and one of the tracks, a pass at a song Gravenites had written called "Born in Chicago," showed up on an Elektra sampler label head Jac Holzman put together. That album, *Folksong '65*, sold an astounding two hundred thousand copies after it was released in September 1965, and "Born in Chicago" became an underground favorite with blues fans on campuses across America before the Butterfield Band's first album had even hit record stores. Five tracks from the first Butterfield sessions appeared on Elektra's 1966 *What's Shakin'* anthology album, a record that also featured recordings by the Lovin' Spoonful and a British pickup band called Eric Clapton and the Powerhouse, which Michael picked up on immediately.

At the beginning, Rothchild managed the Paul Butterfield Band, and they played the Village Gate in New York in early 1965. This may have been when keyboardist Mark Naftalin caught a set by the quartet. As he told writers Jan Mark Wolkin and Neal McGarity in 1995, "In January or February of 1965, Paul and Elvin showed up with the rhythm section they first recorded with, Jerome Arnold and Sam Lay, and they played at the Village Gate, I think it was. I went to hear them and it was some of the best music I'd ever heard in my life, a very pure form of Butterfield—it was all Butter."

Born in Minneapolis in 1944, Naftalin was the son of a professor and politician who was currently serving as mayor of that city, a position he would hold until 1969. Naftalin had picked up experience playing with a Minneapolis blues band called Johnny and the Galaxies before he began his freshman year at the University of Chicago in 1962. He had gotten to know Bloomfield, Butterfield, and Bishop at the school's twist parties, and he'd played piano with them during that period. After graduating from the University of Chicago with a music degree, Naftalin had moved to New York to study composition at the Mannes College of Music. A superb pianist and organist with a sure feel for rhythm-section dynamics, Naftalin would bring a sophisticated rhythm-and-blues sensibility to the Butterfield Band, and he was a subtle, slightly understated soloist in his own right.

Born in Glendale, California, in 1942, Elvin Bishop spent most of his childhood in Iowa before moving with his family to Tulsa, Oklahoma, in the early 1950s. After he won his scholarship to the University of Chicago as a National Merit Scholar finalist, he began attending the university in 1960. Bishop wasn't the extrovert musician Bloomfield was, and he knew it, but he had a knack for playing the kind of parts that kept the band swinging, and he could essay a terse, slangy guitar turn. The tracks Rothchild produced during the spring 1965 sessions caught the band's elegant approach to ensemble playing. As the release date of the record neared, though, Rothchild began to have reservations about the results, and at the last minute he decided that what he had cut didn't represent the band in its fullest sonic or musical capacity. He convinced Elektra label head Jac Holzman to delay the record until he had figured out how to capture what he had heard in Chicago. Holzman gulped hard, because Elektra had already pressed twenty-five thousand copies of the album, but he trusted Rothchild's instincts. Looking for a way to capture the band's power, Rothchild tried recording the band live for four nights at the Cafe au Go Go later that spring, but the results were no more promising than the studio sessions had been.

Heard today on the 1995 release *The Original Lost Elektra Sessions*, what would have been the first Paul Butterfield Blues Band album sounds like a classic collection of modern Chicago blues standards from the likes of Rice Miller (or Sonny Boy Williamson, as he called himself, after another virtuoso harmonica player who'd been murdered in 1948) and Little Walter, with a couple of originals by Butterfield and Bishop thrown in for good measure. The performances are concise, and Butterfield shows off his knack for phrasing. The true heir to Rice Miller and Little Walter, Butterfield acquits himself brilliantly throughout, while "Nut Popper #1" finds Bloomfield dashing off a furious solo that strains at all known limits of electric guitar playing in 1965.

While Rothchild tried to figure out how to record them, the Butterfield Band played as a quartet at New York's Village Gate in late February. Bloomfield may have sat in with them at the Village Gate, and it's likely Sam Lay and some of the other Butterfield band members, along with bassist Bill Lee, backed him at a March 1 demo session for Hammond at Columbia Studios. He was a member of the Butterfield Band, but the group hadn't quite worked out its identity, and Bloomfield continued to perform with Gravenites and Musselwhite at Big John's during April 1965.

No one seems to remember exactly when Albert Grossman began managing the Butterfield Band, but he probably didn't enter into a formal agreement with them until after their appearance at the Newport

Folk Festival in July. Paul Rothchild remembered calling Grossman about managing the band a month or two before the Newport Folk Festival was to start. Grossman agreed to check them out at Newport, and it's likely he viewed the Butterfield Band's Newport shows as their audition for the big time. As it turned out, they passed with flying colors.

It wasn't apparent at the time, but what the Butterfield Band was doing with blues was truly authentic, if that word can be used to describe the aesthetics of any music that has been removed from its original context. But what was the context of blues? For Bloomfield and Butterfield, blues meant more or less the same thing as it did to, say, Keith Richards, Brian Jones, and Mick Jagger of the Rolling Stones—it was a kind of music you could master, if you worked at it hard enough. Bloomfield and his compatriots learned blues in person from Muddy Waters and Howlin' Wolf, while Jagger and Richards learned it mostly from records, though there was a healthy English blues scene that sometimes featured American performers. The context was simply human endeavor and folly. In the hands of anyone smart or dedicated enough to master it, blues could illuminate corners of the world that had previously been dismissed as too crude, shocking, or benighted to bother with. Blues may not have been pop music, but it wasn't exactly folk music either.

In 1965 the folk world had grown to include a sizable percentage of the teenagers and college students in the United States, and it thrived on controversy. When the activists in this generation of kids took time off from arguing about disarmament and integration, they argued about folk music. What was folk, anyway? As did blues fans, folk listeners wanted authenticity, but how did you achieve it, and how did you know when you had witnessed it? You knew when you hadn't seen or heard it, because the antithesis of authenticity was commercialism. Thus, one could sneeringly put down an opponent's favorite performer by saying, "Yes, but that's awfully commercial." Appearing on the dreaded *Hootenanny* television show, which had blacklisted folk saint Pete Seeger, was a particularly heinous crime. (Even though Pete Seeger's own half-brother Mike performed on *Hootenanny*—with the help of Pete himself, who babysat Mike's kids so he could make an appearance with the New Lost City Ramblers.)

The folk music fan's bible, the *Rolling Stone* of its day, was a contentious publication called *Sing Out!* In its columns and letter pages the great issues of folkiedom raged. By 1965 it was apparent that the great authenticity debate had veered completely out of control. Why, some people dared to say that Chuck Berry, who was a rock 'n' roll performer, for heaven's sake, was a blues singer and guitarist! Since some of the readers had heard "Deep Feeling" and a couple of his other blues tunes—backed, incidentally, by the cream of Chicago's blues instrumentalists—Berry was reluctantly admitted to the pantheon by those who were willing to concede that Muddy Waters's electric blues was authentic. That was a tiny minority; the mighty Mud had met with a chilly reception when he brought his all-star electric Chicago band to the Newport Jazz Festival in 1960, and the next year he was obliged to play acoustic and solo. Admitting that Chuck Berry was authentic was only a short step to admitting that the Rolling Stones, who played songs by Chuck Berry and such hard-core blues artists as Slim Harpo and Willie Dixon, were okay, too.

So imagine the confusion when, in the spring of 1965, Bob Dylan, idol of thousands and spokesman for the more artistic, creative, and avant-garde wings of the folkie craze, a mysterious, brilliant figure who was looked up to by the best and the brightest, dared to release an album that was half rock 'n' roll! *Bringing It All Back Home* was, in retrospect, a pretty wimpy sort of rock 'n'roll. But it had electric instruments and, horrors, drums on it, and it sent shock waves through the world of folk, as could be seen from the letters column of *Sing Out!* and its feisty competitor, the *Little Sandy Review*, which was edited by a boyhood chum of Dylan's named Paul Nelson.

This was the *mishegas* that the Paul Butterfield Blues Band, outsiders from Chicago, would blunder into at the 1965 Newport Folk Festival, where Dylan would use members of the band to play his new songs in an electric, rock 'n' roll style that would create controversy among folk fans, blues fans, and rock fans. But first, Michael Bloomfield was about to help Dylan change the course of American popular music.

7

LIKE A ROLLING STONE

Back in 1962 Bloomfield had checked out Bob Dylan's first album, and he hadn't liked it. "I'd bought it, and I didn't think it was very hot," he told Tom Yates and Kate Hayes in 1981. About a year later, during his early Fickle Pickle days, Bloomfield went to hear Dylan at the Bear, a brand-new Chicago nightclub that Albert Grossman was bankrolling. Michael's friend Roy Ruby was working there, playing classical guitar in the evenings. Always a competitive guitarist, Bloomfield showed up at the Bear in April 1963 ready to spar with Dylan, but he came away a fan.

"To open it with a bang, they had Bob open it," Bloomfield told Yates and Hayes. "So I went down there in the afternoon, because a friend of mine worked there, and I wanted to meet him. Really, what I wanted to do was cut him, you know. I wanted to take my guitar, because I was a real good folk guitar player at that time, and I wanted to say, 'Boy, I read your liner notes and I heard your record, and God, I don't think you're saying anything.' He was such a sweet guy, and so charming, and just such a pleasant guy to be with, I spent the whole day jamming with him and singing old songs and whatnot. That night, I heard him perform, and I don't know what it was he had, and I don't know what you'd call it, but it was magic. I was enchanted. It knocked me out, even though it was not especially the kind of music I loved or anything, but he sang this song, 'The Walls of Red Wing,' about a boys' prison, and it moved me. Call it charisma, call it what you want, but he was incredibly appealing."

Evidently, the feeling was mutual, and they reconnected in June 1964 in New York while Bloomfield was there recording with blues-folk singer and harmonica player John Hammond Jr., the son of the executive who had recently signed Bloomfield to Epic. Dylan was there to listen to the band, which included drummer Levon Helm, guitarist Robbie Robertson, and bassist Jimmy Lewis. They were a Canadian rock combo called the Hawks, and they'd paid some of the same kind of dues backing singer Ronnie Hawkins in North American honky-tonks and dives that Bloomfield had in Chicago's rough blues clubs. Playing piano on the session, Bloomfield must have attended closely to Robertson's electric guitar style, which was a brilliant distillation of rockabilly and blues approaches.

In late spring of 1965 Dylan was in New York, ready to record his first all-electric album, and he picked up the phone and called Bloomfield, who was back in Chicago. "I don't know where he got my number," Michael told me. "But he said, 'I'm making a record. Do you want to play on it?' And I said sure, and flew to New York. I didn't even have a guitar case, just a Telecaster and a little overnight bag."

As Dylan remembered it, "We were back in New York, and I needed a guitar player on a session I was doing. I called him up, and he came in and recorded an album. At that time he was working in the Paul Butterfield Blues Band." Dylan met Bloomfield at the airport, and they began driving to Upstate New York, where Dylan had a hideaway in Woodstock. When they got there, they passed what Bloomfield later described as a "big, huge mansion with this old *kacker* sitting out front who looked vaguely familiar." Bloomfield asked Dylan who the man was, and Dylan said, "Oh, that's Albert [Grossman]."

Grossman hadn't yet begun managing the Butterfield Band at this point, but Bloomfield had run into him a few times in Chicago, and he already had a passing acquaintance with the music business impresario. Bloomfield always had a special feeling for Grossman—with his inscrutable mien and intimidating skills as a negotiator, Albert put him in mind of his father. Norman Dayron remembered a meeting between Bloomfield and Grossman at the Bear that had taken place a couple of years earlier. Bloomfield had gone to the club to see Brownie McGhee and Sonny Terry, and he took his guitar along, just in case he got the chance to sit in with them.

"He came into the Bear one night and brought his guitar with him, not in the case, even, just a guitar," Dayron said. "It was a Chicago winter, and Michael came in wearing really torn blue jeans and his bedroom slippers, and he went in there and said, 'I'm the world's greatest guitar player, and I'd like to get in for nothing and see Brownie and Sonny. Brownie is a personal friend of mine.' Albert was amazed, and he let him in."

Now, in 1965, Bloomfield and Dylan began to work on the new songs the latter had written. Dylan confronted Bloomfield with only one rule: "I don't want any of that B. B. King shit," he said. He wanted Bloomfield to emulate the sound of Byrds guitarist Jim McGuinn, who had added ringing Rickenbacker electric twelve-string parts to the band's 1965 versions of Dylan's "Mr. Tambourine Man," "Spanish Harlem Incident," and "All I Really Want to Do." Bloomfield sat listening to Dylan reel off song after song, trying to figure out guitar lines that weren't too bluesy to go along with them.

"I was in Dylan's house for about three days learning the songs," Michael told me. "I had no identification with the material at all. I mean, I had never heard music like this before. When the '60s came and Dick Clark started doing his whole thing, I stopped. By the time we cut the album in 1965 I was into the Beatles, and real into the Stones, but I had no professional session experience, and my ideas about what rock 'n' roll was were pretty unformed.

"It was real strange being with Dylan and his entourage. I'd never been around anyone famous, and I didn't even know how famous he really was. Dylan and Albert Grossman and this guy Bobby Neuwirth, they were beginning to get isolated. Dylan couldn't deal with people anymore, because he was too well known and people would mob him in the streets and shit. And all those people who used to be his buddies, he was getting way famouser than I think he ever thought he'd get—fast. They'd play these little mind-fuck games with everyone they came into contact with, and talked very put-downy to everyone. It was character armor, done in self-defense. I used to marvel at it.

"I remember once being in a room with Dylan and Phil Ochs and David Blue and these people, and they would play their songs and he'd say, 'Well, have you heard this?' and play 'It's All Over Now, Baby Blue' or something that, of course, they had heard, and they knew their stuff just wasn't as good. It was the end for them."

By every eyewitness account, Dylan's *Highway 61* sessions were some of the weirdest in recording history. To begin with, the musicians were mostly the top session men in New York, guys who cut hit rock 'n' roll records in their sleep. Only this time, they were at the whim of a young weirdo who wrote long, abstract songs that even he didn't seem to understand. Al Kooper, whose long string of songwriting credits included penning tunes for everyone from Gene Pitney to Gary Lewis and the Playboys, was to be the guitar player.

"The first time I met Michael was at the Dylan session for 'Like a Rolling Stone,'" Kooper remembered. "No one knew who he was. He was in the [Butterfield] band, but they had no records out. They weren't known outside of Chicago." Kooper was a professional who kept up with things. He had read an article about his fellow session musician in *Sing Out!* magazine, and he knew Bloomfield was reputed to be a hotshot guitarist.

Bloomfield walked into the studio with his Telecaster, which he carried slung over his shoulder. He didn't have a guitar case, and it was raining outside, so his instrument had gotten wet, just like his Schwinn bicycle used to when he left it in a heap on the sidewalk. As Kooper told me, "He just wiped it off with a towel, plugged it in, [and said] 'Let's go,' you know, that kind of thing. So he endeared himself to me right away, with that stunt."

"The session was very chaotic," Bloomfield told Tom Yates and Kate Hayes. "Bob had the vaguest sound. . . . I could probably have put a more formal rock 'n' roll sound to it, or at least my idea of one, but I was too intimidated by that company."

Michael elaborated on his feelings of confusion in his interview with me. "Bob would start singing the songs and we'd start fitting the music around him," he said. "There was no game plan! The day before, he was still writing the songs."

Bloomfield told me that he thought "Like a Rolling Stone" provided a template for a lot of future pop music. Dylan's song also connected with the rock 'n' roll that had come before it, as producer Phil Spector told Jann Wenner in 1969: "[Dylan's] favorite song is 'Like a Rolling Stone,' and it stands to reason because that's his grooviest song, as songs go," Spector said. "I can see why he gets the most satisfaction out of it, because rewriting 'La Bamba' chord changes is always a lot of fun, and any time you can make a Number One record and rewrite those kind of changes, it is very satisfying."

The sound was certainly unique, and it used a convention of contemporary gospel music by pitting Paul Griffin's piano against Kooper's organ. Kooper had switched from guitar to organ during the June 16 session that produced the master take of "Like a Rolling Stone," and he claimed that he was virtually inaudible until Dylan put the organ up in the mix. "That's how I became an organ player," Kooper told me.

With producer Tom Wilson at the helm, Dylan attempted to cut five songs, including "Like a Rolling Stone," on June 15, the first day of the sessions for the album that would become *Highway 61 Revisited*. One of the few black producers at a major record company in 1965, Wilson had graduated from Harvard University, and he'd produced records by avant-garde jazz artists such as Sun Ra, Cecil Taylor, and Donald Byrd in the late 1950s. Wilson had been recording Dylan since 1963, and he had added electric guitars to four previously recorded Dylan songs at a late 1964 session.

Without Kooper, who would come in on June 16 as Wilson's guest, the studio musicians tried to puzzle out "Like a Rolling Stone." Bloomfield acted as bandleader, and he struggled to find an appropriate guitar part for the song. "Like a Rolling Stone" isn't a complicated musical composition, as the many later, more conventional rearrangements of the song make clear. As Spector observed, it's built from the sturdiest of pop materials. "Like a Rolling Stone" is structurally similar to a blues song: the end of each verse allows space for an instrumental lick to comment on the lyrics, as in a Robert Johnson performance.

"Like a Rolling Stone" went beyond all previous essays into folk-rock. It made history as a pop record that pushed Beatles-era rock 'n' roll music into the experimental, long-form directions that would characterize the late 1960s. Wilson caught a remarkable performance, but it's likely that Bob Johnston, the Texas-born producer who stepped in to cut the rest of *Highway 61* after Columbia fired Wilson, fiddled with it after it had been laid down. "I may have gone in there and mixed that thing," Johnston later told writer Greil Marcus. "Wilson would fuck with [Dylan], 'Do this, we gotta do that, this didn't come out.' Everything was wild and scattered, open, until I settled down on it, but that's the way that was."

On the finished recording, which was caught in a single take on June 16, Bloomfield fills the song's spaces with licks that suggest both country and blues. "Like a Rolling Stone" has a groove, but it's an idiosyncratic one—the performance lurches and strains against itself, and the arrangement makes room for Kooper's simple organ lick, Dylan's harmonica,

Dylan's singing, Paul Griffin's ricky-tick piano embellishments, and Bloomfield's guitar. In the song's turnarounds—its transitions from verse to verse and verse to chorus—Bloomfield opens up the sound.

It's in those transitions that you can most clearly hear the country-folk-blues approach Bloomfield devised for "Like a Rolling Stone." Wilson and the Columbia engineers caught the round but slightly roughened sound of Bloomfield's Telecaster, and Bloomfield played in a style that sat ingeniously between McGuinn's and B. B. King's. If Bob Johnston may be the secret auteur of "Like a Rolling Stone," Bloomfield was the musical director, and he knew it all went back to the blues, no matter what.

It is characteristic of Bloomfield that not only did he pretend to forget the title of the album that assured him a place in the center of rock 'n' roll history, but he didn't even like *Highway 61 Revisited.* (Bloomfield also played on Dylan's "Positively 4th Street," cut with Johnston on July 29, and one wonders what he thought about that famous record.) Talking to Tom Yates and Kate Hayes about Dylan, he said, "*Highway 51*, is it called? See, there's a famous blues song called 'Highway 51,' where I'm sure Bob got the title *Highway 61*, and I get 'em mixed up sometimes. I don't think any of it's any good, except maybe 'Like a Rolling Stone' and 'Desolation Row.' But I was too scared. I could've played much hotter. I've heard everything from all those sessions on the bootleg albums, stuff that never came out on the album. I don't think any of it's that good."

Bloomfield didn't play on "Desolation Row," which featured Nashville session musician Charlie McCoy on acoustic guitar. Outtakes from the sessions included a first pass at "Can You Please Crawl out Your Window" that was accidentally released as "Positively 4th Street" on a mislabeled single, and a Dylan-Kooper-Bloomfield improvisation called "Killing Me Alive" that had lyrics that showed up in "Just Like Tom Thumb's Blues." Virtually all of this material has been released by now, of course.

8

DYLAN AND NEWPORT

The whole Chicago crew followed the Butterfield Band to Newport. And why not? The cream of America's folk talent would be there, and with a performer's pass or any type of backstage pass, you could hang out with them, shoot the breeze, pick up licks, and generally make the scene. It was shaping up to be a big moment for the band, and Paul was a little nervous about appearing there. His Chicago friends, including Nick Gravenites and Barry Goldberg, would act as a support group. As Nick Gravenites said later, "We all got in our cars and drove back east to Newport."

With the help of Bloomfield and his other hired guns, Dylan had turned "Like a Rolling Stone" into a pop record that you wanted to listen to over and over. Columbia had released the single on July 20, two days before the 1965 Newport Folk Festival was set to begin. At Newport with Dylan and the Butterfield Band, Bloomfield would apply his virtuoso guitar to some of Dylan's latest and most compelling songs, and the result was music that was both populist and musically advanced, a combination of qualities that folkie ideologues and purists had previously thought incompatible.

Bloomfield wasn't exactly a musical purist—he liked everything from George Jones and Jerry Lee Lewis to Cecil Taylor and Big Joe Williams. An intellectual who analyzed what he heard from a musicological stand-point, Bloomfield found country, soul, blues, and the Beatles completely compatible. He respected what the Newport board of directors was trying to do, but he had reservations about their intentions, and he thought there were better places to hear folk and blues music.

"For years, the Newport Folk Festival was a really good musical service," he told Tom Yates and Kate Hayes. "It brought a lot of real good music to the ears of a lot of people that may not have heard it, though it wasn't, in my opinion, the best folk festival that you could see. I think the University of Chicago probably had the best folk festivals that were going on in America at that time, but Newport was no slouch." Newport's board was composed of folk musicians and scholars—Alan Lomax, Theodore Bikel, Pete Seeger, Jean Ritchie, Ralph Rinzler, and Peter Yarrow.

Lomax was a musicologist and writer who had been championing the working-class aspects of blues and folk since the 1930s. He would present blues in a scholarly context at the 1965 Newport festival, while Peter Yarrow, of the bestselling commercial folk group Peter, Paul and Mary, would champion the work of such folk-pop songwriters as Gordon Lightfoot, Donovan, and Dylan himself. In fact, it was Yarrow who suggested to his fellow Newport board members that they extend an invitation to the Paul Butterfield Blues Band, to Lomax's displeasure. The Butterfield Band hadn't yet recorded their first album, and they were still almost completely unknown outside of Chicago. Lomax hadn't heard their music, but he was suspicious of them from the start, since they had been put on the program by Yarrow and Grossman, with the help of Elektra.

With Gravenites sitting in, the Butterfield Band made their Newport debut on Friday afternoon at Lomax's workshop on blues history, where they began their set with Little Walter's "Juke." They continued with "Look over Yonders Wall," a version of a 1945 song by Memphis pianist James Clark. Titled "Look on Yonder Wall," the song had been cut in 1961 by Elmore James. Lomax probably knew "Look over Yonders Wall" as well as the Butterfield Band did, but he gave them an offhand introduction that led to a now-legendary fight between him and Albert Grossman.

"He introduced us in this very scathing way—something to the effect that Newport has finally stooped so low as to bring this sort of act on the stage," Bloomfield told Tom Yates and Kate Hayes. Bloomfield observed how strenuously Albert Grossman came to the band's defense: "He said, 'Listen, man. How can you give these guys this kind of introduction? This is really out of line. You're a real prick to do this.' And they got into a fistfight, these two sort of elderly guys. I was screaming, 'Kick his ass, Albert! Just stomp him!'"

In fact, Lomax prefaced his introduction with a continuation of his lecture about the history of the blues, and he made it clear that he thought white people had no business playing it: "Us white cats always moved in, a little bit late, but tried to catch up," he said. Finally, he introduced the band. "I understand that this present combination has not only caught up but passed the test," Lomax said. "That's what I hear—I'm anxious to find out whether it's true or not. We have here tonight, highly recommended, already the king of Chicago, which is a big, uh, tribute: Paul Butterfield." He finished by saying, "Anyway, this is the *new* blues from Chicago," and then the band lit into "Juke."

The subsequent fight between Lomax and Grossman has become part of the lore of the 1965 Newport Folk Festival. Paul Rothchild, who was there on behalf of Elektra and was helping Joe Boyd and Yarrow run sound, had a similar recollection to Bloomfield's: Grossman asked Lomax, "What the fuck kind of a way is that to introduce a bunch of musicians? You should be ashamed of yourself." Lomax retorted, "Do you want a punch in the mouth?" and Grossman shot back, "I don't have to take that from a faggot like you!"

Both men were rotund, and they began feebly punching at each other and rolling on the ground. It was quite a spectacle. Blues songwriter Willie Dixon, a former Golden Gloves boxer, looked on with amusement. Documentary filmmaker Murray Lerner was at Newport that year with his crew, and they caught the scene for the 1967 film *Festival.* Contrary to the legend, it appears that the two men began fighting after the set was over, not during it—*Festival* clearly shows Grossman beaming away during the performance, without a scratch on him.

Although the Butterfield Band played their collective asses off, Gravenites thought they received "a mixed reception. It was just ingrained in the people in that audience, the years and years of controversy over whites playing blues. Not folk-style blues—*serious* blues." Geoff Muldaur thought they were superb, "the most important thing to happen at Newport in 1965," he later said. The reporter for the *Quincy Patriot Ledger* described the Butterfield Band as a "group half way between the Righteous Brothers and the Rolling Stones," and took note of the crowd's excited "writhing and shouting."

Years later, Michael was still angry about what had happened there. "When we came to Newport, we brought an electric band, and we played what to us was the music that was entirely indigenous to the neighborhood—to the city—that we grew up in," he told Tom Yates and Kate Hayes. "There was no doubt in my mind that this was folk music, absolutely. This was what I heard in the streets of my city, out of the windows. It was what the people listened to, and that's what folk art is to me, what people listen to."

In fact, neither the Newport board nor the folk fans who came to the festival were categorically opposed to the idea of electric instruments. John Lee Hooker had played an electric guitar at Newport in 1963, while Johnny Cash had appeared with guitarist Luther Perkins in 1964. At the 1965 festival, Lightnin' Hopkins would perform with an electric guitar. What some fans found confusing was the relationship between what was called folk and what was termed commercial pop music. Cash was a Nashville country star, but he was as much a folkie and song collector as Bloomfield or Pete Seeger, and such country songwriters as John D. Loudermilk, Billy Edd Wheeler, Dallas Frazier, Marijohn Wilkin, and Roger Miller were busy writing what amounted to modern folk tunes. Judy Henske's 1963 version of Wheeler's "High Flyin' Bird" had been a minor hit for Elektra, and Richie Havens would introduce Wheeler's tune to a new generation of folk-rock fans on his 1967 debut album for Verve Records.

Havens appeared at the 1965 festival as well, performing Dylan's "Maggie's Farm" at a songwriting workshop that also featured Gordon Lightfoot, Donovan, Ian and Sylvia Tyson, and Dylan. The folk scene was changing quickly, as Yarrow, who had put together the Contemporary Songs workshop, couldn't help but notice. New songwriters such as Ian Tyson, Dylan, Donovan, and Lightfoot were taking folk conventions and turning them to their own purposes, just as the Nashville tunesmiths were doing.

On Friday morning, Bloomfield hosted a blues workshop that included Mississippi John Hurt and Reverend Gary Davis. Geoff Muldaur, who had known Joe Boyd since they were teenagers together in Princeton, was aware of Bloomfield. Not many others were, though. Eric Von Schmidt noticed Bloomfield's name on the list of performers who would be participating in the workshop. "You ever heard of Mike Bloomfield?" Von Schmidt remembered asking Muldaur. "He said, 'Oh, he's a great guitar player.' That was all I knew."

The Butterfield Band played another set on Saturday afternoon at the Blues and Harmonica workshop, and it offered a taste of what was to come on Sunday night when members of the band would back Dylan on three of his new electric songs. Their amped-up performance drowned out the autoharps of Maybelle Carter and Mike Seeger, who were leading a folk workshop near them. The set started off with a shuffle titled "Elvin's Blues," which gave Bishop a chance to show off his chops. Bishop didn't take the kind of chances Bloomfield did during the band's three Newport performances, but he proved himself a perfectly credible soloist with a fine feel for blues classicism.

Bloomfield had looked on with pleasure at the fight between Lomax and Grossman, and he later zeroed in on the element of hypocrisy in the way folkies recast American music in their own image. Talking to Tom Yates and Kate Hayes, he remembered Lightnin' Hopkins's 1965 Newport appearance. "It was real weird, because it was such a scam: they had Lightnin' Hopkins there, who had played electric guitar for years and years, and who was sitting there with his processed hair and his pimp shades, and he had this slick mohair suit on, and I think he came out, man, in bare feet, with overalls," Bloomfield said. "I mean, he just acted like a farm boy." (At the Friday morning blues-guitar workshop, Bloomfield introduced Hopkins as "my favorite blues singer, the king of the blues.")

Lerner's film *Festival* also included some amazing performances by Son House, and juxtaposed interviews with him and with Bloomfield, who offered explanations of the blues aesthetic that were only superficially dissimilar. Drumming out a loose beat with his fingers, House improvised a talking blues: "You wants to see 'em, wonder where they at," he intoned. "You don't know whether to cut their throat or to cry again. That's the blues." Meanwhile, Bloomfield laid out his background as a child of affluence. "It's very strange, 'cause I'm not born to blues, you know," he said. "It's not in my blood; it's not in my roots, in my family. Man, I'm Jewish, you know. I've been Jewish for years."

House seemed to understand what was happening at Newport and in the folk music scene of 1965, as aficionados such as Bloomfield cut through class barriers to appreciate blues and the men and women who had created it. "But this old-time stuff, that was out before he come here," House said about Bloomfield. "And so, then when he see it, then that's new to him." As for Bloomfield, he appreciated what his associate Paul Butterfield was doing with the blues tradition. "You can quote me on this, man," Bloomfield said. "Butterfield's somethin' else. He feels it—he's in there, all the way. . . . There's no white bullshit with Butterfield. . . . If he was green, it wouldn't make any difference. If he was a planaria, a tuna fish sandwich, Butterfield would still be into the blues."

One of the landmarks of the Newport festival grounds has always been Nethercliffe, the large white common house where performers can go to tune, rest before or after a performance, and generally socialize and hang out. After the Butterfield Band left the stage of the Blues and Harmonica workshop on Saturday afternoon, Grossman called them all to Nethercliffe. "What they were doing was bringing various people that could play electric into the house," Gravenites recalled. "And Bloomfield was there, Dylan was over in the corner, and Michael knew all the chords and would audition these people. If they didn't know what to do, bam! he got somebody else. It was amazing. Bloomfield sitting there, auditioning each guy, showing everybody the arrangements, and Dylan would come over and clarify some chord or something. It was an historic moment, and Michael was its concertmaster."

Dylan had arrived at Newport Friday night, so he hadn't seen the Butterfield Band's performance that afternoon. He had played a workshop set on Saturday afternoon that had drawn over five thousand people. Talking to a *Time* magazine reporter on Saturday, Dylan had named his favorite bands of the moment: "For me right now, there are three groups: Butterfield, the Byrds, and the Sir Douglas Quintet." Barry Tashian, a rock 'n' roll guitarist and singer who was playing in a Boston band called the Remains, and who had recently played electric guitar with Richard and Mimi Fariña at a Cambridge radio station, recalled meeting Dylan as the pop star made a stop at a concession stand. "I said to him, 'Who's gonna be in your band tomorrow, Bob?'" Tashian said. "And he didn't know me, so he started puttin' me on. And he said, 'Oh, let's see—I've got Clark Terry on trumpet, Jack Teagarden on trombone.' I was just crushed at the time. I went, 'Uh huh,' and I kinda backed away, because I wasn't ready to laugh and say, 'Right.'"

Dylan probably got the idea to use the Butterfield Band musicians from Grossman, who told Dylan about the stir they'd caused at their

Friday performance. Lomax and the rest of the Newport board, minus Yarrow, had called an emergency meeting to discuss banning Grossman from the grounds, but George Wein refused. Grossman was managing Gordon Lightfoot, Ian and Sylvia, Odetta, the Fariñas, and Peter, Paul and Mary, not to mention Dylan, and Wein didn't want to alienate him. Meanwhile, Grossman had run into Al Kooper, who came to Newport every year, and he told Kooper that Dylan was looking for him. Kooper joined the Butterfield Band and Dylan's entourage on Saturday night at Nethercliffe to rehearse Dylan's material.

With Kooper on keyboards and Bloomfield serving as guitarist and bandleader, the group began working out the three Dylan songs they would perform the next night. Sam Lay had heard "Like a Rolling Stone" on the radio, but Jerome Arnold, who didn't know who Dylan was, found the song's changes hard to grasp. Goldberg was there, and he was eager to play, since he'd come to Newport hoping to sit in with the Butterfield Band but had been turned down by Rothchild, who wanted to keep the group a quintet. Meanwhile, Gravenites made himself comfortable in the big house. Writing in *Blues Revue* thirty years later, he remembered putting his feet up on one of the mansion's coffee tables, only to have them kicked off by Bob Neuwirth, one of Dylan's entourage.

The Butterfield Band had been scheduled to perform on Sunday afternoon at the New Folks showcase, but a rainstorm soaked the stage, and Peter Yarrow told the crowd that they would play a set that night, before Dylan was scheduled to go on.

There has been plenty written about that Sunday evening set at Newport. Some say there erupted a cacophony of booing that nearly deafened those not already deafened by the band. Others maintain that despite the disapproval writ large on the face of the Newport establishment, the majority of the crowd loved it. Dylan arrived for his sound check early that evening, and he wore a pop star's outfit: a pistachio-colored shirt with white polka dots.

One legend that has arisen out of Dylan's 1965 Newport set has to do with with how the music sounded to the audience. In the standard accounts of that night's performance, the Newport technicians were defeated by the demands of loud, electric music. However, Joe Boyd and Paul Rothchild had arrived at Newport a day early to check microphone levels and equalization. They knew how loudly Bloomfield and the Butterfield Band liked to play, and they were determined to make everything sound as clear as possible.

What made Dylan's electric set sonically problematic wasn't the ineptitude of the technicians. The Newport stage was raked—that is, it sloped toward the audience. There were no stage monitors in those days, and the PA speakers were set at the sides of the stage. Dylan's vocals came through the PA speakers, but there was no way to feed the electric instruments into the PA. Anyone sitting directly in front of the stage heard the amplified sound coming right at them, while Dylan's voice came only through the PA speakers. For many in the audience, it made for a bizarre listening experience.

The Butterfield Band hit the stage at eight o'clock Sunday night. They played a brilliant set that ended with "Born in Chicago," the song Gravenites had brought to the band. Sam Lay drove the performance with a display of tactful but powerful drum work that subtly pushed the beat with artfully placed sixteenth-note patterns. Bloomfield paced Butterfield during "Born in Chicago" with slurs and bent notes that often landed hard on the first beat of every measure without ever impeding the flow of the music. It was a summation of everything they had learned during their apprenticeships in Chicago.

"I thought Paul Rothchild did a good job with the sound," Joe Boyd remembers. Rothchild and Boyd marked each channel's levels on the soundboard with a fluorescent pen and checked the equalization dials above the faders. Boyd went back to the stage to look one last time at the microphone and amplifier positions, and signaled with his flashlight that everything was ready to go, and Peter Yarrow got ready to introduce Dylan and his band.

Bloomfield plugged his 1964 Telecaster into an Epiphone Futura amp and checked his tuning, and Yarrow began his introduction, which was interrupted by the cheers and howls of the audience. "Ladies and gentlemen, the person that's gonna come up now has a limited amount of time," he said. "His name is Bob *Dylan!*"

What Bloomfield played in the next five minutes would mark a turning point in the history of electric guitar. His performance on "Maggie's Farm" was a radical move, but it didn't come out of nowhere, though he played louder than just about any electric guitarist before him. With Lay, Arnold, Kooper, and Goldberg providing a rough groove, Bloomfield played variations on a simple riff that harked back to Elmore

James's 1961 song "Stranger Blues," itself a reworking of the Mississippi Delta blues standard, "Rollin' and Tumblin'."

During "Maggie's Farm," Bloomfield becomes Dylan's second voice. He sits so hard on top of the beat that it screams, and what he plays amounts to a sardonic running commentary on Dylan's song. Bloomfield approaches atonality in a couple of places, but his playing on "Maggie's Farm" sits squarely within the blues tradition. It's not hard to understand why some people in the audience were confused, because what Bloomfield gave them on the evening of July 25, 1965, was the future of rock guitar.

Eric Von Schmidt remembered Bloomfield's performance as a deliberate act of provocation. "It was obvious that Bloomfield was out to kill," he said later. "He had his guitar turned up as loud as he could possibly turn it up, and he was playing as many notes as he could possibly play. I thought it was terrible. . . . I admire his music, but at the moment he was just a note machine." Von Schmidt almost got the point: Bloomfield did play a lot of notes, but they were the right ones.

"We backed up Bob Dylan, who had a hit single with 'Like a Rolling Stone' at that time," Bloomfield told Tom Yates and Kate Hayes. "I thought he'd be well received. The guy's got a hit, there's all these people there who obviously love him, they probably came more to see Bob Dylan more than anybody else in the whole festival. I mean, they booed him."

When you study Lerner's *Festival*, you hear booing combined with a loud, collective murmur—the sound of an audience who has heard something they can't quite describe. As Peter Yarrow recalls, the Newport audience was composed of genteel people. The legend of Newport says that everyone hated what Dylan and his electric band played that night, but that's not true, either. "It was Godawful loud," Maria Muldaur remembered. "To me it was exciting . . . but lots of people just freaked out."

Dylan and the band got through "Like a Rolling Stone" and a new song called "Phantom Engineer," which would show up on *Highway 61 Revisited* as "It Takes a Lot to Laugh, It Takes a Train to Cry." Al Kooper, who thought some of the crowd booed Dylan because of the brevity of the set and not because of its content, remembered that Arnold and Lay got the beat turned around during "Phantom

Engineer." As he said later, "I thought it was a dreadful performance, myself. I didn't think it was historic."

Talking about the 1965 Newport Folk Festival fifty years later, Peter Yarrow remembers Dylan's set as an experiment that had gone wrong. "The only song that worked at all was 'Maggie's Farm,'" he says. "I was mixing it at the time, so I know what it sounded like. It sounded horrible. There was so much leakage that it was ridiculous."

In Yarrow's estimation, the controversy over Dylan going electric had everything to do with Dylan's intentions, not his use of amplified guitars. "Looked at in retrospect, why would it be OK for the blues singers to have amplification?" he asks. "Well, it was OK because that was part of the way they performed anyhow. So where do you draw the line? The point was, it wasn't a line. It was the spirit with which something was shared."

Backstage after it was over, Pete Seeger was livid. Dylan went out and played "It's All Over Now, Baby Blue," and "Mr. Tambourine Man," accompanying himself on acoustic guitar, but the deed was done. The final part of the Dylan-at-Newport legend is that Seeger threatened to cut the cables to the PA with an ax. This may be true. Boyd thinks that the story of Seeger and the avenging ax started because Seeger had used an ax in a performance with the Texas Work Song Group, an ensemble who played at Newport that year. They performed one song while swinging axes at a tree stump. Other observers have pointed to the fact that Yarrow referred to Dylan's guitar as "his ax" before Dylan came back out to perform his two acoustic numbers. Paul Rothchild claimed to have seen Seeger carrying an ax, while Theodore Bikel remembered Seeger saying, "I feel like going out there and smashing that fucking guitar" as the band rocked out. Seeger finally retreated to a car parked on the grounds, where it was quiet. As George Wein recalled it, Seeger said, "That noise is terrible! Make it stop." Wein replied, "Pete, it's too late. There's nothing we can do."

9

BUTTER DAYS

The Butterfield Band was energized by their Newport experience, and they loaded their equipment into their van themselves, since roadies were unknown in those days. They knew they had some work to do in the studio in New York. As soon as they had caught their collective breath, they prepared to cut the album that would be called *The Paul Butterfield Blues Band*.

Bloomfield rejoined Bob Dylan and producer Bob Johnston in New York on July 29 to cut more tracks for Dylan's new album. The band included organist Al Kooper and drummer Bobby Gregg, and they cut "Tombstone Blues," a tune that added and subtracted measures in the manner of the old, eccentric Delta blues artists Bloomfield and Butterfield had studied in Chicago. Bloomfield played a beautiful obbligato on the song, complete with slurs and bends that reinforced a Dylan lyric that mentioned Ma Rainey, Cecil B. DeMille, and Galileo. The sessions for *Highway 61 Revisited* ran through early August.

The *Highway 61* sessions over, Michael was approached by Albert Grossman. Dylan wanted Bloomfield in his touring band, and Butterfield wanted him, too. Harvey Brooks, who played bass on some of the *Highway 61* sessions and would go on to perform in Dylan's road group, remembered how Bloomfield weighed his options. "Dylan had some gigs coming up—we were going to do Forest Hills [New York] and the Hollywood Bowl," Brooks said. "But Michael was going to stay with Butterfield, because he felt that was his obligation and that's what he should do. . . . He said we'd go on and be stars and everything, but he was going to play the blues."

As Bloomfield told me, "With Bob, I'd have no identity. I didn't even know that. All I knew was that I didn't understand what was happening. At the same time, I was also offered a gig to be the guitar player on [the TV variety show] *Shindig!* Jimmy Burton took it. I didn't want to do that either. The producer of the show was a guy named Jack Good, who'd come to Chicago, and he was an Englishman and a blackophile and really dug hanging out at blues bars with me. But I couldn't imagine going to Hollywood and doing that thing, either. So I told Albert, 'Man, I'm a bluesman. I'll go with Butterfield.' And I played with Butter and didn't play with Dylan, and we were cookin'. We wailed from then on."

The Butterfield Band had played New York's Cafe au Go Go two days after the Newport festival ended, and they performed at a series of dates in Massachusetts in early August. They settled in for a three-night run at Cambridge's Club 47, which had recently moved to a new location on Palmer Street. It was a well-appointed space with stone and brick walls and oak tables with slatted wooden chairs. Club 47's manager, Jim Rooney, had served on the board of directors for the Newport Folk Festival. As Rooney later wrote, "The sound in that small room was unlike anything we had heard before. We were charging $1 at the door and were paying the band $100 per night."

They continued to play at the Cafe au Go Go in late August and early September, and Bloomfield did session work with Peter, Paul and Mary, Judy Collins, and Chuck Berry during this time. Meanwhile, Mark Naftalin, who had attended the Butterfield Band's January performance at the Village Gate, sat in with them on piano at one of their Cafe au Go Go shows. "I had spent that summer trying to get involved with professional music," Naftalin told Jan Mark Wolkin and Neal McGarity. "I had taught myself Fender bass and I was trying to get myself into a band as a bass player because I didn't see much of a market for keyboard players—it was the Beatles era—and I got a couple of gigs that way."

On September 8 Naftalin went to the Butterfield Band's session at Mastertone Recording Studios at 130 West Forty-Second Street. "I dropped by the session, hoping for a chance to sit in on organ, which was the only keyboard on the scene," Naftalin remembered later. "Someone, probably Paul Rothchild, said that they might try organ later in the session. I was too impatient to hang around. I went home and came back the next day, sometime in the mid-to-late afternoon. On this occasion Elvin was late for the session. This was four-track recording, so they put me on his channel, and we played an instrumental."

The track ended up on *The Paul Butterfield Blues Band* album as "Thank You Mr. Poobah." Naftalin had never played Hammond organ before, but he acquitted himself well enough that Rothchild and the band invited him to stay for the rest of the nine-hour session. As Naftalin remembered, "Sometime during the session Butterfield asked me if I would join the band and go on the road with them to Philadelphia that weekend. This was just days before I might have gone back to school, because nothing had been happening. So I wound up playing on eight of the eleven selections on that album, playing Hammond organ. Hammond wasn't an instrument I knew much about, so if it sounds like I had sort of an unimaginative approach to it, that's why."

Naftalin is being overly self-deprecating. When *The Paul Butterfield Blues Band* hit the record stores in October 1965, the last thing people were worried about was his approach to the organ. The very opening lines of the record knocked listeners for a loop from which they would not recover until the album ended. Nick Gravenites's lyrics for "Born in Chicago" went to the core of the toughness Bloomfield had sought since adolescence, and spoke to thousands of those who had had the urban experience or wanted it in words of realism and caution: "I was born in Chicago / In 19 and 41 / My father told me / 'Son, you had better get a gun.'" In every way, "Born in Chicago" was a brilliant updating of the Chicago blues tradition, and it ended with this line: "Things just don't seem the same."

All of this was delivered against a hard electric background totally unlike anything the folk or the rock 'n' roll audience had ever heard. It was a shocker. It even had a boxed reminder on the back cover that read, "We suggest that you play this record at the highest possible volume in order to fully appreciate the sound of the Paul Butterfield Blues Band." Pete Welding's liner notes placed the record into a modern context: "Putting aside for the moment Butterfield's long intimacy with the culture that produced the music that he performs so brilliantly and his equally long apprenticeship in the style, it is apparent that the musical idiom itself is much less bound up in a maze of socio-cultural factors than is the country blues of another time and place." Elektra released the album's "Mellow Down Easy" and "I Got My Mojo Working" on a single in October. *The Paul Butterfield Blues Band* went only to Number 123 on the *Billboard* chart, but its influence far exceeded its sales.

The album was a good balance of original material by Butterfield, Bloomfield, and friends, and blues classics by Little Walter, Muddy Waters, Sonny Boy Williamson, and Willie Dixon. True, the Rolling Stones had recorded these people's music before, but it hadn't sounded like this. Butterfield's harmonica had the expressiveness of a saxophone, Lay and Arnold worked as if their lives depended on it, and over it all was the swooping, ecstatic guitar of Michael Bloomfield, who, it was noted, appeared "courtesy of Columbia Records."

The response was phenomenal, if not in sales then in the controversy it engendered in the press and among musicians. Julius Lester, a respected black journalist of the time who played folk music on the side, attacked the record savagely. Lester's review appeared in the June 1966 issue of a small, short-lived jazz magazine called *Sounds & Fury*, which had begun publication a year before. Lester had written a book titled *The Folksinger's Guide to the 12-String Guitar as Played by Leadbelly* with Pete Seeger, and he was critical of white blues musicians. "Despite reports to the contrary, Paul Butterfield sounds like a young white boy trying to play and sing Negro music," Lester wrote. "I wonder if these same people would try to become cantors as readily as they attempt the blues."

Essentially, Lester was accusing the Butterfield Band of stealing music that didn't belong to them—though he knew that the group contained two black musicians, Sam Lay and Jerome Arnold. "I hope one day the Butterfields will realize that you can't walk into another man's house and cook the meal that he would cook on *his* stove," he wrote. "If you try it, the man might not like it." Lester's accusations infuriated Bloomfield. "He really put it down, and he said it was just a watered-down version of the blues," Bloomfield told Dan McClosky. "I met him in New York, and I made a point of meeting him, saying, 'Hey, man, listen, you don't know how many gigs I've played with black cats. You know, how many cats have took me to be their protegés. But you know, he's right—it was a cultural ripoff."

But given the fact that Paul Butterfield, Michael Bloomfield, and Elvin Bishop had been welcomed by black musicians at their Chicago houses and clubs, Lester's charge made no sense. The history of rock 'n' roll up to that point had been full of collaborations between white and black musicians, and those collaborations produced great music despite the racism and oppression blacks had found in cities such as Memphis, Los Angeles, and Chicago. Lay and Arnold had taken the Butterfield gig partly for the money—as Lay remembered later, "Myself and Jerome Arnold left [Howlin'] Wolf's band together to go work for Butterfield. We was looking for the money part of it." What could be more American than that?

Lester's review prompted a long response from *Sounds & Fury*'s editor, Ralph Berton, in which Berton cited the example of Cab Calloway, who had done a cantor routine onstage in the 1930s that Jewish audiences relished. And, Berton said, Louis Armstrong had played with white trombonist and singer Jack Teagarden for years.

For the first time in the history of popular music, the white kids who had appropriated a black form were actively promoting the black artists whose music they played. Welding bent over backward to say that in the liner notes: "So individual and fully assimilated is his approach that, listening to him sing and play, the question of his aping Negro style or specific Negro artists never arises," he wrote about Butterfield. The originators were named and given credit for their music right where anybody could see them. And at the time, all of the classic Chess albums Little Walter and Muddy Waters had made were available for any of the fans who wanted to go and buy them. A lot of us did just that, and discovered for ourselves the dark sensuality of Waters's music, the astonishing harmonica styles of Little Walter and Sonny Boy Williamson, and the bawdy good times of Howlin' Wolf.

There were no radio stations to play this music when it appeared, no way for much of its intended audience to check it out, but slowly the word spread. The Butterfield album became a symbol, among folkies, of having crossed a Rubicon that said, *I accept America's music as it is, not as it is interpreted for me.* Michael Bloomfield became the name on everybody's lips. How did he play guitar like that? We waited for the band to tour.

———————

In retrospect, Michael made the right decision to go with the Butterfield Band. It must not have seemed like it at the time. Bob Dylan was selling albums hand over fist, while the Butterfield Band got a lot of good words in the rock press, such as it was at the time, mostly in *Hit*

Parader, whose Jim Delehant ran a series of 1967 articles titled "Mike Bloomfield Puts Down Everything." *Crawdaddy* reviewed the band's first Elektra single in early 1966, and *Variety* reviewed one of their Chicago performances in its June 1966 issue. But their album wasn't exactly setting the charts on fire. Bob Dylan was touring the world and staying in first-class hotels, drawing first-class hangers-on, while the Butterfield Band traveled in a Ford Econoline van and set up their equipment themselves.

Still, *The Paul Butterfield Blues Band* got through to fans and musicians alike. The band made music that was tough but accessible, and "Born in Chicago" laid out the blues ethos in a way that any garage-band musician or aspiring blues guitarist could relate to. Fritz Richmond, who had been present when Rothchild was mixing the record at Mastertone Recording Studios in New York, was on the road with the Kweskin Jug Band in late 1965, just after the record hit stores. They couldn't afford to stay in hotels, so they depended upon the kindness of their friends when they hit a new town.

"The way we would get those parties going was to play records," Richmond remembered. "We would carry around the records that were very good to serve this purpose, and I carried the Butterfield album. That was worth about two bottles of whiskey, as far as getting a party going. That album and the Junior Walker *Shotgun* album were wonderful for that."

The Butterfield Band was on the road almost constantly in the early days. "We had an apartment in the Village, at 10 Christopher Street, a basement apartment we never lived in," Susan told me. "We were on the road pretty much constantly until almost '67." When Susan said "we," that's just what she meant—she and Michael, and usually Michael's dog, a big mutt named Harry, would drive in their own car along with the van.

Life on the road, too, was different than it is today. "It was right at the point before they started getting crazy with the money and before it got into that whole superstar thing," Butterfield told me. "We were out there, very honestly, just working hard playing. We were very into the music, not so much into the Hollywood of it all. I think that protected us in a certain way, that naïveté or something," Certainly doing all your own equipment work and driving your own van to play for $1,500 to $2,000 a night would tend to shrink a swelled head.

Still, the band had some of the typical rock-band problems. Bloomfield remembered Butterfield as a "despot, as far as the money was concerned," and Sam Lay also recalled how Butterfield tried to take the lion's share of the proceeds in the group's early days. "The first few jobs we played after we recorded, Butterfield gave us a little money," Lay said. "Bloomfield didn't like that, and he raised all kinds of hell. Butterfield came back the same night after Bloomfield raised so much hell about it, and he paid us more than double."

Michael's best friend on the road, besides Susan, was Mark Naftalin. In terms of the group dynamic, this was probably a good thing, since Naftalin was the outsider in the band. After the group played at the Philadelphia Folk Festival on September 11, they returned to Chicago to begin a six-week run at Big John's. Naftalin and Bloomfield would walk along Wells Street together, smoking joints. Deeply introverted, extremely reticent, and highly intelligent, Naftalin had a dry sense of humor. He didn't get along well with Butterfield at all, although Paul insists that he looked up to him and to Bloomfield. "To me the band was a warm family, and I felt altogether accepted, though sometimes musically inadequate," Naftalin said later. "I retain a vivid memory of Paul looking at me over his harp with such an intense expression of what I thought was disapproval that I later sat on the curb and shed private tears. I think he was trying to get me to play right, and God knows I was trying."

"None of us were really close," Susan told me. "Michael was often the peacemaker, although there weren't too many fusses. We were separate—so separate that I wasn't aware the whole time that Elvin hated Michael's guts. When we'd stay at a place, Mark and Michael and I would go for dinner. Paul usually had a girlfriend and went with her, and Elvin went somewhere by himself."

Elvin Bishop was definitely not happy with things. "Elvin had a very hard time, especially since Michael was a better guitar player," Butterfield told me. "Elvin was pretty much like the second guitar player, and Michael played most of the leads, and for good reason. So there was a rivalry on Elvin's part, if not on Michael's. Elvin worked hard, but you could feel it, the jealousy. I think that's why he was a very introverted guy, and now he's very extroverted, outspoken. I think he went the other way with it, overcompensated from being so subdued for so long."

And while Susan was having the time of her life, Michael was making a discovery that would stay with him from then on. He hated touring. Hated it. Eternally wired, he had suffered from insomnia for years. It would keep him up for days, and although he was enough of a pro to keep it from interfering with his playing, he didn't like it at all. Still, there was nothing he could do about it. The Butterfield Band was a draw, an attraction, and they spent as much time as they could touring a circuit that started on the East Coast, hit Detroit and Chicago, and then went to the West Coast.

Something else was brewing in the band, and it would exert a tremendous influence on the musicians who would hear the Butterfield Band's West Coast shows in 1966. During the group's six-week run at Boston's Unicorn club in late November, Bloomfield and Naftalin were given two sugar cubes of LSD. "On one of our nights off, we took it," Naftalin remembered. "Early in the trip we ventured onto the wintry street, without a destination—without, in fact, the ability to conceive a destination. . . . Around daybreak Mike joined me in the kitchen, and we tried to keep things going by smoking some joints. This was when he told me that he had had a revelation and that he now understood how Indian music worked. On our next gigs, while we were still in Boston, we began performing the improvisation that we called 'The Raga' for a while, until it was given a name, 'East-West.'"

People had talked about Indian music before that epic piece, and words like "raga-rock" got tossed around whenever the Beatles' "Norwegian Wood" or the Kinks' "See My Friends" came on the stereo, but this was some serious music.

Michael described it perfectly to Tom Yates and Kate Hayes. "'East-West' was such a radical departure melodically, structurally, and chordally from the rock 'n' roll leads and licks that were being played at that time," he said. "It was a long, long series of solos using scales that just had not been played by rock 'n' roll guitar players. It broke a lot of new ground, gave you a lot of new ways to play in a rather simple mode. I was playing scales and things that no other guitar player had ever thought of. But believe me, I knew they were not my scales. They were things I'd heard on John Coltrane records and guys that played a lot of modal music. Pre–'East-West' I'd been listening to a lot of Coltrane and Ravi Shankar and guys who played modal music. The idea was not to see how far you could go harmonically but to see how far you could go melodically or modally. The other things on the *East-West* album, other than 'Work Song' and 'East-West,' were just sort of typical guitar leads that to me isn't as good as the stuff that I did on the album before that, the blues stuff that was on there. But I think those two tunes certainly broke a lot of new ground for other guitar players."

As the band began to work out what would become "East-West," Sam Lay fell ill. He had the habit of going out into the Boston winter chill directly from their Unicorn shows, and he developed pleural effusion, a serious lung condition. Lay played his last date with the Butterfield Band on November 27 at New York's Town Hall. With Lay recovering in Chicago's Cook County Hospital, Paul Butterfield hired Chicago drummer Billy Warren to take his place. Warren joined them for their show at Detroit's Chess Mate Gallery a few weeks later, but Butterfield decided his style wasn't right for them.

Butterfield, Bishop, and Bloomfield had sat in with Billy Davenport in 1964 and 1965 at shows around Chicago. Davenport was born in Chicago in 1931, and he began his career as a jazz drummer influenced by Gene Krupa and Big Sid Catlett before he switched to blues in the mid-1950s. Before he joined the Butterfield Band, Davenport had played with Junior Wells, Otis Rush, Fenton Robinson, and Magic Sam in Chicago. Bloomfield and Butterfield got Davenport on the phone the Sunday after they had finished their Detroit show and convinced him that he was making a smart move, and Davenport traveled to Detroit from Chicago that night with eleven dollars in his pocket.

"When I first started I was all on edge because it was the first time, you know, that I had ever played with a mixed band, for one thing, and I didn't really know how it would work out at all," Davenport told *Crawdaddy* magazine's Paul Williams in 1966. "And what it is, well, it worked out wonderful for me, I mean everybody respects me and I respect them. And what they got is mine if I need it and everything." A well-trained, versatile musician, Davenport would play a major part in developing "East-West" and the new material the band created in the next six months.

Davenport flew with the Butterfield Band to Los Angeles on New Year's Day 1966. Their first California engagement was opening for the Byrds at the Trip, a club next door to the Playboy building, at 8572 Sunset Boulevard. They played the Trip through the end of January and moved to the Whisky a Go Go in early February. By this time they had developed "East-West" more fully, as live performances from the period document. In 1996 Mark Naftalin released three performances from 1966 and 1967 on a collection titled *East-West Live*. On their twelve-and-a-half-minute rendition of the tune recorded at the Whisky a Go Go in February 1966, the band locks into the song's syncopated two-bar riff while Bloomfield plays an extended solo that straddles the line between blues and raga. Davenport and bassist Jerome Arnold switch to a straight four-four beat, and Butterfield plays a harmonica solo that manages to be bluesy without breaking the mood of the song. It's a remarkable performance that clearly anticipates the later work of the Grateful Dead and the Allman Brothers.

The Butterfield Band's 1966 shows in Los Angeles and San Francisco would turn the heads of the California rock musicians. "I remember I moved out here at the beginning of the hippie boom," Nick Gravenites told me. "None of the shows [concert promoter] Bill Graham put on were really serious until the Butterfield Band showed up, because they were the hotshots from the East, people who were already accomplished electric musicians. Most of the hippie bands that were playing in this area were the result of a lot of acid and not too much expertise. So when the Butterfield Band came, it became real evident that these people were just children, learning how to twang. The Butterfield guys had been playing this shit for years on records and stuff, and they could really play it. They influenced many musicians. It showed them the way—here's what's happening, here's what's possible. Work at it, apply your musicianship, and practice, and you can do this."

During this period, Bloomfield also incorporated a fire-eating act into the band's sets. Naftalin remembered Bloomfield showing off his kit, which included a wand, rags, and white gas. "He said it was easy," Naftalin remembered Bloomfield telling him. "'All you have to do is keep your lips wet and make sure you keep breathing out.'"

The band's San Francisco shows also caught the ears of a young Mexican-born guitarist named Carlos Santana, who had cut his teeth playing the music of B. B. King, Chuck Berry, and Little Richard in rough-and-tumble Tijuana clubs. After moving to San Francisco in 1962, Santana had started to attend shows at the Fillmore Auditorium, a rock venue that promoter Bill Graham had opened in late 1965.

"We all used to wait for [Bloomfield] to take his solos," Santana remembered. "As much as we loved Paul Butterfield and Elvin, all of us were always anticipating, 'What is Michael going to do, man?' Just the way he put his finger on it—you get a chill and it gets you excited, you know." Country Joe McDonald had a similar experience when he saw the band at the Fillmore in April. "Michael was playing a Telecaster, which I'd never seen anybody play before. He used it like a prop. He'd knocked the chrome plate off the bottom, where the strings are from the bridge, and it was very impressive."

"East-West" in particular was a remarkable piece of music. Over thirteen minutes long in the version that they recorded for the *East-West* album with engineer Ron Malo at Chess Studios that summer, it wasn't anything that would startle a jazz fan, as Michael said, but to rock ears it was an amazing piece that kept unfolding until it reached a throbbing climax, a perfect soundtrack to the times. And their version of Cannonball Adderley's "Work Song" was the same thing, only funkier. It was all improvisation except for the melody, with the band stretching out to nearly eight minutes. This was unprecedented in rock 'n' roll in August 1966, when the record came out.

Aspects of "East-West" can be traced back even further than the band's LSD-inspired experiments with Indian music in Boston. The two-bar riff that begins the song came from a Gravenites tune called "It's About Time" that he and Bloomfield had been playing since 1964. Another element of "East-West" was derived from Latin music and from the moves of the shake dancers the band often played for in Chicago clubs, as Elvin Bishop explains. "The bass player in the Butterfield Band, Jerome Arnold, didn't play jazz and he didn't know anything about Indian music," Bishop says. "If you listen to it, the bass part he plays is the type of beat they'd play behind a shake dancer. That's all it was." What tied the disparate parts of "East-West" together was Davenport's drum pattern, which he played in a bossa nova style.

Of course, those weren't the only songs on the record. Elektra didn't mind having prestigious artists like the Butterfield Band on the label, but a hit single would have been nice. They knew this stuff had potential, and they weren't as sure about some of the acts they were signing. Elektra had signed Love, a Los Angeles pop-rock band that was led by a pair of songwriters named Arthur Lee and Bryan MacLean. Love would make the lower rung of the charts in spring 1966 with a crazed version of Burt Bacharach and Hal David's "My Little Red Book." That summer, Elektra signed another Los Angeles band, the Doors. The label pressed up one thousand copies of their first album and then didn't release them for months, until they'd gotten some feedback from the fans as to whether this was anything worth bothering with. Hoping for a hit single, Elektra let the Butterfield Band hang out in Los Angeles, where they recorded Monkees guitarist Michael Nesmith's "Mary, Mary" during the summer. The Monkees cut their own version at the same time, but they wouldn't release it until January 1967.

"We got real hot for a while to cut commercial records," Michael told me. "We went with these guys who used to cut records for the Stones, Bruce Botnick and Dave Hassinger. We cut 'Mary, Mary' and a song called 'If I Had My Way,' which never came out. All sorts of weird attempts to make rock 'n' roll singles. We really wanted to do that, but it never happened." The group would also cut a fine single called "Come On In" in September that flopped miserably after it was released that fall, perhaps as much because of Elektra's innocence in the world of pop music as the Butterfield Band's lack of commercial expertise. "Mary, Mary" was an interesting foray into pop music, but it didn't become a hit.

East-West was a mixture of commercial attempts, blues, and experimentation. Heard today, it stands up as some of the era's most adventurous and accomplished rock music. Other bands were attempting similar blues-rock fusions in 1966. Producer Tom Wilson, who had moved to Verve Records after leaving Columbia the previous year, recorded a band called the Blues Project, who featured the guitar work of Steve Katz and Danny Kalb and the keyboards of Al Kooper. Their November 1966 album *Projections* would sport an avant-garde version of Chuck Berry's "You Can't Catch Me." But it was *East-West* that laid the foundation for the Grateful Dead's *Live Dead* and much of the Dead's subsequent work, and it anticipated by five years the Allman Brothers Band's *At Fillmore East* and *Eat a Peach*.

In July 1966 the Butterfield Band was performing at the Cafe au Go Go in New York City when Michael Bloomfield first saw Jimi Hendrix play. "The first time I saw him was when he was Jimmy James, and he was with the Blue Flames at the Cafe Wha? in New York," Bloomfield told me. "I was playing across the street and I was the local hot guitar player on the street with the Butter Band, and he was just across the street, unknown. I went over there one night, and man, he wouldn't even shake hands. I mean, he knew how bad he was. He got up there.

He had a Twin; he had a Strat, the first fuzztone that ever came out, and there were jets taking off. There were nuclear explosions and buildings collapsing! I never heard anything like it in my life. And it was an off night for him, too. I was sitting right in the front row and he was doing it right to me, like a machine gun. 'You like this, man?' *B-bb-bbb-room!* He was just mowing me down. Oh! Talk about burning!

"Every time we played together, it was pretty hip. . . . I remember once playing with him, taking this long solo, and then I looked over, and I heard these insane sounds, and he was playing with the toggle-switch of his guitar, and a knob and his bar, and he was tapping the back of the guitar and it sounded like sirocco winds on the desert."

The band continued to tour, Michael grew more miserable, and though there were still plenty of triumphs live—Michael told me about hearing tapes of "versions of 'East-West' that were forty minutes long that were unbelievably coherent all the way through"—this version of the Paul Butterfield Blues Band was about to become history.

10

FLYING THE FLAG

The Butterfield Band returned to the Fillmore in October, just before they were set to travel to England to play two weeks of dates with a troupe of English blues singers that included Georgie Fame, Eric Burdon, and Chris Farlowe. Their equipment hadn't arrived when they landed in London, so they had to make do with borrowed instruments for the first week. Albert Lee, who held down the guitar chair in Farlowe's band, lent Bloomfield his Gibson 355 until the band's gear showed up.

Bloomfield had listened hard to the sound Eric Clapton had gotten on John Mayall's *Blues Breakers* album with an instrument that Bloomfield's New York friend John Sebastian was also using at the time. It was the Gibson Les Paul Standard, a guitar that Gibson had discontinued manufacturing in 1961 because jazz guitarists found it too heavy and expensive. Sebastian's band, the Lovin' Spoonful, kept a rehearsal space at the Albert Hotel, where the Butterfield Band roomed while they were in town. Lee attempted to locate one for Bloomfield during the Butterfield Band's monthlong stay in England, but he wasn't successful. After their equipment arrived, Bloomfield continued to use the 1956 Gibson Les Paul goldtop he had bought earlier that year.

The band jammed with Cream on October 19, and Bloomfield met Eric Clapton again at a club in Leeds a few days later. Joe Boyd, whom Jac Holzman had appointed head of Elektra's new London office, escorted Bloomfield and the Butterfield group to the Marquee Club for a performance by the Move, a brilliant Birmingham, England, pop-soul-psychedelic band who drew upon the harmony-rich, guitar-laden

West Coast pop of the Byrds, Moby Grape, and Buffalo Springfield. Then, after the Fame tour ended, the Butterfield Band played a series of dates on their own.

They did an interview with the *International Times'* Simon Barley on November 14 at Edmonton's Cooks Ferry Inn. The exchange between Barley and the band was particularly lively. "The blues is basically a Negro form," Barley said. "Can the white man really play it?" Naftalin replied, "You have ears, don't you? You heard Paul play." As usual, Bloomfield was opinionated and very quotable. Barley asked him about the Chicago blues scene, and Bloomfield described the way audiences had begun to favor the likes of B. B. King, Junior Parker, and Bobby Bland over the old, Delta-style musicians the Butterfield Band had studied under. "The blues scene in Chicago is dying, getting less and less every day," he said. "It's getting throttled because the cats can't make any money. . . . I'm telling you, man, blues is dying among the Negroes of Chicago."

Barley's *International Times* piece did a remarkably good job for any publication in 1966 of analyzing, however inadvertently, the way white fans and musicians still tended to look at blues as a purely folk process that was untouched by commercial aspirations. It gave Bloomfield ample room to speculate about the future of the blues. "How will the blues fit the evolutionary process of pop music," Barley wondered. "Will pop be more influenced by the blues now?" Bloomfield had an answer: "Blues will become like hillbilly music. There will be a centre for it, devotees and blues radio stations just like there are for folk music now. Blues won't get any bigger than it is now because the majority of the white people are not hip to the social reasons that predominate to make blues."

On November 18 they gave a superb performance of "Droppin' Out" on the *Ready, Steady, Go* television program—one of the great, neglected pop-blues moments of the mid-1960s. Butterfield gives a suavely exuberant vocal performance, Billy Davenport rolls through the song's triplet rhythms, and Bloomfield rips off a fluid solo that ranks with the best playing he ever did. It stands with the best work the psychedelicized English blues-pop musicians were doing at the time. The Butterfield Band flew home a couple of days later.

Bloomfield's English visit gave him a chance to hear—and meet— some of the country's finest blues-influenced rock musicians, and he appreciated their imaginative recastings of American blues and soul, as he told *Hit Parader*'s Jim Delehant shortly after he returned to the United States. "I've heard English cats who are extremely talented," Michael said in Delehant's excellent January 1967 piece on Bloomfield. "Jeff Beck of the Yardbirds, the kid with the Spencer Davis Group, Steve Winwood—he's unbelievable. There's another kid—he's on that Elektra *What's Shakin'* album we're on—Eric Clapton." Michael amplified this statement in 1981 for Tom Yates and Kate Hayes. "I heard [Clapton] on the Mayall *Blues Breakers* record. I knew that he couldn't play the far-out way like on 'East-West' and stuff like that, I knew his mind wasn't anywhere into that at all. But as far as straight blues, he was as good as they got, he was right there with B. B. King and Albert King."

Bloomfield told Yates and Hayes that he admired Clapton's work on the *Blues Breakers* track "Have You Heard" and on 1970's *The London Howlin' Wolf Sessions*, which Norman Dayron produced. According to Bloomfield, Clapton regarded his playing on "Have You Heard" as his best on record to that date: "[Eric] once told me, 'Man, I'll never top this. I mean, no one will ever top this. It's as bad as it gets. You can just play B. B. King records all day; this is just up there with him.' Eric told me that once, and he was right." But Bloomfield didn't like Clapton's work with Duane Allman on the 1970 album *Layla and Other Assorted Love Songs*. "I think Derek and the Dominos is shit. I think 'Layla' is shit. I don't like it. I don't know who's Eric and who's Duane, I don't know which one's playing which."

Bill Graham, who was booking acts into his Fillmore Auditorium, had met Bloomfield and the rest of the Butterfield Band in 1966. Graham was a tough, intelligent, detail-obsessed businessman who Bloomfield felt was hilariously out of place in peace-loving San Francisco. He'd given fellow rock promoters Chet Helms and John Carpenter, who had brought the Butterfield Band to the Fillmore for its first San Francisco date, a lesson in practical business that Harold Bloomfield would have appreciated. Seeing how positively the San Francisco rock audience had reacted to the Butterfield Band's opening night at the Fillmore, Graham got on the phone early enough the next morning to catch Albert Grossman in New York, and Grossman granted him the options on the next couple of years of their Bay Area performances.

"They hit it off like two long-lost brothers," Gravenites said. "I mean, they loved each other. And they were respectful of each other." Like Michael Bloomfield, Graham was a funky, speed-rapping Jew. He had endured the privations and terrors of World War II in his native Germany before arriving at Ellis Island in 1941. As the two men traded street wisdom and got to know each other, Graham began to ask Bloomfield about the origins of his guitar style. Graham was a Latin music fan who knew next to nothing about rock 'n' roll and blues. In particular, Bloomfield talked in glowing terms about B. B. King, who in 1967 was virtually unknown to white audiences. Taking Bloomfield at his word, Graham booked King into the Fillmore in February on a bill that included the Steve Miller Blues Band and Moby Grape. Along with Otis Rush, Howlin' Wolf, and Muddy Waters, all of whom played the Fillmore that year, King would introduce young listeners to the glories of electric blues.

Bloomfield quit the Butterfield Band on February 25, the day before King was to make his Fillmore debut. Someone had overbooked them into three shows that day in Boston and Cambridge, and that was too much for the sleep-deprived Bloomfield to take.

The band had already walked out on Butterfield during a Los Angeles engagement. According to Bloomfield, the reason was simply Butterfield's reluctance to pay them what they felt they deserved. Ira Kamin, a friend of Bloomfield's since their teenage days in Chicago, had been studying the band's interactions from up close, and he thought the source of the disagreement had something to do with Butterfield's bad temper—he said that Butterfield had physically abused both Elvin Bishop and Bloomfield—and with Bloomfield's musical ambition. Naftalin, meanwhile, thought that Bloomfield wanted to give Bishop an opportunity to display his talents. Whatever the reason, Bloomfield quit, and that was that.

"I think he was probably sick of it," Susan told me later. "I think he was trapped in the Butterfield Band. I think he wanted something else, maybe a different kind of music. I remember everyone was really shocked."

Butterfield blamed the traveling and the relationship between Bloomfield and Bishop. "One thing was that the traveling was getting to him," he told me about Bloomfield. "In his own mind, he wanted to start a thing on his own. . . . He didn't leave in any kind of huff. I mean, I don't think he enjoyed playing with Elvin very much, partially because Elvin, at the time, had a bad problem keeping time. The rivalry was more from Elvin's side, anyway."

Although he said he left the band to give Elvin more space, Michael knew that wasn't the reason. One thing was that touring developed into a full-fledged nemesis, and there was also his desire to grow musically. "I wanted a band with horns," Michael told me. "By that time I was like a professional musicologist. I was really into studying American music, and I found that the kind of blues and music in general that I loved best was this kind of horn music. It was Kansas City jump music. It was Texas shuffle music, or whatever. I wanted a band with horns. I wanted Elvin to play lead, and he wanted to play lead. It couldn't go the way it was anymore. We weren't smart enough to think like [the Allman Brothers Band's] Dicky Betts and Duane Allman, that you could really just split it down the middle. I don't think Elvin was quite up to doing that then, anyway, although God knows he got better later."

Immediately after the split, Michael retired to his Christopher Street apartment in Greenwich Village, but he couldn't sit still. He started to play sessions wherever he could get them, and with his reputation, he could get any sessions he wanted. Mitch Ryder decided he wanted Bloomfield on his 1967 *What Now My Love* album after hanging out with him at the *Highway 61 Revisited* sessions. "[Producer] Bob Crewe told me he wanted the best guitar player, so I told him I'd got one," Ryder told me. "I guess he was good, but what I mainly remember is that he played so damn loud! He kind of had to be pushed into playing, but he got it done." Ryder remains a fan to this day.

Bloomfield had also played on Peter, Paul and Mary's 1965 *Album*, and he contributed slide guitar to the Chicago Loop's 1966 single, "(When She Wants Good Lovin') My Baby Comes to Me," a Crewe production that made Number 37 on the *Billboard* chart that fall. The keyboard player on the record was his friend from Central YMCA High School, Barry Goldberg.

Goldberg was born in Chicago on Christmas Day in 1942, and his family moved when he was six months old from the city's Albany Park neighborhood to the Edgewater district on the far North Side. Like Harold Bloomfield, Goldberg's father had benefited from World War II. "During the war, he made a lot of money making the straps for the walkie-talkies for the U.S. government," Goldberg remembered. His mother had been a child actress and was an avid pianist. "She turned me onto the boogie-woogie style. The first song I remember was 'Chattanooga Shoe Shine Boy' by Red Foley, and we had a housekeeper that would play gospel music a lot."

A fan of Jerry Lee Lewis and Chuck Berry, Goldberg got his initiation into folk music and blues from Bloomfield, who invited him to perform at the Fickle Pickle one night. "I said, 'I don't know that much about folk music,'" he said. "'All I know is "Michael, Row the Boat Ashore."' Michael said, 'Well, you can play that in a boogie version, and you can play a straight version.' So I went down there and I played this song in about twenty different styles, and nobody knew the difference." With Bloomfield leading the way, Goldberg sat in with Howlin' Wolf's band at Silvio's in the early 1960s, playing piano with Hubert Sumlin and drummer Fred Below. By 1963 Goldberg was playing cover versions of James Brown and Jackie Wilson songs at a Rush Street club called the Rumpus Room with Robby and the Troubadours, a band led by singer Robert Vidone.

By the time Bloomfield left the Butterfield Band, Goldberg had become a seasoned musician. Hanging out at the Albert Hotel one evening in early 1967 after they played a Mitch Ryder studio date—Goldberg had been on the session that produced Ryder's 1966 "Devil with a Blue Dress On" single—Bloomfield broached an idea for a new band to Goldberg. As Goldberg told me, "He said, 'I have this incredible idea of an all-American music band playing every conceivable type of American music with American roots—rock 'n' roll to blues to Stax to Spector—all the elements of American music in a band.' I said, 'Well, it sounds like a dream come true.'"

"They were in New York, and I was in Chicago, and they came back all excited about this fabulous band they were going to put together, and I didn't want to go," Susan told me. "I was sick of the music business, but they talked me into going to California." The music on the cutting edge was happening in San Francisco, and the Electric Flag, their new all-American band, would be the cutting edge of San Francisco music.

With money provided by Albert Grossman, who had committed himself to financing the band's move west, Nick Gravenites rented a house for the group on Wellesley Court in Mill Valley, a quiet town nestled at the base of Mount Tamalpais across the Golden Gate Bridge from San Francisco. Gravenites had been managing a nightclub in

Chicago, the Burning Bush, and working on a case of incipient alco-holism. His business partner, Jeff Spitz, had been killed in a motorcycle accident, and the Burning Bush had money problems that some people Gravenites preferred not to work with wanted to fix. He had left in 1966 for Mill Valley, where his Chicago friend Ron Polte now lived as he managed the Quicksilver Messenger Service, Marin County's top band. In California, Gravenites told me, he "didn't have to work or do nothing. If I needed cash they'd give it to me. I could just take it easy and do what I wanted to do. And then I got a call from Bloomfield, who said he was quitting Butterfield's band. He said he was gonna form a new band, and did I want to be the lead singer, and I said sure. So he told me to rent a house we could all live in and started shipping musicians out west."

Back in New York, Michael had enlisted bassist Harvey Brooks, who had worked with Al Kooper in New York before playing on some of the *Highway 61 Revisited* sessions. The group also welcomed saxophonist Peter Strazza, with whom Goldberg had played in Robby and the Trou-badours. Then Bloomfield and Goldberg began looking for a drummer. Their original choice was Billy Mundi, who had been playing with the Mothers of Invention. It was Harvey Brooks who took Bloomfield and Goldberg to their future drummer, Buddy Miles, at a Wilson Pickett performance during one of disc jockey and promoter Murray the K's "Music in the Fifth Dimension" shows at Manhattan's RKO 58th Street Theatre in late March. The weeklong extravaganza featured the Blues Project, the Young Rascals, and the Blues Magoos, along with Cream and the Who, both of whom were making their North American debuts. The headliner was Mitch Ryder. Murray Kaufman's wife, Jackie the K, was in charge of directing the fashion shows that filled in the gaps between acts. Back at the Albert Hotel after the show, Bloomfield and Goldberg fed Miles Oreo cookies while they talked up the attributes of the young girls in San Francisco. They immediately agreed that Miles fit their concept perfectly: "Our plan was that he could be the star of San Francisco and have anything he wanted—which is basically what happened," Goldberg said. Pickett took exception to the poaching, but Buddy was the kind of guy who needed to be a star.

The musicians began arriving in California. "Then these people started showing up," Gravenites told me. "I remember when I met Buddy Miles. Christ! He was like Baby Huey! Buttons popping off his overcoat, weighed about 300 pounds. Oh, my God! Then I met Harvey Brooks, a huge, huge Jew from New York, a 250-pounder. Where did he get 'em? And the trumpet player, he was like six foot three, weighed 195. All together, we looked like the Fearsome Four, all of us big, big guys."

Actually, Nick may have been the second choice for the Electric Flag's vocalist, because Mitch Ryder remembered Goldberg and Bloomfield trying to talk him into leaving the Detroit Wheels. He tactfully declined because he wanted to stick with them, but the thought of Ryder being in the Flag is a fascinating one.

The musicians settled into the comfortable ranch-style house on Wellesley Court and began working on their new songs. "The first tune we worked out was 'Groovin' Is Easy,'" Michael told Dan McClosky. "Nick wrote it, and we worked it out. We worked all the parts out but we never played it as a band until we had every part worked out. And all of a sudden, I said, 'OK, man, now we're gonna play this tune from beginning to end,' and the sound just blew our minds. All of a sudden, we knew we had a dynamite band, and man, it was just a fantastic feeling then."

11

"MIKE BLOOMFIELD PLUGS IN HIS GUITAR AND HIS FLAG"

Few bands in the history of rock 'n' roll were anticipated quite so eagerly as was the Electric Flag. The reasons are largely historical. During the period that the Butterfield Band was making its impact, the nature of American pop music changed radically. As late as 1966, the records being bought were pop tunes in which the entire package—arrangement, melody, lyric, production—were of a piece, but the music that Michael Bloomfield and his cohorts were playing sacrificed novelty of arrangement and presentation for a jazz-like emphasis on soloing and improvisation. Pop records had previously been danceable three-minute pieces of fluff, but they were now, thanks in part to Bob Dylan, worthy of being listened *to*, and listened *into*, for their lyrical and improvisational complexities.

It was turning into an era of guitar players, virtuoso guitar players at that, and this was a brand-new development. Of course, the technology available to amplified guitarists had never been as conducive to virtuosity as it now had become, but that hadn't stopped bands like the Ventures and Johnny and the Hurricanes and six dozen or so surf bands from playing primitive guitar instrumentals. No, the turnaround to the focus on the guitarist, the fans putting the guitar player in the spotlight, must be laid to the incredible influence that Michael Bloomfield's work with the Butterfield Band—and with Dylan—had on musicians and the musically aware public.

Before Michael, there were lead guitarists in bands, but you never heard people discussing the fabulous solos of Keith Richards, George Harrison, or even Eric Clapton of the Yardbirds. It was the music that the Butterfield Band made that pushed bands like Cream, the Jimi Hendrix Experience, and, later, dozens of white American and British blues bands like Canned Heat, the Steve Miller Blues Band, Chicken Shack, Fleetwood Mac, Captain Beefheart and His Magic Band, and the Siegel-Schwall Band into looking beyond the hit single and the three-minute pop tune.

The man who started it all, the very first bona fide American guitar hero, had given up the job that had made him famous and was putting together his own band. The fans waited with bated breath, not quite knowing what to expect.

A few weeks after everybody got settled in on Wellesley Court, Albert Grossman appeared in San Francisco to sign the contracts, and Gravenites got to see up close how persuasive he could be. "He came out with contracts," Gravenites remembered. "He had a recording contract. He had a personal management contract. He had publishing contracts. I was perfectly willing to sign the recording contract and the personal management contract, but then he told me I had to sign over my publishing to him, too." Grossman threatened expulsion from the band, and Gravenites relented. "The contracts didn't exist for the things I was supposed to be getting paid on," he said. "It was a huge mistake."

The new band's first recordings were done for producer Roger Corman's 1967 film *The Trip*, an exploitation movie about the effects of LSD and anomie on a young Los Angeles television-commercial director played by Peter Fonda. Written by Jack Nicholson, the film also starred Susan Strasberg, Bruce Dern, and Dennis Hopper. The group traveled to Los Angeles in April to rehearse their new material, and they used a house that Gram Parsons, a Florida-born folk and country singer who was working with a group called the International Submarine Band, was occupying. Bloomfield had gotten to know the band's guitarist, John Nuese, during his Butterfield Band days, and it was from Nuese that Bloomfield had acquired his Gibson Les Paul goldtop guitar in a trade for his 1964 Telecaster. The International Submarine Band had signed with Corman to do the soundtrack for *The Trip*, but their

Bakersfield-style country-rock seems to have been deemed insufficiently atmospheric, and Bloomfield's group got the job.

Albert Grossman decided the band should make their debut in June at the Monterey Pop Festival, a showcase for new rock bands that producers Lou Adler and John Phillips had organized. Right up until it was time to play the festival, Bloomfield's group called themselves An American Music Band. It was Gravenites's cohort Ron Polte who provided them with the sobriquet that they thought suited their concept: "Ron Polte had this flag that started waving when you plugged it into the wall," Goldberg remembered. "It was an electric flag. And he actually gave us that name: the Electric Flag. That's where that came from."

For the Electric Flag, Monterey was going to be a big deal. Short of the Beatles and the Rolling Stones, every group that mattered would be there. The Who, fresh off their North American debut at Murray the K's "Music from the Fifth Dimension," was going to play. Jimi Hendrix was bringing his British band, the Experience, to the festival, and Janis Joplin, the exciting Texas-born blues singer who fronted one of San Francisco's most popular bands, Big Brother and the Holding Company, was going to sing. And Stax Records star Otis Redding would meet "the love crowd," as he put it, from the stage.

Another thing about the Monterey Pop Festival was best summed up by an insider who once told me, "People think that the action at Monterey was on the stage. Wrong. The action was in the bar, where every record executive in the United States was making deals with the bands that were playing." At long last, it appeared that the record business was going to pay attention to the incredible explosion of mutated pop music that America's youth was performing and dancing to, and the executives who gathered at Monterey weren't going to leave until they had scored, preferably big.

Grossman invited both Atlantic Records' Jerry Wexler and Columbia Records' Clive Davis to the festival. Davis had recently become the president of Columbia, and he was looking for new rock 'n' roll bands for the label, as was Wexler for Atlantic. In retrospect, it seems reasonable to suggest that the Electric Flag might have better served themselves by signing with Atlantic instead of with Columbia, since Atlantic executives Wexler and Ahmet Ertegun's savvy business sense and sure musical instincts had helped to create some of the soul music that the band was attempting to take in new directions with material like "You Don't Realize," Bloomfield and Goldberg's homage to Steve Cropper and Otis Redding.

"For my part, I was impressed enough with the idea of Bloomfield's Electric Flag to pitch them," Wexler wrote in his autobiography. "Bloomfield, who had a wide-eyed and simplistic manner, was enthusiastic, and said he'd been raised on Atlantic artists. All he had to do was mention my interest to his agent, the inscrutable, eccentric, infamous Albert Grossman." Bloomfield came back to Wexler with Grossman's answer. "I was certain that he'd be interested in having Bloomfield on our label, but I was wrong," Wexler wrote. "'Grossman says we can't go with you because Atlantic steals from the niggers' is what Mike said to me the next day, naively quoting his manager." Grossman and the Electric Flag signed with Davis. It was his first acquisition of a rock band, and he paid $50,000 for them, high dollar at the time.

Bloomfield liked to talk about his Monterey experience as a watershed in the evolution of his already skewed relationship to the idea of stardom. Striving to become revered and famous was fine for some people, but Bloomfield thought of himself as a great musician who was good at organizing other musicians, and he had a very well-developed sense of the way fans tended to miss what was truly important when they naively compared pop musicians' intentions with their actual accomplishments. The Flag's Monterey reception reinforced his notion that the mass audience tended toward the kind of blind, unhearing idolatry that made Bloomfield extremely uncomfortable. "We played abominably, and they loved us," Bloomfield told *Rolling Stone*'s Jann Wenner in a February 1968 interview the magazine planned to run over two issues in April to mark the release of the Flag's first album. "I couldn't understand, man, how could a band play that shitty and have everyone dig them?" he said. "I said, 'Well, it's festival madness.' Monterey will remain a straight, jive pop phenomenon. You know, if we'd gone on first, we would have bombed. We went on last."

Peter Strazza believed that the band had gotten sidetracked by jumping from San Francisco to Los Angeles to finish their work for Corman, and there was all the rock 'n' roll action around Gram Parsons and his scene, which included visits from Nico, a former model who was now singing with a band Tom Wilson had been producing for Verve Records, the Velvet Underground. Nico faithfully piloted the Electric Flag's van from the Hollywood Hills to the United Artists studio on Santa Monica Boulevard and back again every day. "*The Trip*—well, that's good, because we had full control of it," Strazza said. "We didn't have anyone else meddling. Mike produced it and mixed it, because that's before we were signed with Columbia, so Mike got what he wanted on it." Strazza thought the band was underrehearsed for Monterey. "We were ready—but not for 50,000 people," he said. "We didn't have everything down the way we should have, because we were messing around with *The Trip* too much."

For Harvey Brooks, Monterey was a new experience, and he enjoyed it. "You looked around, and you saw people smiling and having a nice time," he said. Meanwhile, Goldberg thought it was an average set: "It was definitely better than most of the bands that were there, Quicksilver or any of that stuff. The people loved it, which amazed me, because I didn't think it would go over that well. Michael was terribly nervous. A lot of that might have been nervous energy, insecurity and not getting a good monitor."

Bloomfield was indeed nervous at Monterey, as you could tell from the overly sincere way he introduced the band's first number, but his lack of showbiz patter was endearing. "Dig yourselves, 'cause it's really groovy, man," he told the bemused crowd. The group kicked into "Over-Lovin' You," and they turned in a crisp performance that showed off Miles's vocal chops. Jerry Wexler must have noted the way the audience grooved on their version of Stick McGhee's old Atlantic hit, "Drinkin' Wine, Spo-Dee-O-Dee." Maybe Bloomfield just couldn't bring himself to believe that the rock audience was capable of appreciating a man like Stick for who he was.

"All of a sudden there's a lot of drugs," Harvey Brooks said about the period right after Monterey. "Reefer was like cigarettes. There's a lot of heroin. The heroin seemed to be coming from the horn players. That seemed to be where it generated from, because that sort of materialized when they materialized." In fact, Marcus Doubleday, who had gotten the trumpet slot at the recommendation of guitarist Larry Coryell—they had played together in a Seattle instrumental band called the Dynamics—had come into the band with a heroin habit. Strazza and Goldberg soon followed suit.

"Marcus Doubleday was a junkie, which they hadn't known, and Barry Goldberg had had trouble with dope for years off and on," Susan told me. "I remember that Michael didn't know about Marcus, and he'd say, 'Gee, that new guy sure sleeps a lot.' He was just the new guy. Then Barry brought Peter Strazza, who was heavily into dope, and a bum from Chicago—a nice guy, but still a bum—named Ronnie Minsky, to act as road manager. By the time they got to L.A., between Minsky—who was pushing it—and Doubleday and Peter, I don't know if Peter got strung out first, or Barry, but the dope was there. And then they got to L.A., and there was Owsley and his acid."

Heroin split the Electric Flag in half even before it got going. Susan confirmed that Michael used to tell her he had infrequently used heroin since around 1964. Whatever the reason, his wife noticed a change, as did his friends. "When he started getting into heroin, he lost himself," Michael's friend Ira Kamin said. "He never really came out of that. It's true that he was an insomniac, but it's kind of like a vicious circle." Looking back later, Susan said much the same thing: "Drugs were Michael's downfall. Back then, I never would have said what I believe now, which is that drugs change people, and drugs make people do things they normally wouldn't do." The drugs seemed unavoidable, and Michael had always been a thrill seeker, but the Electric Flag had other problems that also became obvious from the beginning.

For Harvey Brooks, the drugs were a big problem, but the Electric Flag's inability to get it together was also partly a consequence of the way Bloomfield pitted his loud, aggressive sound against the other elements of the band. "The horn players were great players, but I think that we had serious tuning problems," he said. "Michael had a tuning problem. We didn't have electronic tuners then, and I think the tuning problems drove the horn players completely nuts." As Brooks noted, Bloomfield wasn't inclined to change his strings every day, and his setup wasn't ideally suited to the demands of a big band. He played at extremely high volume through a Fender Twin amplifier, and sometimes daisy-chained it and a Super Reverb together for extra power. Brooks thought the band never really established a good balance in their live performances.

When it came time to begin recording in July, the same kind of technical issues got in the way. The producer Columbia had gone with was John Court, a business associate of Grossman's who was half of the entity known as GrosCourt and whose previous credits included albums by Peter, Paul and Mary, Gordon Lightfoot, and Richie Havens. Bloomfield found him lacking, as he told Jann Wenner in 1968. "No, he's not that hip to rock for all those years," he said. "The sound is not as good as it could be for all those records, not as good as a Stones record, as good as a Beatles record, as good as a Motown or Stax record." Bloomfield had better taste than Columbia Records, as he explained to Wenner: "I would like to be personally produced by Jerry Ragovoy in New York. He's one of the greatest soul producers I've ever heard. . . . I think Jim Stewart, if not better, would be just as good. Or perhaps Jerry Wexler would be groovier."

The first product of the band's recording efforts was a single released with a picture sleeve that featured a black-and-white photograph of the Electric Flag. I remember getting my copy of "Groovin' Is Easy" / "Over-Lovin' You" soon after it appeared in late October 1967, and I remember my amazement at the sheer physical size of the musicians in the photograph—there was the massive Buddy Miles, who was grinning with a Siamese cat in his arms. Behind him stood Bloomfield, who held a flag at a slightly disrespectful angle and looked every bit the leader of the band. Authorship of the A-side song was credited to Ron Polte, who had given the Electric Flag their name.

"Groovin'" featured a superb Gravenites vocal, Cass Elliot and Buddy Miles's background harmonies, and a brief instrumental interlude that contained a Bloomfield riff that he played in a sort of raga-meets-Celtic mode, but it sounded like somebody's twisted idea of a three-minute pop song. Goldberg and Bloomfield's "Over-Lovin' You," the B-side, was a soul tune that sounded like a slightly more ornate version of the records Arthur Conley and Wilson Pickett were currently cutting in Memphis and Muscle Shoals, Alabama. The single went nowhere on the charts, but it was a worthy first try.

As production proceeded on the band's first album, *A Long Time Comin'*, Bloomfield spent time at Columbia's San Francisco studio trying to get Court and the Columbia engineers to listen to Sam Phillips's Sun productions, Beatles records, anything to shake them loose. It was to no avail. Later, Bloomfield credited Columbia's Roy Segal, who mixed *A Long Time Comin'* and allowed Bloomfield to make suggestions, with helping him implement some of his production ideas.

Still, the album expressed Bloomfield's vision, even if the production made it sound more like a pastiche of soul styles than it really was. THE ELECTRIC FLAG IS AN AMERICAN MUSIC BAND, read the headline on his short liner notes. "American music is not necessarily music directly from America. I think of it as the music you hear in the air, on the air, and in the streets; blues, soul, country, rock, religious music, traffic, crowds, street sounds and field sounds, the sound of people and silence."

As for how representative an album of American music it really was, that's open to speculation. Certainly there wasn't any country music on it, nor any country blues, but there was plenty of America, 1967 turning into 1968, and in living stereo. The band's romp through "Drinkin' Wine, Spo-Dee-O-Dee" effectively revived the song for every bar band in the country, while Bloomfield played a great solo on "Texas." The album also included the San Francisco Sound of Barry Goldberg's "Sittin' in Circles" and a psychedelic workout, complete with the dubbed-in voice of Lyndon Baines Johnson, called "Another Country." In fact, the solemn voice of the thirty-sixth president of the United States introduced *A Long Time Comin'*: "I speak tonight for the dignity of man," Johnson began, but his speech was cut off by the sounds of a raucous party and the band's kick-ass version of Howlin' Wolf's "Killing Floor," on which Gravenites set a vocal standard he's rarely surpassed.

Goldberg and Bloomfield's nod to Cropper and Redding, "You Don't Realize," took the Stax Records style into territory that the average pop fan could appreciate. The music on *A Long Time Comin'* may have represented soul more than it did any other American style, but its attempt to take that style into supersonic, modern territory was as American as you can get.

For many, the album's highlight was a tiny fifty-second throwaway tacked on to the record's end—Michael and his electric guitar, peacefully picking away on "Easy Rider." Some think it is his finest recorded moment, and it definitely fits in with the best he ever did. Gravenites always said that the best music Bloomfield played with the Electric Flag was done after hours, when no one was listening.

The sound of the album is the sound of a band, but that is actually the magic of electronics. When the band was recording the album, they all moved into different houses around Mill Valley. Susan remembered the first three or four months as close to ideal, where the worst problem was Buddy Miles parking the Continental he'd insisted upon when he joined up, disappearing with the keys, and blocking the hilly driveway to the band's house. "He was just a sweet little kid," Susan told me. "He liked shrimp, and he'd take a whole bologna and a jar of mayonnaise and dip the bologna into it and eat it."

With the album done, it was time to take the band—volatile egos, drug problems, and all—on the road. "Our record wasn't a giant hit, wasn't a million-seller," Gravenites said. "We weren't at the upper echelon, Sonny & Cher or Three Dog Night. We were stuck at that middle rhythm-and-blues level, you know, and we were doing a lot of marginal gigs."

Grossman dispatched an associate of his named Ronnie Lyons to act as one of the Flag's tour managers. A native of the Bronx, Lyons had previously gone on the road with the Butterfield Band and with another Grossman act, the Paupers, a Canadian rock band led by Skip Prokop. The Paupers had played at Monterey, but they hadn't made much of an impression. The Electric Flag didn't travel in high style in late 1967, as Lyons remembers. "We had what you could call a schlepper moving in the truck all the equipment, and I would drive the guys in a station wagon," he says. "Albert told me to go to the Flag because he was afraid of the horn players. I wouldn't stay in the same hotel with them."

When the band played the Fillmore in late August 1967 on a bill with Cream, which was making its West Coast debut, Lyons witnessed an example of Bloomfield's indifference to the niceties of show business. "They were headlining, and Cream was [on] the bill," Lyons says. "Michael runs up onstage and tells the audience about Eric Clapton: 'This is the greatest guitarist you'll ever hear.' And Michael was the great guitarist, you know, and he goes up and says how great Eric Clapton is before the Flag even took the stage. It infuriated me."

A month later in Huntington Beach, California, Brooks, Goldberg, Bloomfield, and Gravenites were arrested on narcotics charges (pot, not heroin) at their motel. They had been getting high in their motel room and playing records late one night, and they attracted attention from their fellow guests. Goldberg got probation, and police dropped charges against the other three.

Shaken, Goldberg left the band in early December. An Ontario musician whom Goldberg knew, Mike Fonfara, took his place, but he proceeded to get busted while the band was finishing up the album. Fonfara was replaced by Herbie Rich, who had been there from the beginning. Rich doubled on saxophone and organ until Stemzie Hunter was hired at the beginning of 1968.

Grossman called an emergency meeting of the band in spring 1968 to discuss firing Strazza and Doubleday. Drug dealers had held up Strazza at gunpoint in Detroit after a show in March, and Grossman had endured enough. Strazza and Doubleday stayed on, because bookers wanted the full band, but Grossman had lost faith in them. Another factor in the band's demise was the gulf between Buddy Miles's desire to clown around onstage as the band's soul music showman and Bloomfield's need to abjure virtually all show business concessions. In the end, it turned out that Miles had lied about his age when he signed Grossman's contracts. He had been nineteen when Brooks, Goldberg, and Bloomfield pulled him away from the force field of Wilson Pickett. Miles went to court and got out of the agreements, and Bloomfield left the band after their June 8 show at Bill Graham's recently opened New York City venue, the Fillmore East.

Gravenites chalked it up to the drugs, the pace, and the band's tenuous sense of identity, and to the fact that Bloomfield and Miles had such different views of how to present the band's music. Buddy loved being a star, but Bloomfield despised the very idea of being adored as a star and not as a musician. The situation also had something to do with Bloomfield's state of mind. His relationship with Susan had been deteriorating since they moved to California, if not before.

12

SUPER SESSION

When he told me about leaving the Electric Flag years later, Michael Bloomfield was still visibly upset. He echoed a lot of what Nick Gravenites said when I had asked him why Bloomfield had quit. He couldn't handle being the band's de facto manager, and business affairs had sailed way out of his hands. He claimed that people were buying houses and charging them to the Flag. "We were getting stale," Bloomfield said. "We were playing the same shit over and over. We weren't writing new songs. We were trying to live up to a mystique, trying to get this super-exciting wham-bam show which, for me, lost the meaning of what we were about. It began to be un-good." The pressures had come from every direction. Columbia had made it known that they thought the burly Gravenites wasn't exactly a pop icon, even though Gravenites was a very good singer who could also come up with material as potentially commercial as "Groovin'." It turned out that Gravenites had written the song under his friend Ron Polte's name.

The whole thing had been a lot of stress and hassle that had produced an album Bloomfield wasn't entirely happy with, and being on the road while having to contend with Miles's showboating and Columbia's demands affected his playing. "Michael was an extremely spotty player," Gravenites said. "We would give extremely mediocre performances. Sometimes, Michael couldn't hit a note—I mean, it would just be embarrassing. Other times, you'd go flying through the air with greatest of ease."

There were other things that were keeping Bloomfield unhappy. By the time he came off the road, Susan had spent a lot of time getting to know people in Mill Valley, like Nick's girlfriend Diane, and for the first time since high school she had plenty of women friends. It began giving her some perspective on her marriage, and it began to occur to her that things weren't as they should be.

"A number of years before, I had started feeling sort of trapped," she told me. "Here we were, I was twenty-five, and we had married at nineteen, and it was not really anything having to do with the music business or anything at all, except that I'd been married, and I didn't want to be married anymore." There were physical confrontations, and on one occasion, Michael tried to run Susan down with a car, which meant, considering how painfully shy and undemonstrative he usually was, that he was well over the brink. Susan got a divorce and moved back to Chicago in December 1967. Michael flew home that Christmas, but they weren't able to reconcile.

Chicago was even worse, and Susan returned to California in the summer of 1968 to find that Michael had moved to Lagunitas, a remote community about thirty miles north of San Francisco in Marin County. According to Susan, he was shooting heroin and doing nothing to speak of. His brother Allen came out for a brief visit.

"I was mostly interested in getting my life together," Susan told me. "I wanted to get out of Chicago, and I came back to Mill Valley because I knew I could stay with Michael. Then I got my own apartment, and he got me a car. He found a check for $100 made out to me in his wallet, and Nick took him to the vehicle auction at San Quentin and they bought me a car, which we shared for a while."

Meanwhile, the Electric Flag was going through its own traumas. By the time *A Long Time Comin'* hit stores in April, the Flag was almost finished, and the record struggled to Number 31 on the *Billboard* chart.

Hit Parader's Jim Delehant reviewed "Groovin' Is Easy" in April 1968, just before the album hit stores, and he thought the group was heading in the right direction. "The failure of the Electric Flag's first single, 'Groovin' Is Easy,' on Columbia is by no means the fault of the Electric Flag," Delehant wrote. "Lack of air play was one factor, and being just another group added to Columbia's hundred-odd artist roster didn't help much either. But the Electric Flag will happen if their super-star egos continue to think as one. (Groups do have a bad habit of breaking up, you know.)"

Delehant interviewed Bloomfield for his piece, and as usual, the leader of the Electric Flag had plenty to say about his latest musical concept. "You won't believe it," he said about "Groovin'." "It sounds like 400 pieces. All the influences in production I've ever had come out in it . . . Phil Spector, Bob Crewe, George Martin." Bloomfield waxed rhapsodic to Delehant about gospel music and Fats Domino, put down the Rolling Stones—"Jagger can't sing. He sings better than me, but he can't sing," he declared—and talked about a new tune the band was working on, a tribute to the sound of Memphis's Stax Records. "One of the songs I'm working on will be 'Dedication to Steve Cropper.' He's a beautiful cat," Bloomfield said.

Also in April, just as *A Long Time Comin'* hit, *Rolling Stone* published the interview Wenner had done with Bloomfield two months earlier. Bloomfield could always talk at length about virtually anything, and Wenner got the full force of his opinions about the accomplishments of the San Francisco rock bands. As much as Bloomfield admired Ken Kesey's novels or savored a tab of Owsley acid, the San Francisco scene had certain drawbacks, as far as he could see. The Butterfield Band had come to the Bay Area in 1966 wearing their sharp continental suits and Italian shoes, which they quickly discarded for clothing more appropriate to the local climate. Everyone liked to play mind games, and that was fine with Bloomfield. "I like to play mind games, too," he said in a later interview. "I play Jewish mind games." It was a clique that he couldn't penetrate: "What it comes down to is that they're nice folks. But we were not part of that scene."

What it came down to, he told Wenner, was that he thought the San Francisco bands, from the Grateful Dead to the Jefferson Airplane to Country Joe and the Fish, were amateurs, folkies who played the kind of licks that Bloomfield had gone beyond in high school. "I have all his works," he said about the Airplane's Jorma Kaukonen. "When he plays blues, he plays it sloppy. Or he doesn't play blues, he plays different melodies." The singers were just as bad. "I don't dig Pigpen trying to sing blues, it's not real blues," he told Wenner. He excepted two San Francisco groups from this Olympian judgement. One was Mother Earth, a soul-blues band led by Tracy Nelson, who had celebrated New Year's Day 1965 with Bloomfield and his friends in Chicago at Magoo's.

The other was Moby Grape, who expertly played roadhouse-style psychedelic country-rock and wrote concise songs. Bloomfield always had good things to say about the Grape's lead guitarist, Jerry Miller, and he appreciated the band's professionalism and solid blues and rock 'n' roll chops. He just thought they were a bit too slick.

In the Wenner piece, Bloomfield got around to talking about his own style. "You know, I like sweet blues," he said. "The English cats play very hard, funky blues. Like Aretha sings is how they play guitar. I play sweet blues. I can't explain it. I want to be singing. I want to be sweet." He praised the Stax musicians for their ability to "[bother] to find the best possible" singers and material, and told Wenner he liked Merle Haggard, Tammy Wynette, Lonnie Mack, Jimmy Hughes, and Wayne Cochran. And, of course, he extolled the virtues of B. B. King and Jimi Hendrix. "His few albums are among the best albums ever recorded in the world," he said about Hendrix.

Ralph J. Gleason, a veteran jazz journalist who had started *Rolling Stone* with Wenner the previous year, shot back at Bloomfield in a May 11 column titled "Stop This Shuck, Mike Bloomfield." In many ways, Gleason's polemic was similar to Julius Lester's earlier dismissive review of the Butterfield Band's first album. "No matter how long and how good he plays, Michael Bloomfield will never be a spade," Gleason wrote. Meanwhile, the San Francisco musicians were exploring their own style, which was a white style, Gleason thought: "The white sons of middle-class America who are in this thing are not ashamed of being white."

Many *Rolling Stone* readers were appalled at Gleason's racist line of reasoning, and those old enough to understand jazz and know something of its history were more than a little puzzled at his curious division of the music along racial lines. Gleason failed to see that the white musicians who composed the San Francisco scene of the mid-1960s were folkies who paid homage to American vernacular styles that were almost as declassé as the blues: bluegrass and country music. Jerry Garcia revered Bill Monroe and Merle Travis, and so did Bloomfield. As Bloomfield's brilliant Delta blues–style solo on *The Trip*'s "Gettin' Hard" had demonstrated, mastering the secrets of a musical idiom wasn't a matter of race; it was a matter of being able to listen and perform correctly. Bloomfield liked the old blues musicians as fallible human beings, and he respected them as equally fallible professionals and artists, and that was where he was at. Gravenites shot back a response to Gleason titled "Stop This Shuck, Ralph Gleason!" that appeared in *Rolling Stone*'s May 25 issue. "Mike is from Chicago and Chicago has over one million black Americans living there and it is virtually impossible to live in the city and not become a little black in your heart and soul," he wrote.

Talking to *Rolling Stone*'s Jann Wenner in June 1968, Steve Cropper and Stax keyboardist Booker T. Jones provided a professional critique of "Groovin' Is Easy." Jones thought it sounded like a Stax record. "They did a lot of things in that one like we might have done them," he said. "The horns have a good sound and the guitar player plays very good." Cropper approved of Bloomfield's blues style: "He doesn't play frantic or try to overplay like a lot of people do."

In June Michael returned to Mill Valley without the Electric Flag. They recorded a second album without him, but it went nowhere, lacking its star.

In May, not long before he played his last date with the Electric Flag, Bloomfield had gotten a call from Al Kooper, who had stayed in touch after they had gotten through with Dylan's *Highway 61* sessions. Kooper had left the Blues Project to put together a new group, Blood, Sweat & Tears, a big band that was similar to the Electric Flag, and he had gone on to do A&R for Columbia in New York. Kooper thought Bloomfield hadn't been recorded properly: he believed part of the problem was that Bloomfield had never been placed in a studio environment that was relaxed enough to suit him.

Bloomfield and Kooper had played piano on a couple of tracks on Moby Grape's recently released *Grape Jam*, a collection of instrumental tracks that Columbia had packaged with the band's *Wow*, a set of tongue-in-cheek country-rock. Kooper figured Bloomfield would thrive in a situation that was something like a jazz jam session where select players got together and improvised. "I got him on the phone, and it turned out he was not doing much of anything," Kooper said. "'Why don't we just go on in the studio,' I proposed, 'and fuck around and jam. Columbia'll put it out, and big deal.' 'Okay,' he says, 'but let's do it in California.'"

Kooper and Bloomfield went into Columbia Studios in Los Angeles on May 28 for a two-day session with Barry Goldberg sitting in on electric piano with drummer Eddie Hoh and bassist Harvey Brooks, who had spent the previous day tripping on psilocybin. "I think I was coming down by then, so I was feeling pretty good," Brooks remembered. Kooper played organ and, on a San Francisco–style folk-jazz jam called "His Holy Modal Majesty," a keyboard called the Ondioline, and Bloomfield turned in some of his best work on record. Kooper didn't get the second day out of Bloomfield, who fled in the night for Mill Valley. Around nine the next morning, someone called Kooper from San Francisco: Did Michael make the plane? What plane? Kooper asked. He walked to Bloomfield's room. "Dear Alan, couldn't sleep well . . . went home . . . sorry," Bloomfield's note read. Kooper finished the second day of *Super Session* with guitarist Steven Stills. Bloomfield and Kooper's collaborations would be marked by disappearances and dramatic reappearances that would become part of Bloomfield lore.

"I think those were scams," Bloomfield told Tom Yates and Kate Hayes about *Super Session* and *The Live Adventures of Mike Bloomfield and Al Kooper*, which they recorded at the Fillmore Auditorium in September. "I think that Kooper had a good idea by calling something 'super.' 'Superstar, super-this,' so they could sell records."

"I'll tell you how he felt about those albums," Kooper countered. "He felt like he was the street, and I was the slick guy. He admired my slickness and sort of wished he could motivate himself to get into some of that. The last thing I ever expected was that *Super Session* would sell, I tell you. I went into Tower Records the day it was released, and I just saw those records sailing over the counter, and I thought, uh oh." It got Michael his one and only gold album, a fact that disgusted and pleased him to the end.

Pleased by the way copies of *Super Session* were being briskly transferred to record buyers—released in late August, the two-record set climbed to Number 13 on *Billboard*'s pop album chart—Kooper and Columbia had decided to record Bloomfield in the same setup, only in front of an audience at the Fillmore over three nights. From this came the *Live Adventures* album, which was even more of a nightmare. "I had stage fright, I couldn't sleep for days," Bloomfield told Tom Yates and Kate Hayes. "Basically what it was, it was selling a product by its name, not really by the content. It was a huckster's idea that worked.

The music's not that invalid. In a way, some of the *Live Adventures* stuff, 'cause it's riskier, is even more valid."

Once again, Kooper assembled a rhythm section: drummer Skip Prokop and Bloomfield's Marin County neighbor John Kahn on bass. The first two nights in September 1968 went perfectly, with Bloomfield turning in some of his most subtle and incisive playing on superb versions of Ray Charles's "I Wonder Who" and "Mary Ann."

Once again, Kooper got an early-morning phone call. It was from Susan, who wanted to let him know that Michael was in the hospital, being sedated in an attempt to get him to sleep. Kooper steeled himself to face Bill Graham, who screamed at him before calling Susan to continue screaming at her. She was having none of it. "It was more important that Michael get better than play that stupid show," she said later.

Kooper called Elvin Bishop and Carlos Santana to fill in (it would be Santana's first appearance on record). *The Live Adventures of Mike Bloomfield and Al Kooper* has its longueurs, but Bloomfield does justice to Albert King on a version of King's "Don't Throw Your Love on Me So Strong" that runs 10:50 and never flags for a second.

Kooper was determined to put the *Super Session* concept on the road, at least for a while. Kooper had gone into business with a music business manager named Stanley Polley, who had recently negotiated a deal with Columbia's Clive Davis for singer Lou Christie, one of Polley's clients. Kooper brought Allen Bloomfield on board as Polley's assistant after Allen showed up with his camera at a Chicago gig. Allen wasn't a professional photographer, but Kooper used his new employee's talents in other ways. "I remember one time we were headlining at the Boston Garden—a huge place, totally sold out, and no Michael," Kooper told me. "So I panicked, and I got a guitar, put it on Allen, and said, 'Go out there and pretend that the amp doesn't work,' figuring that one Bloomfield was as good as another, and that we could buy some time that way. He's just about to go up there, and here comes Michael like nothing was wrong."

Although what Kooper was trying to do onstage was more in line with the musical-appreciation idea that Bloomfield preferred for his performances, no sooner had Bloomfield done it to his apparent satisfaction than he bowed out of the collaboration. He retired to Mill Valley, with nothing to show but a gold record.

Bloomfield didn't end up with the original artwork for the cover of *Live Adventures*, painted by none other than Norman Rockwell. Michael had showed up for Rockwell's preparatory photograph session in late December very relaxed, having borrowed his brother's coat, which yielded a collection of random pills that Allen had stashed in one of its pockets. Bloomfield put his arm around Rockwell and told the painter he was missing a great opportunity to depict America at its liveliest. "Ah, Norman, you got to come to San Francisco and paint," he said. "It's like Jerusalem. There's women nursing their babies in the street. It's incredible. You'll get some great paintings." Rockwell eventually sent the original painting to Columbia, displayed in an old-fashioned frame. Kooper later said that he looked for opportunities to steal Rockwell's portrait from where it was hanging in the office of Columbia's art director, John Berg, but he couldn't get away with it. Sometime later, Berg sold the painting, and Kooper tracked the buyer down, just for his own satisfaction. The whole thing made Kooper depressed, and that was as much as he wanted to know about it.

13

UNPLUGGING

Bloomfield lent his guitar and his production skills to a variety of side projects in 1968. His old friend Mark Naftalin had moved to Marin County early in the year after leaving the Butterfield Band. Naftalin wanted to get back to playing piano, his favored instrument. He got the job of arranging and playing piano on Mother Earth's *Living with the Animals*, an album that featured Tracy Nelson's superb blues-soul vocals and a funny song about comic book heroes by band member Powell St. John, "Marvel Group." After moving from Wisconsin to San Francisco, Nelson had formed Mother Earth in 1967 with Ira Kamin and two Texas musicians, George Rains and Wayne Talbert. *Living with the Animals* fit into the same ultra-American category as *A Long Time Comin'*—Nelson sang "Down So Low," a song she had written about her recent breakup with guitarist Steve Miller, and the group also essayed two Allen Toussaint tunes and Willie Dixon's "My Love Will Never Die." Bloomfield contributed a solo to the record's cover of Memphis Slim's "Mother Earth."

Bloomfield also sat in on two records by Talbert, who would cut three albums of Ray Charles–influenced soul. One of them, 1969's *Dues to Pay*, was a pixilated version of the kind of music the Flag had done, complete with strange percussion, avant-garde saxophone solos, and production by New Orleans–born session musician Mac Rebennack, who had recently adopted the stage name of Dr. John. Bloomfield's fills and solo on the *Dues to Pay* track "Funky Ellis Farm" recalled the glories of his work on *Highway 61*—Talbert was no Dylan, but the song sounded like a Texas-fried version of "Maggie's Farm."

At the end of 1968, Bloomfield and Gravenites undertook another outside project. Gravenites had met Janis Joplin and her Big Brother and the Holding Company bandmates Peter Albin and James Gurley a few years earlier during his days as a folk music performer in San Francisco. Hanging out at a North Beach folk music bar called the Coffee Gallery, Gravenites had gotten to know the aspiring folk musicians. Gravenites ran into them again in Chicago in 1966, when they did a series of performances at Mother Blues for audiences who weren't ready for their untutored variation on blues. Joplin and Big Brother recorded their debut for Mainstream Records, a jazz label run by producer Bob Shad, to raise enough money to get back to San Francisco, where Big Brother began playing at venues such as the Avalon Ballroom. They signed with Albert Grossman and went to Columbia Records a few months after they appeared at the Monterey Pop Festival.

Joplin left Big Brother in September 1968, and Grossman directed Gravenites and Bloomfield to rehearse her new group, the Kozmic Blues Band, which featured Big Brother guitarist Sam Andrew and a brace of musicians that included keyboardist Goldy McJohn and Jerry Edmonton from the hard-rock group Steppenwolf. "They came in, and Michael took the time to make everyone feel good, and they whipped that band together really quick," Andrew said. "We had other music directors who were totally unessential. Michael was really the one who put it together." There was also heroin in the picture, as Andrew remembered. "Our connection was in a hotel maybe four or five blocks away from where we were rehearsing. He and I and Janis were always going out to buy heroin and stuff. It was a real confused time."

The Joplin entourage traveled to Memphis just before Christmas to play Stax-Volt's annual Yuletide Thing. With Bloomfield acting as musical director, they rehearsed at the Stax studios on East McLemore Avenue Friday afternoon before the show and attended an evening cocktail party Stax president Jim Stewart threw for the Yuletide revelers at his house. Grossman was present to make sure everything went well the next day.

On assignment from *Rolling Stone*, Stanley Booth was backstage with Bloomfield, Steve Cropper, and Duck Dunn when the Bar-Kays, a Stax group who had re-formed after all but two of their members perished with Otis Redding in a plane crash the previous year, came onstage Saturday in zebra-striped flannel jumpsuits. "Bloomfield's eyes widened," Booth wrote. "It was the first sign of the cultural gap that was to increase as the evening progressed."

As Booth heard it, Joplin and her band didn't go over well with the thirteen thousand black Memphians and mostly teenage whites who had crowded into the Mid-South Coliseum to see her on a bill that included Eddie Floyd, Isaac Hayes, Carla Thomas, and Wilson Pickett. "They can all play, but not blues," he wrote. "Certainly not Mike Bloomfield, whose music is, like Paul Butterfield's, a pastiche of incompatible styles. One Memphis musician suggested that three months at Hernando's Hideaway, the Club Paradise or any of the Memphis night-spots where they frisk you before you go in might give them an inkling as to what the blues is about."

Booth was being a bit unfair to Bloomfield, who had certainly seen his share of potentially dangerous activities during his days in the Chicago clubs, and Booth was also making the mistake of thinking that Chicago blues and Memphis blues were the same thing. But his assessment of Bloomfield's style pointed to some of the difficulties that Bloomfield and his associates had faced in their efforts to combine soul and blues in 1968. They hadn't been completely successful, but each of the records he and Gravenites and Naftalin had contributed to that year contained some excellent music. They would keep working on it.

As 1969 began, Bloomfield and Gravenites took on a project that was close to their hearts. They had admired Otis Rush since their Chicago days, and Rush's guitar style had deeply impressed Bloomfield. He convened with Naftalin and Gravenites in Muscle Shoals, Alabama, in mid-February. "We were trying to get Otis out of the blues bag and into something more contemporary, which we thought would help his career and get him more money," Gravenites told me. "We went to Muscle Shoals at Michael's insistence, so he could meet his heroes, the guys who played on all those great tracks for Aretha Franklin and Wilson Pickett."

The sessions for Rush's *Mourning in the Morning* took place at FAME Studios, where Wilson Pickett, Clarence Carter, and Arthur Conley had been cutting superb soul sides with producer and owner Rick Hall and a band that included drummer Roger Hawkins, guitarist Jimmy Johnson, and keyboard player Barry Beckett. Young Nashville-born guitarist

Duane Allman had also been working at FAME, and Bloomfield was aware of his reputation. The Muscle Shoals rhythm section usually included bassist David Hood, but he was replaced on the Rush session by Jerry Jemmott, who had played on the recent FAME sessions that produced Wilson Pickett's "Hey Jude," a track that included a superb blues solo by Allman. Jemmott had played with Bloomfield the previous December at the Fillmore East, and some of those performances would be issued in 2003 as *Fillmore East: The Lost Concert Tapes*.

Rick Hall wasn't there for *Mourning*, and Birmingham-born song-writer and percussionist Mickey Buckins engineered the session. During breaks, he and Bloomfield talked about records, and he remembered how enthusiastically Bloomfield and Gravenites threw themselves into their work as the album's producers. "They loved it here," Buckins says. "Matter of fact, I couldn't hardly get 'em to go home at night. We'd just be fried out, you know, and Mike and Nick just wanted to sleep on the floor in the studio. Mike and I were both blues freaks, of course, and I said, 'Can you turn me onto some good, old blues that I know you've got that I've never heard?' He said, 'Man, as soon as I get through with this and get back home I'll start sendin' you cassettes.' But it never took place."

The session gave everyone a chance to trade licks and compare notes, and Naftalin remembers how relaxed everything was in Alabama. "They were very welcoming of us," he says. "They were real friendly, nice people—Jimmy Johnson, Barry Beckett, Roger Hawkins. They were fine folks. I had a get-together with Barry Beckett after one of the sessions, in the evening, and we exchanged ideas. He showed me some things, and I showed him some things I did."

Still, the South in 1969 must have been a strange place for two big-city Chicago musicians to visit, as Gravenites says. "When we got there, Michael said, 'Hey, where are all the black people? What do they do—hide 'em all behind the billboards?'" *Mourning* featured a Memphis horn section that was led by Gene "Bowlegs" Miller. "The horn players came in and they did 'Gambler's Blues,'" Gravenites laughs. "And Jesus, they finished the horn section and goddamn, the whole band—Otis, everybody—got down on the rug and started throwin' the dice."

In later years, Gravenites said he and Bloomfield were shocked to discover that the Muscle Shoals players that Hall was using at FAME weren't getting what they saw as the musicians' fair share of the profits from Hall's enterprise. "We couldn't believe it," Gravenites told me. "We were saying, 'Guys, you gotta come to San Francisco just to see what happens. Anybody who can twitch in rhythm is getting a recording contract and making all kinds of bucks.'" No doubt Johnson and the rest of the session band listened with interest as the San Francisco musicians extolled the virtues of moving west. But the members of the Muscle Shoals band had been unhappy for some time. They left Rick Hall in late March 1969, after Hall made a new distribution deal with Capitol Records that awarded them no more remuneration than they'd been getting before. David Hood said that the group flew to New York in mid-March to meet with Jerry Wexler, who agreed to lend them money to renovate Muscle Shoals Sound, their new studio at 3614 Jackson Highway in nearby Sheffield. The Muscle Shoals rhythm section stayed in Alabama.

Mourning in the Morning didn't turn Otis Rush into a soul star, but he acquitted himself well throughout, as did Naftalin, Allman, and the Muscle Shoals musicians. According to Gravenites, part of the problem was Bloomfield's lack of focus. "He couldn't produce a turd," he told me. "He could amuse people, be funny, show 'em stuff, but to actually sit down and control it and put it all together into a piece of product—he couldn't do it." The other problem was Bloomfield and Gravenites's material, which wasn't up to the standards of Muscle Shoals, Memphis, or Nashville. Buckins, who had been collaborating with tunesmith George Jackson to come up with first-rate material for soul singers Candi Staton and Clarence Carter, could have helped them out. Otis Rush didn't think it represented his talents. "It was a little bit too much of Bloomfield's and Gravenites's ideas and not enough of mine," he told *Guitar Player*'s Dan Forte in 1987. "I don't think the public accepted it, because it wasn't me." Neither reviewers nor record buyers much liked *Mourning* when it appeared in 1969, and Atlantic Records dropped Rush from their label soon afterward.

By early 1969 Norman Dayron had moved up at Chess Records. After starting out doing whatever Leonard and Phil Chess needed him to do, including emptying the trash and packing up records, he had become an apprentice engineer in 1965. The very bright Dayron busied himself picking up tricks and techniques from Chess's engineer, Ron Malo, who had recorded the Butterfield Band's *East-West* in 1966, just before Chess moved its operations from 2120 South Michigan Avenue to their new eight-story facility at 320 East Twenty-First Street. Like Leonard Chess's son, Marshall, Dayron had a sensibility that was somewhat different from that of Chess staff producers Charles Stepney and Bobby Miller. According to Dayron, Stepney and Miller had each done his duty to Leonard and Phil by checking out the Rolling Stones when the Stones recorded there in summer 1964, and both declared the band lacking and thus unfit for further consideration. Malo would engineer the Stones' Chess sessions.

Dayron was working with Marshall Chess in 1969 to bring Chess into the rock era. Bloomfield had come up with an idea that Dayron and Marshall liked: record Muddy Waters at Chess with Otis Spann and a host of great session players. Marshall pitched the idea to his father, and he even had a title, courtesy of Michael: *Fathers and Sons*. Dayron cut it that April in Chicago with a band that included Stax bassist Donald Dunn and, on harmonica, Paul Butterfield. *Fathers and Sons* serves as a serviceable introduction to Waters's music, and Butterfield plays well on it, but Dayron later said that he believed Bloomfield felt suppressed by the concept.

In fact, Michael tried to board a plane leaving Chicago to avoid playing the second day of recording sessions for the album. Norman quickly dispatched his girlfriend, Jo McDermot, to the airport, where she snatched Bloomfield from the gate. In the final recording, you can hear hints of Bloomfield's constraint, but he gets off some good licks on "Can't Lose What You Ain't Never Had."

Bloomfield and Gravenites had started off 1969 by recording three nights' worth of shows at the Fillmore West, Bill Graham's new twenty-five-hundred-seat venue at Market Street and South Van Ness Avenue in San Francisco. Released that October, *Live at Bill Graham's Fillmore West* was an attempt by Columbia Records to export the excitement of groovy San Francisco to the benighted provinces. A jam album, it met Michael's lowered expectations for such an event, but it proved to be a superb testament to Gravenites's talents as a singer and songwriter. The group, who billed themselves as Michael Bloomfield and Friends, turned in a brilliant performance of Gravenites's funk tune "It's About Time," and Bloomfield took an impressive solo turn in "Carmelita Skiffle." Several performances from the Fillmore West shows would appear on Gravenites's 1969 solo album, *My Labors*. He'd done some studio work with Quicksilver and arranged to fill out the rest of the album from the Fillmore album's leavings. The live stuff on *My Labors* sounds even better than the performances that turned up on *Live at Bill Graham's Fillmore West*, particularly "Gypsy Good Time" and "Moon Tune," a Howlin' Wolf tribute. "Holy Moly" is a psychedelic soul-funk song that sounds like the work the Dells were doing at Chess with Stepney at the same time. Bloomfield plays superbly throughout *My Labors*.

Michael Bloomfield and Friends would go through a dozen or so different incarnations, and it would be Michael's primary forum until his death. The *Live Adventures* band had comprised Al Kooper, bassist John Kahn, and drummer Skip Prokop, while *My Labors* featured Kahn, Gravenites, and Naftalin, who were augmented by a horn section and organist Ira Kamin. With his various friends during the first half of 1969, Bloomfield played the Fillmore and the Avalon Ballroom in February, recorded with Muddy and Spann at Chess, and recorded his first solo album, *It's Not Killing Me*.

Produced by Gravenites with help from Michael Melford, who had played in a bluegrass trio with Bloomfield and Ira Kamin in Chicago, *It's Not Killing Me* is a typical rushing-in-every-direction-at-once Bloomfield mess. The record has its charms as Bloomfield's first foray into the kind of easygoing studio rock that Ry Cooder would perfect on *Boomer's Story* and *Paradise and Lunch* a few years later. As a country-blues vocalist, Bloomfield was no Hank Williams or Gram Parsons or even Keith Richards, but he wrote some interesting and self-revealing songs for *It's Not Killing Me*. "Good Old Guy" contains a concise description of the man who wrote it: "He mostly kept to himself / He was shy and pretty funny / He stayed awhile and then he left."

Bloomfield's music for *The Trip* and 1973's *Steelyard Blues* is his best soundtrack work, but *Medium Cool* is the most significant film he scored (he split chores with Frank Zappa), and that includes Bloomfield's notorious later work with Norman Dayron for Andy Warhol's 1977 film *Bad* and a series of films overseen by San Francisco pornographers the Mitchell Brothers. Scored by Bloomfield and Friends in spring 1969, *Medium Cool* was written and directed by Haskell Wexler, a great cinematographer and the son of Bloomfield's great-uncle Simon

Wexler. Shot in Chicago in 1968, the film covers a lot of ground—Wexler combines documentary footage of the Democratic National Convention and the police crackdown that accompanied it with a narrative that encompasses the role of the media, black militancy, southern immigration to Chicago, and the brute power of Chicago itself. Bloomfield created an ominous surf-guitar instrumental to accompany the film's opening sequence, which takes place on an exit ramp on the Eisenhower Expressway.

Barry Goldberg had made an appearance in Sheffield, Alabama, in early November 1968 to record tracks for *Two Jews Blues*, which appeared in spring 1969. Goldberg had begun cutting *Two Jews Blues* a year earlier in Los Angeles with a band that included Bloomfield and drummer Eddie Hoh, and his sojourn in Alabama gave Goldberg the chance to record with bassist David Hood and guitarists Eddie Hinton and Duane Allman at Quin Ivy Studios, where Percy Sledge had cut the epochal soul single "When a Man Loves a Woman" three years earlier. Goldberg remembered how graciously Mickey Buckins and Eddie Hinton escorted him and his wife, Gail, around the Muscle Shoals area.

One afternoon after he finished up, Goldberg visited Duane Allman and Wilson Pickett at Pickett's hotel room. Pickett had forgotten about the annoying way Goldberg and Bloomfield had recruited Buddy Miles out from under him the year before. He and Allman were listening to a dub of a tune they had just cut with Rick Hall at FAME—it was "Hey Jude." "There was Duane and Pickett—they were jumping up and down on the bed like little kids, listening to the cut and screaming," Goldberg said. Bloomfield overdubbed his guitar parts for *Two Jews Blues* in sessions in Los Angeles.

In June 1969 Bloomfield and Gravenites organized the New York recording session for Janis Joplin's first record with the Kozmic Blues Band, *I Got Dem Ol' Kozmic Blues Again, Mama!* Bloomfield guested on four tracks. Sam Andrew, who also played on the album, said later that he could tell who was really listening by the way fans asked him about the record. "They'll say, 'Was that you playing on 'One Good Man'?' I'll say, 'No, that was Michael,' and they'll go, 'I knew it! I knew it!'"

At the end of 1969, *Rolling Stone* reviewed Bloomfield's *It's Not Killing Me* in less than glowing terms. "Bloomfield's singing should never have been released," David Gancher wrote in the magazine's November 15 issue. "His playing is a caricature of itself; it sounds stale, full of instrumental mannerisms and little else." Gancher also took time to dismiss two recently released albums that featured Bloomfield and Friends, *Live at Bill Graham's Fillmore West* and Gravenites's *My Labors*. "Bloomfield is a strange dude," Gancher noted. "When he's in the right room with the right people, he can be great."

Miles Davis took a slightly more nuanced view of Bloomfield's recent work in an interview with Don DeMicheal that ran in *Rolling Stone* in December. Davis trenchantly analyzed the difference between the way black musicians approached music and the attempts by white musicians to imitate their style. "I know some guys who'd be corny motherfuckers if they didn't have some other guys with them, and both of them are black," he told DeMicheal. "But one of them is almost corny and one is super hip; you put the two together and they get even. . . . In other words, you could put Mike Bloomfield with James Brown and he'd be a motherfucker." The thought of Bloomfield in James Brown's band is intriguing, but Mr. Brown would have taken more out of Bloomfield's salary for not shining his shoes than the notoriously ill-dressed guitarist could ever have paid. It is interesting to imagine what Bloomfield could have brought to Davis's *Bitches Brew*, which featured Harvey Brooks, or the trumpeter's 1970 album *A Tribute to Jack Johnson*, which sported a Bloomfield-like turn from English guitarist John McLaughlin.

Bloomfield ended 1969 with a guest appearance on Brewer and Shipley's *Weeds*, a Byrds-style folk-rock record that featured Gravenites's production along with backing by Naftalin, Bob Jones, John Kahn, and Ira Kamin. Michael added unobtrusive licks to the *Weeds* version of Dylan's "All Along the Watchtower." Minus Bloomfield, Michael Brewer and Tom Shipley would cut again with Gravenites and most of the same musicians on the following year's *Tarkio*, which yielded the duo's biggest hit single, "One Toke over the Line."

"After the Fillmore album, Michael decided that he didn't want to play the big places anymore, and he wanted to get back to the roots and play clubs and joints," Gravenites told me. "I'd heard about this place, the Keystone Korner, and was gonna check it out as a club we could possibly play in. We met the owner, Freddy Herrera, who was about ready to give up the ghost. He'd tried music; he'd tried topless, bottomless, everything. He'd lost his house, and he was about to go under."

The Keystone Korner started its life as Dino and Carlo's, a small North Beach bar that featured performances by local musicians and performers who were starting out. Before Herrera bought Dino's in 1969, singer-songwriter Harry Chapin and San Francisco rock band the Flamin' Groovies had played pass-the-hat shows there. Gravenites and Bloomfield told Herrera that they would make the Keystone Korner a regular stop if Herrera would let them counsel him on whom to book. With their help, the Korner became a popular club. "We told Freddy to get Elvin Bishop to play there, and he filled the joint," Gravenites said. "Elvin brought John Lee Hooker, and eventually Elvin moved into the back room, lived there for a while." Bloomfield and Gravenites performed irregularly at the Keystone Korner from late summer 1969 until 1972, when Herrera sold it to Todd Barkan. Under Barkan's management, it became the jazz club San Francisco had lacked since the days of the Beats.

Gravenites summed it up. "It was like that old TV show, *The Millionaire*, the guy with the check," he said. "We walked in there and saved his ass and didn't even know it. Two little angels. Blues angels. Ha ha ha."

Bloomfield stopped playing for a while in 1970. In another one of the dramatic reversals that became part of Bloomfield lore, his mother, Dottie—everybody called her Dottie—got dressed up one night that summer and sought out B. B. King, who was playing in Chicago at Mister Kelly's, a fancy nightclub on Rush Street. Bloomfield told Dan McClosky that she told King, "You know, Michael doesn't want to play anymore. His hands are getting rusty. It's terrible." In response, "B. B. King, you know, he wrote me a letter. He called me on the phone and said, 'You've gotta keep those fingers in shape. You must do this. You can't just fall apart. You just can't let what you've got go to hell like that.' My God, the next time I had a chance to see B. B. King, I was embarrassed to face this man who had meant so much to me. I so much wanted to be like him, play like him, and like he knew that I didn't want to." "It's like an old spiritual song," B. B. told his errant student. "It may not come when you want it, but it's always right on time."

Around the same time a party of guitarists that included Carlos Santana and Terry Haggerty, the guitarist for the San Francisco band the Sons of Champlin, visited Bloomfield at his house on Carmelita Avenue in Mill Valley. Like his mother and B. B. King, they had heard he wasn't doing much playing. "And they told me, 'Man, you ought to be ashamed of yourself to charge admission at the door to see you, because you're a fucking joke, you're a laughingstock,'" Michael told *Guitar Player* magazine's Tom Wheeler in 1979. "'We used to *learn* from you. . . . You're a fraud. You can't even *hold* a guitar anymore.' And I just said, 'Hey, I'm not into that anymore. I'm into watching the *Tonight Show* and shooting dope. I'm into stoned leisure.' But they wouldn't let up. They sat down, and they said, 'Now listen to us play, man.' And they played. Hag started playing and, oh, my God, he was better than I ever was. It was unbelievable. From then on, I vowed, never again. If you're going to get up in front of people, God knows you better be good. That those guys would do that, to come over, to come down on me so hard, to get the balls to do that . . . it so moved me that these people wanted to see me playing again . . . it affected my heart tremendously. What nice guys, what gentlemen. They got me back into guitar."

Suitably chastised, Bloomfield applied himself anew. He was probably just rusty, because he admitted to Tom Wheeler that "there was no prolonged period like this—it was more of an on-and-off thing."

As Miles Davis's early-1970s work with McLaughlin and former Chess session guitarist Pete Cosey demonstrated, Bloomfield's electric guitar innovations had become part of rock, blues, and jazz. Leading Cream through their extended versions of such blues tunes as "Spoonful" and Skip James's "I'm So Glad," Eric Clapton helped advance the guitar-hero mode, just as Bloomfield had done by recording "East-West" with the Butterfield Band. Clapton had gone on to front Derek and the Dominos. Jeff Beck had recorded 1968's "Love Is Blue," a superb instrumental version of André Popp and Pierre Cour's Paul Mauriat–recorded song. Jimmy Page had left the Yardbirds to form Led Zeppelin, and inspired a whole generation of electric guitarists by adding flash to licks that Michael had first made popular.

Johnny Winter, who had received a lucrative contract from Columbia Records partly on the strength of Bloomfield's endorsement (Winter had performed with Bloomfield and Al Kooper at one of their December 1968 shows at New York's Fillmore East) began making albums that combined T-Bone Walker–style guitar with heavy metal, and moved up to headlining huge arenas. Duane Allman and Gregg Allman had assembled the Allman Brothers Band, who invented a southern variant on the blues-based rock of the Butterfield Band's *East-West* and the leisurely jams of the Grateful Dead.

There were others: the barely competent Grand Funk Railroad's Mark Farner, the speed-flash virtuoso Alvin Lee, the Hendrix clone Robin Trower, and the eccentric Peter Green. There were straight bluesers: Rory Gallagher, Mick Taylor, Kim Simmonds, and Henry Vestine. All had different styles, all flirted with the blues to a greater or lesser extent, and every single one of them, if they were speaking honestly, would acknowledge a debt of some magnitude to Michael Bloomfield.

Bloomfield's blues playing represents a fine expression of the Mississippi-to-Chicago style. Bloomfield often sounds like Muddy Waters, right down to the dramatic shakes and microtonal shifts he employs. He also sounds, most obviously, like B. B. King, and when Bloomfield famously described his style as sweet, he meant the way he used sweet notes—the sixth, ninth, and thirteenth notes of the major scale, to be precise—to color his melodies. You can hear Otis Rush and Chess guitarist Jody Williams in his playing as well, and while Bloomfield didn't choose to play like Curtis Mayfield, Steve Cropper, or Bobby Womack, he could also negotiate the demands of rhythm guitar accompaniment that Cropper, Womack, and the brilliant Missouriborn session guitarist Reggie Young perfected in Memphis, Muscle Shoals, and Nashville. Bloomfield was a consummate blues soloist, but he could play virtually any style of American guitar.

Bloomfield's domestic and romantic situation during the first half of the 1970s was complicated. He had met a fifteen-year-old high school student named Christie Svane in 1969 at the Fillmore West, where she was helping out in the kitchen. Bloomfield came in to say hello to the Fillmore's cook, Ron Butkovich, and Svane was struck by Bloomfield's wide stride and open-bodied walk. The way he carried himself, his aura, reminded her of Allen Ginsberg, she said later. After the show, everyone went back to Svane's father's house in San Francisco, and Bloomfield crashed on the spare bed. In the morning, Svane discovered he'd gone back to Mill Valley.

They met again in 1971 on the night the Fillmore West closed. They drove with her brother and Dan McClosky to the top of Mount Tamalpais, near Bloomfield's house. They watched the sun rise and, as she told me later, "We really fell in love right there." She went back to high school in Davis the next day. Bloomfield told her about his heroin addiction, which Svane said later was a warning sign. "He told me all these horror stories about how the walls were weeping, with blood running down them, and hallucinations of the radiator turning into a wolf. . . . Having said all that, he then said, 'You know, heroin is the best thing in the world. It's better than sex.' Which didn't mean anything to me. I didn't know about sex from personal experience at that point."

At the end of 1971, Michael's ex-wife, Susan, reappeared in Mill Valley. She had been living in Europe and had had a son with another man. Landing in Chicago, she had talked to Dottie, with whom she was close, and Dottie suggested she go out to help Michael and bought her a plane ticket. Susan moved into Michael's new house on Reed Street, where she would live for the next six years. The house sat on a hill near the Kentucky Fried Chicken on Miller Avenue, with a driveway so steep that you needed a good emergency brake if you were going to visit.

It was at Michael's house in 1973 that Susan met Bonner Beuhler, a young Mill Valley resident and good friend of Toby Byron, who had met Bloomfield while Byron was still in high school. Gathering his courage, Byron knocked on Bloomfield's door one afternoon in late 1968, and Michael came out in a T-shirt, groggy from being awakened. Byron enlisted Bloomfield and his current Friends to perform at a November 1969 benefit show at Tamalpais High School in Mill Valley. Byron did road work for Michael in 1971, and in early 1972 Michael asked him to move into the house on Reed Street and work for him booking gigs, moving equipment, driving him to shows, and overseeing many of his recording sessions. "It was also the beginning of an awareness about a whole lot of other stuff beyond music, in culture, whether it be Lenny Bruce or Johnny Carson or loose women or drugs or whatever," Byron said about their relationship.

In 1973 a romance developed between Byron's friend Bonner Beuhler and Susan. "I'd go over to the house, Michael would get up around noon, Susie would make breakfast, and he took to his room a lot," Beuhler told me. Bloomfield had settled into a daily routine. "He was a voracious reader, and he'd sit there and read, or watch TV and practice guitar," Buehler recalled. "And then it would be dinnertime and he'd roll a joint, then sit down and watch TV." Bloomfield took them on excursions into San Rafael to buy magazines. There were Billy Swan and Merle Haggard records to savor, books to devour. Everyone gathered around on Saturday night to eat fabulous dinners and drink beer and laugh at the antics on television. "He was like the king," Susan said. "Not in a bad way, because everyone—and there were a lot of us circulating around us—got a lot from him."

Family life had its good points. Susan's son, also named Toby, wasn't Michael's, but Michael begged her to pretend he was. Sitting around the tube with Bonner, the two Tobys, and Susan, it was easy to feel that you had a family, so why not pretend that you did? And if Bonner and Susan were beginning a love affair that would result in marriage a few years later, so what? There were clubs in San Anselmo, just up the road, and over in Berkeley, a forty-minute ride, not to mention the Keystone Korner, in case he wanted to play. Downtown in Mill Valley was the world's greatest record store, Village Music, which sold every kind of music in the world. It was where all the musicians shopped, so the customers were cool and wouldn't bother you with idolatry or bullshit.

And Bloomfield still toured fairly extensively during the early-to-mid 1970s. He played dates in Seattle, Chicago, Vancouver, Halifax, and Toronto, and he performed at the Under the Sun Festival in Madison, Wisconsin, in July 1973 with a band that included Naftalin along with James Brown drummer Clyde Stubblefield, who sat in at the gig. Later that summer, he played two nights at Tulagi in Boulder, Colorado. The reporter for the *Colorado Daily*, Deborah Osment Ryan, caught up with Bloomfield in Boulder. "Well, you see, there is the particular road that you're supposed to take—engagements in Vegas and Tahoe, your own TV show," he told Ryan. "I can't see myself as Shields & Yarnell or Donny and Marie [Osmond], so I just refuse to hustle."

It was an easy life. Who cared that in 1973, *Crawdaddy* felt it necessary to headline an interview by songwriter-groupie Lotti Golden WHATEVER HAPPENED TO MIKE BLOOMFIELD? Who cared that a reader looking for an answer would have to conclude, "Not much"? In 1974 I interviewed Mike Bloomfield for a piece in *Creem* magazine that, in the end, they never ran. They figured it was all over for him.

There was time. And there were shades to keep at bay.

14

TERMINALLY MELLOW

What happened to Michael Bloomfield over the final half-decade of his life was partly or perhaps even mostly a matter of the drugs, as Susan and Ira Kamin and almost everyone else thought, but that was almost too obvious to mention, and anyway, his situation had to do with a number of other things that they realized Michael wasn't very adept at managing and that may have in fact eluded the grasp of the most fastidious careerist. Some of his difficulty obviously had to do with his relationship to his parents and to his money. His bohemianism and disregard for mere objects was an understandable result of that, but it seemed a bit excessive, even for a folkie who was also a rock star. His habits would land him, for example, in serious tax trouble in 1974, when Susan discovered that he hadn't filed returns of any kind between 1968 and 1972, his prime years as an earner.

Harold Bloomfield bailed him out of that mess, and Susan spent two years with Michael's accountant, a very nice lady, before they got it all straightened out. It transpired that Michael wasn't amassing any mountain of money through the largesse of the Bloomfield family, because he and Allen and his two cousins received income from the trust their fraternal grandmother had set up: proceeds from the interest on Michael's 25 percent, about $50,000 a year. That wasn't insubstantial in 1974 terms, but Michael had to pay tax on it, and he had needed more in 1971 to buy his house on Reed Street in Mill Valley. His father arranged for that, because Michael needed a house. So there was access, and that certainly must have been in the back of his mind.

As for the career, Gravenites said that the reason for its decline was also obvious but, again, a function of Bloomfield's vexed relationship to simple things that a musician of his seriousness could hardly be expected to willingly attend to. "He never took care of his business," Gravenites said. "He never followed up on stuff." When it came to the music, Bloomfield was usually all there—as Gravenites said, he tended to be the last person to leave the rehearsal, and he worked harder on getting the music right than anyone. Bloomfield's experiences with Dylan and Bobby Neuwirth and the other members of Dylan's entourage, and the brutal way some of them had all put down the formerly hip folk stars, like Phil Ochs and David Blue, who had fallen by the wayside as Dylan reinvented songwriting in the 1960s, reinforced his already advanced notion of the way the music business and fame got in the way of everything, especially friendship. As a deep musical thinker and consummate guitarist, Bloomfield inspired his fellow musicians, but he himself needed inspiration, a little competition, a compatriot who could keep him honest, more than most musicians do. I asked Allen Bloomfield point-blank if he thought Michael deliberately picked musicians who were somewhat beneath his level, meaning some of the nonplayers he sometimes used from the Group days to his 1970s work with Norman Dayron in nowhere studios with never-could-be sidemen. Many of the musicians Bloomfield worked with, from Mark Naftalin to Bob Jones to Nick Gravenites and Harvey Brooks and Marcus Doubleday, were very excellent players and singers, but Allen understood the question. "If he were put on a stage with Robbie Robertson or B. B. King or Albert King, it would possibly be too anxiety-provoking for him, and he gets real nervous," he said. "He surrounded himself with a comfortable group of players that he could pretty much direct. In some way, it took away the pressure and the challenge that he would've had to have risen up to."

———————

Bloomfield was candid about most aspects of his life, but he'd lie when it came to junk. In interview after interview during the 1970s, he'd talk about how glad he was to be off junk, and then go right back to doing it. He could be very articulate about it, as he told Tom Wheeler in their 1979 interview. "Heroin gave me pimples," he said. "And I put the guitar down, didn't touch it. See, a junkie's life is totally, chronically fucked. You either eat and move and be productive, or else you're a junkie. There's no choice. Or at least there wasn't for me." According to Toby Byron, Bloomfield also exaggerated his drug use in the name of good storytelling. Byron said that, aside from sleep issues, Bloomfield was healthy and off drugs in the first half of the 1970s. For example, Michael would put orange juice, banana, raw egg, and Tiger's Milk into a blender for breakfast, and he also did a lot of swimming.

15

WHATEVER HAPPENED TO

Over the next five years, Bloomfield lent his talents to a number of studio projects, including his second solo album, 1973's *Try It Before You Buy It*, and the same year's *Triumvirate*, recorded with John Hammond Jr. and Dr. John. He also cut 1974's Electric Flag reunion album, *The Band Kept Playing*.

Try It Before You Buy It stands among the best work Bloomfield did during this part of his career. Once again, he gave a good-natured nod to New Orleans R&B and the Meters–style funk. His singing had gained confidence, and the combination of his guitar and Naftalin's elegant piano accompaniment made for a relaxed but never indolent collection of good songs. It's one of Bloomfield's most enjoyable and accomplished records. Columbia rejected it for release in 1973, and the complete version of *Try It* wouldn't be issued until 1990.

As Hammond said later, Bloomfield played well on *Triumvirate*—for a supergroup record, it's very relaxed—but Columbia's head of A&R, Kip Cohen, resigned in 1974 after Clive Davis was fired, and the album went nowhere. It was an honorable effort in the vein of the Meters' contemporaneous *New Directions* and *Trick Bag* albums, and the trio even did well with King Floyd's "Baby Let Me Kiss You" and a Muddy Waters blues shuffle, "Just to Be with You." Hammond went back to playing solo, and Bloomfield re-formed the Electric Flag.

Bloomfield called Barry Goldberg in New York to enlist him in the task of reviving the Flag, and the keyboardist flew with his wife to California in spring 1974 to woodshed with the band. The reborn group, which included Roger "Jellyroll" Troy, a veteran of numerous

King Records sessions in Cincinnati, went to Miami in mid-1974 to record *The Band Kept Playing*. They had finally gotten the chance to work with Atlantic Records, but Jerry Wexler and engineer Tom Dowd found Buddy Miles impossible to control. As Wexler said later, Miles got into a disagreement with Dowd on the first day of recording at Criteria Studios. One of the greatest recording engineers in history, Dowd had put an ambient mike over Miles's drum set, and Miles took exception to Dowd's setup. By the time Wexler got to the studio, Dowd was gone. Wexler said that Miles "featured himself as the man who knew everything." Wexler and his crew had to go into the studio every day before the session and erase Miles's bass parts, which the drummer had overdubbed in place of Roger Troy's. *The Band Kept Playing* was a curiously empty, soulless record by a great group of soul and blues musicians. "People had gotten really tight and weird and crazy," Goldberg said later. "It didn't work out."

In the mid-1970s, while Bloomfield toured with his Friends and enjoyed relaxing at home with his extended family, his spirit was large upon the land. It was more than just the sound of his guitars—it was the guitars themselves. Inspired by the example of Freddie King and Eric Clapton, Bloomfield had begun playing his famed 1959 Les Paul Standard sunburst-design guitar in 1967. It featured wonderfully hot pickups that enabled a guitarist who was turned up high enough to sustain notes like crazy. The Les Paul Standard was an unpopular model among rock guitarists until Bloomfield used it in the Butterfield Band. Bloomfield's example inspired Jeff Beck, Jimmy Page, and Johnny Winter to begin playing Standards. Gibson resumed manufacturing the Standard in 1968, and today vintage models command prices as high as seven figures. In 2009 Gibson manufactured a limited edition of Michael's Les Paul Standard that reproduced the famous guitar right down to the mismatched volume and tone knobs and the scratch above the tailpiece.

It's part of Bloomfield lore that he lost his Les Paul Standard in the 1970s, but the exact date remains uncertain. Bloomfield's housemate Toby Byron remembered seeing Bloomfield's Les Paul Standard in their Reed Street domicile in 1975. According to Byron, it's likely that Bloomfield lost his famed Sunburst in late 1975 or early 1976.

Bloomfield performed with Muddy Waters, Johnny Winter, Dr. John, and Buddy Miles for producer Ken Ehrlich's July 1974 *Soundstage* tribute to Waters. The *Soundstage* show gathered some of the black musicians—Waters, Guitar Junior, Junior Wells, Pinetop Perkins, Willie Dixon, Koko Taylor—from whose fountain Bloomfield had drunk. It also reminded viewers that Gravenites and Bloomfield had learned their lessons directly from Waters and the other Mississippi-to-Chicago musicians who had invented the style in the 1940s and '50s. Nick was there, and he walked over to the ultra-cool, commanding Waters and said, "Remember me? The man with the money?" It wasn't a race-relations thing at all.

During our 1974 interview, Michael talked to me about what he wanted to happen in the future. Things had changed since he retreated to his house on Reed Street. For one thing, the Chicago blues scene Bloomfield had known in the 1960s had been transformed. Big John's had closed in 1966, and the building had been razed to make way for a high-rise apartment building, the Americana Towers. Silvio's had burned to the ground in April 1968 during the civil unrest that followed in the wake of Martin Luther King's assassination. Howlin' Wolf drove with his wife to look at the site after things had calmed down, and she said he wept. (Silvio's owner, Silvio Corazza, would die in 1975, and Howlin' Wolf would die the following year.) Leonard Chess had died in 1969 after he and Phil sold the label to the GRT Corporation for $6.5 million dollars. Newly out of a job after the Chess deal went down, Norman Dayron had moved to Mill Valley in the early 1970s. Dayron would produce a series of records with Bloomfield over the next decade.

"As long as I mature as an artist, my life is not in vain," Bloomfield told me. "This is what I'm here for. It used to be just that, but now it's two things. The other is that I have a good time every day and do not end up like no Jimi Hendrix. I do not want to be put in the position where I am not the complete master of my own destiny at all times . . . I definitely do not want to be a cog in nobody's machine unless it's gonna make me a rich motherfucker."

It was a familiar refrain. Bloomfield talked about the demands of show business, the way that some artists, such as Duke Ellington, Elton John, and Totie Fields—Bloomfield always had wide-ranging interests—could become "beloved entertainers" out of a compulsion to perform, which he didn't have.

"I also want to be solvent," he said. "I've influenced millions of musicians. I'm a good musician, and I want to keep being a good musician. But I want to be solvent.

"But one thing I am not going to do, man, is I am not going to work to become an idol again. Toby [Byron]'s always saying 'Build your name up again, blah blah blah.' Man, lookit: I saw hundreds of times I coulda been there, and I never thought it was that important. There are sides of my ego that I'm sure would love to see it happen, being on the cover of *People* magazine and talk on Johnny Carson and all of that. That is not what I'm shooting for, because I am sure that the price you pay for that, for my personality, would be too great a price.

"I used to be a very crazy guy, and I had pain for almost every day for years and years and years. It never stopped. I don't know if you've ever been crazy or ever really lost your mind to the degree that you hurt every day, *physical*, man, so that you would do anything to stop it. Now that is a distant memory."

He'd just completed the sessions for *Try It Before You Buy It* in early 1973, and in fact gave me a cassette of the album when I left that day, but he cautioned me that it wasn't as good as he'd wanted it to be. "If only I could do another album, make it a double record so I could have lots of guitar playing in all styles, and write more songs, I would be really happy," he said. "I hear music and think of it in my mind, and I know how I want to hear it. All these sonorities and all the sounds everyone is capable of, and I live it all, in a way. It all comes through the radio, man. It all comes from the air, you know, and it all feeds into me. I think I know the sonorities and the melodies and the chords that are really beautiful, that you would find really beautiful and that most anyone would. I would like to put out a record that had those sounds on it. And I will. Oh, if I could only do just one that would make me as proud as the Beatles probably were with *Sgt. Pepper* or Jimi Hendrix was with *Axis* or I was with the first Butterfield album . . ."

He thought I didn't hear the pain in his voice, that I missed his brushing tears from his eyes. He was wrong.

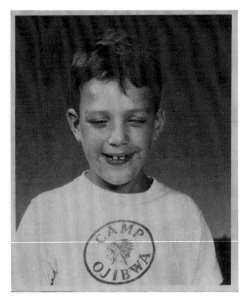

Top Left: Michael at Camp Ojibwa. Top Right: Dottie, Michael's mother.
Bottom: Michael (second from right) and Allen (right) vacationing in Arizona, circa 195

Top: Harold Bloomfield. Bottom: Big Joe Williams.

Michael with Sunnyland Slim at the Fickle Pickle, 1963.

ᴏᴘ: Michael (left) with his oldest friend, Roy Ruby, playing on the street two doors down om Big John's, in front of the Trails, at the corner of North Avenue and Wells Street in hicago, 1964. Bᴏᴛᴛᴏᴍ: At Muddy Waters's house, interviewing Muddy for *Rhythm and ues* magazine, 1964.

Top Left: From left to right, Charlie Musselwhite, Michael, Mike "Gap" John-son, and Donna Koch at Big John's, on Wells Street in Chicago, October 1964. Top Right: From left to right, Sid Warner (only his arm is visible), Mike "Gap" Johnson, Michael, Charlie Musselwhite, and Donna Koch, at Magoo's on Chicago's North Side, January 1965. According to Donna Koch Gower, this would be the last night they played the club. Michael kept playing blues when the club owner wanted rock 'n' roll. Bottom: Delmark Records recording session, March 3, 1964. From left to right, Hammie Nixon, Sleepy John Estes, Michael, Yank Rachell.

Michael with John Hammond Sr. (BOTTOM) at his 1964 demo session.

"Like a Rolling Stone" recording session.

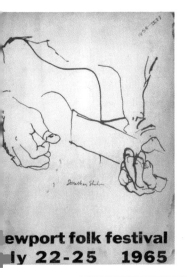

ewport folk festival
ly 22-25   1965

ewport. BOTTOM RIGHT: Michael and Paul Butterfield.
BOTTOM LEFT: Pete Seeger introduces the Paul Butterfield Blues Band.

The Paul Butterfield Blues Band at Newport, July 23, 1965.

...ichael and Dylan rehearsing at Newport, July 25, 1965. Top: From the Newport film *...stival!* produced and directed by Murray Lerner. Bottom: Sam Lay on drums, Jerome ...rnold on bass, Al Kooper on organ.

BOTTOM: The Butterfield Band, Monterey Jazz Festival, September 17, 1966.

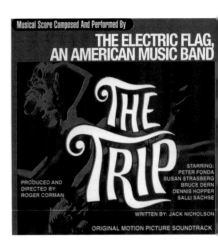

The Electric Flag, an American music band, 1968. From left to right, Harvey Brooks, Stemzie Hunter, Michael, Buddy Miles, Marcus Doubleday, Peter Strazza, Nick Gravenites, Herbie Rich.

Electric Flag sessions at Columbia. UPPER LEFT: Nick Gravenites. UPPER RIGHT: Barr[y]
Goldberg. BOTTOM: Left to right, Michael, Buddy Miles, Harvey Brooks.

Top: The Electric Flag flies at the Fillmore Auditorium, San Francisco, 1967.
Bottom: Michael and Eric Clapton, backstage at the Earl Warren Showgrounds, Santa Barbara, California, February 24, 1968. The bill: Cream, James Cotton Blues Band, Taj Mahal.

Top: The Electric Flag at the Trauma club in Philadelphia, March 1, 1968.
Bottom: Michael and B. B. King at the Fillmore East.

CENTER: Al Kooper, Norman Rockwell, and Michael at the photo session from which Norman Rockwell would paint the cover art for *The Live Adventures of Mike Bloomfield and Al Kooper* (BOTTOM).

TOP: *Super Session* live at the Boston Garden, 1969. BOTTOM: Michael rehearsing Janis Joplin solo band in Memphis at the Stax studios for the Stax Records Christmas party, December 21, 1968. Left to right: Brad Campbell, Roy Markowitz, Janis, and Michael.

TOP: Michael takes a bow during *Super Session* at the Boston Garden, 1969.
BOTTOM: Bloomfield eats fire.

ROLLING STONE/NOVEMBER 9,

MIKE
BLOOMFIELD
TRY IT BEFORE
YOU BUY IT

Harvey Brooks and Mike Bloomfield down South

ELECTRIC FLAG IS BUSTED: 'THE LENNY BRUCE RIFF'

had been signed to play
of the Mexican gardener
he film version of Terry
en's book, Candy. The
er is not the one with the
Marlon Brando and Rich-
urton are also in the film.

On the Move

Move have now signed
A&M Records in Los An-
They were the second Eng-
p signed — Procul Har-
ng the first. Denny Cor-
&M man for both groups,
coming to L.A. later to
o record them at A&M's
track studios.

and Benefit

ce for the benefit of the
ill be held this Sunday
Winterland. Grateful
g Big Brother and the
Company are heading
which includes the
er Messenger Service,
arth and Blue Cheer.

Salvation

, formerly New Sal-
ry Ramone, shortly be-
concert in record
tours.

In the same week the Grateful
Dead were busted, and, like Moby
Grape, on the eve of their first
record release, most of Mike
Bloomfield's band, the Electric
Flag, were arrested on narcotics
charges. It happened at a Hunt-
ington Beach motel near the
Beach club where the Flag

were listening to tapes.
Their bust was one of a series
of raids in Orange county that
week. The band reports, however, that the officers were not
at all hostile, just uptight.
Bloomfield, et. al., return to
Huntington Beach for a prelim-
inary hearing on Oct 24. After
that they are headed for gigs and
ding sessions in New York.
bands of fate,"
different

ᴏᴘ Rɪɢʜᴛ: Susan. Bᴏᴛᴛᴏᴍ: The Paul Butterfield Blues Band reunion at Winterland in
an Francisco, February 1973. Left to right, Elvin Bishop, Michael, Mark Naftalin, Paul.

Mark Naftalin and Michael.

16

RECORDS FOR MONEY, RECORDS FOR FUN

I had been trying to see Michael play as often as I could. Because I lived in the Bay Area, there were plenty of opportunities, but I missed a lot of them, including the dates Bloomfield and Gravenites had played with Sunnyland Slim in area clubs in late 1972 and early 1973. I did get to see Naftalin, Bloomfield, and Gravenites—the old Chicago crew—do a series of shows that were almost always good and very often great. Bassist and singer Roger Troy had joined the Friends in 1973 and the new incarnation of the Electric Flag shortly after.

Troy brought a lot to every situation, but getting the Flag together again had been a distasteful experience for almost everyone involved. With the record going nowhere, they played dates through the first couple of months of 1975. Gravenites said later that Buddy Miles was going through "absolute insanity" during 1974. Everyone was either crazy or in it for the money.

It's typical of Bloomfield's career that in 1976 he released what he considered his best record, *If You Love These Blues, Play 'Em as You Please,* and what may be his most derided effort, KGB's *KGB.* The latter was a misguided attempt to capitalize on the supergroup concept that Al Kooper had created for Bloomfield in 1968. At Toby Byron's suggestion, he and Barry Goldberg took Bloomfield to meet manager Elliot

Roberts, who owned a company called Lookout Management, in his L.A. office. Roberts, with David Geffen, had managed Joni Mitchell and Neil Young before starting Asylum Records in 1970. "The guy looked across the table and said, 'Boys, let's put a super group together,'" Bloomfield said. "I told him he was crazy. Al Kooper had invented the term—super group, super session—and it was a pure scam. It was filthy lucre."

On paper, the group had its merits: singer Ray Kennedy had written lyrics for "Sail on Sailor" with Beach Boys head Brian Wilson; Brooklyn-born drummer Carmine Appice had played with Vanilla Fudge, a rock-soul group, and with guitarist Jeff Beck; and Ric Grech played bass for British avant-garde blues band Family and for supergroup Blind Faith before he joined Traffic in the early 1970s.

Before he joined the newly created firm of Kennedy, Goldberg, and Bloomfield, Appice had played drums on the sessions for Beck's 1975 album *Blow by Blow*, only to have his parts replaced by Richard Bailey's. Appice had wanted equal billing with Beck, but the guitarist demurred. "I was hangin' out with Ric Grech, thinking that if [the Jeff Beck record] didn't happen, I might need to do something else," Appice says. "My lawyer told me about this band, and he said they're looking for a bass player and a drummer. When we met Michael, they played, and it sounded good and all."

Elliot Roberts put forward the initial offer for the right to record KGB, which started a bidding war for the band. They signed with MCA and prepared to cut the record. Lookout even arranged for the band to perform at a Hollywood showcase for record label executives, and MCA threw a party for them featuring waiters dressed like Russian Cossacks. "We went into the Village Recorders to record, on Santa Monica, and Michael just said he wasn't coming," Appice says. "So we hadda get a session guy to play guitar on the basic tracks, and then we had to take it up to San Francisco so he could put his parts on. He couldn't sleep. I don't know if he could sleep anywhere else, but we had to do the tracks without him."

Appice also noted some of Bloomfield's other eccentricities. "He was like a schizophrenic guy," he says. "I can just visualize him, the way he'd walk around with his head sort of down. He never stood straight up. He was quickly walking around and changing directions, with a white T-shirt on." The condition of Bloomfield's car and house impressed Appice as well. "His car musta had a foot high of trash on the floor," he says. "You couldn't get in the backseat and sit there with your feet on the floor, because of all this trash in there." But he thought Bloomfield played superbly.

The record could have done well, but Bloomfield sabotaged the release from the beginning. "We were the number-one most added record on the radio, a big push comin' on and everything," Appice says. "We all did interviews, and Mike did an interview with Robert Hilburn of the *Los Angeles Times*. He told Robert Hilburn that no way would he have ever played with a band like this, and that this was just put together by the big management company just to get big money from the record company. It totally blew the whole thing."

Bloomfield left the band, and Grech soon followed suit. Talking to *BAM* magazine's Terry Marshall in 1976, Bloomfield explained what had happened. The record was a "completely fabricated bullshit trip for a lot of money, where everybody was sort of burned," he said. During the interview, he described currently popular guitarist Peter Frampton as a "junior Eric Clapton or junior Michael Bloomfield."

Appice would later assist Bloomfield on the soundtrack for the Mitchell Brothers' *Sodom and Gomorrah*, and he and Michael attended the film's San Francisco premiere. He never worked with Bloomfield again.

Bloomfield believed his best work was on an instructional record for other guitarists, and indeed, *If You Love These Blues, Play 'Em as You Please*, recorded in 1976 for *Guitar Player* magazine, has plenty of merit and earned him his only Grammy nomination. He may even have been right, because *If You Love These Blues* is a very listenable record, right down to Bloomfield's vocals, which at their best do approach the level of Ry Cooder's similar efforts. The album is both a document that students can take as a lesson book and a record a nonplayer can enjoy without reservation.

The album reflected Bloomfield's new approach to performing. As he told Tom Yates and Kate Hayes in 1981, he had developed a new method of guitar playing. "I had worked out a style of guitar playing that was as much country-blues style that you play with your fingers, the sort of orchestral, one-man-band sound, that was mixed with as much hot-licks lead guitar," he said. "It was just an equal mixture of it, and I'd also learned how to sing by then. From that period, which was around '76, '77, from then on, it's just been a progressively hot period for me. I'm still in the middle of it." Despite the common perception that he never again played as well as he had in 1967 and 1968, Bloomfield plays about as fluently as he ever did on the track "WDIA," the record's tribute to, or lesson about, B. B. King's Kent Records style. He sounds like he's earned the right to sing about what the blues has done to him.

The Electric Flag and KGB experiences had given backbone to Bloomfield's resolve to reinvent himself. After he unburdened himself to the press in early 1976 about the machinations of the KGB deal, Bloomfield composed a remarkable letter to Elliot Roberts. "Elliot, BANDS are individuals grouped or bonded together for a common purpose, a common aesthetic, more than just the dollars," he wrote. "ELLIOT MAN, you have no idea what I DO as a musician or entertainer, and it's plenty weird." He explained to Roberts that he was like Ry Cooder, Jesse Ed Davis, and Leon Redbone—artists who could make a living by staying faithful to their aesthetic and by playing music that remained true to an idiom that pop music could only imitate. "I was wrong to take the money. I was wrong not to walk out of your office the first or second time I met you and you referred to me as a loser and those people I play with as losers," he wrote. He was sorry to negate their investment in him, but he had to back out.

Meanwhile, Bloomfield continued a long-distance relationship with Christie Svane. She had left California to go to college in Vermont, and she would conduct her romance with Bloomfield from afar for most of the decade. Susan made a change as well, moving out of the Reed Street house in 1976 to live with Bonner Beuhler. "When I married Bonner, part of me was scared that I had given up my family, which was Michael and his family," she said. "It was pretty scary there for a little bit."

After he completed *If You Love These Blues, Play 'Em as You Please*, which had been financed by *Guitar Player* magazine through their books and records division, Bloomfield began recording with Norman Dayron. Bloomfield's work with Dayron documents a rich period in the guitarist's anti-career. Far from being a diminished performer in his last five years of his life, Bloomfield exhibited a very high level of mastery of the guitar. And on such late-1970s recordings as "I'm Glad I'm Jewish" and his 1977 live version of Randy Newman's "Uncle Bob's Midnight Blues," he fleshes out his guitar skills with a newly discovered flair for singing.

What comes through in the recordings that Dayron made of Bloomfield from 1976 until his death is Bloomfield's outsized—and wonderful—sense of humor. Bloomfield wrote a number of songs in a country-music style in the 1970s. Demo versions exist of such potential Nashville classics as "Soaping Dolly Down" and "Do It with Jerry Lee." In his live performances Bloomfield covered Tom T. Hall's "That's How I Got to Memphis" and Wayne Kemp's "The Image of Me," a 1968 hit for Conway Twitty.

Dayron's work with Bloomfield has its detractors. One of them is Nick Gravenites, who thought Dayron encouraged Bloomfield's disdain for music business thieves to little effect. "Maybe Norman didn't feed on Michael's cynicism, but he reinforced it," Gravenites said later. "And there's a big difference between knowing someone is a thief and doing something about it. . . . Norman contributed activism—actually going out and fucking the record companies. The result was, probably, that they felt good about doing it. But it resulted in a lot of schlock product, a lot of stuff that didn't really represent Michael's best interests."

Al Kooper agreed, but thought that Bloomfield had abdicated control. "I don't think Michael gave a fuck," he said. "Going to put out another record—great, like that. I don't think he cared very much about them."

Dayron defended the albums he made with Bloomfield. "For Michael, the truth is that those albums were a natural self-expression of what he wanted to do," he said. "He didn't feel there was any market for what he really wanted to do. . . . Maybe they are controversial, but they are incredibly valuable, because Michael put his whole heart and soul into them." In Dayron's view, Kooper and the other critics of Bloomfield's later work simply missed the point: that was what Michael wanted to do.

An enthusiastic piano player himself, Bloomfield worked with a series of estimable keyboardists that included Al Kooper, Barry Goldberg, and Mark Naftalin. If Kooper attempted to provide a producer's context for Bloomfield on *Super Session*, Goldberg brought songwriting chops and soul music sensibility to his collaboration with Bloomfield. A superb blues accompanist, Naftalin dueted effectively with Bloomfield during the 1970s. Bloomfield enjoyed his collaborations with such versatile musicians, producers, and songwriters, but he did what he wanted to, as Dayron said. Goldberg also remembered Bloomfield's self-willed approach. "He was so charismatic that everybody just wanted to hang out with him," said Goldberg. "He opened up a lot of doors for musicians that maybe weren't really at the top of their game."

Norman Dayron recalled how Bloomfield allowed pianist Jon Cramer to play on the 1980 sessions for *Cruisin' for a Bruisin'*. "He had Jon Cramer play the piano, and they did this song, 'Snowblind,' about cocaine," Dayron said. "Cramer was interesting. He was another one from Chicago, from a wealthy family. . . . But as a producer this was a horrible experience, because here was something that was, in my view, so difficult and so lame and so painful I didn't want it on the album." As their careers demonstrated, Kooper, Naftalin, and Goldberg were first-rate musicians. Bloomfield's generosity toward his friends sometimes caused him to lower his standards, but it also demonstrated his humanity.

From 1976 on, Bloomfield mostly played live around the Bay Area, with occasional trips to New York, where he was a big draw at the Bottom Line. He also made a few trips to Canada and Europe. One of his favorite working situations was playing acoustic guitar with Mark Naftalin in emulation of the great piano-and-guitar duets that were the rage in blues during the 1930s, when Big Maceo and Tampa Red, Scrapper Blackwell and Leroy Carr, and Cripple Clarence Lofton and Big Bill Broonzy recorded in that style.

"I felt that Mike and I were a guitar-and-piano team that could hold its own with the greats," Naftalin told me. "Not to compare myself with the greats as a piano player—nobody speaks with the true blues voice like one who comes from the true blues background. But we were a remarkable combination. I think there's plenty of evidence of that." Naftalin would perform with Bloomfield until close to the end.

17

LOVE AND DEATH

"I'm sorry," Mark Naftalin said when I interviewed him at his San Rafael house on a cold, rainy night in 1981. "But when I think of Michael, all I think of is the pain that was in him, and that is in me residually." That was the refrain I heard from Michael's friends when I asked them about the last years of his life.

Always adept at devising new ways to avoid going out of the house, Bloomfield in the late 1970s had become even more unreliable about making shows than in 1969, when he had tried to leave Chicago rather than attend the second day of Dayron's *Fathers and Sons* sessions at Chess. Gravenites, Naftalin, Bob Jones, and Steve Gordon, who operated the Savoy nightclub in San Francisco, had also been the victims of his dilatory mode of creation.

For Naftalin, who had faithfully and sensitively accompanied Bloomfield during the 1970s, it wasn't a matter of Bloomfield's seriousness as an artist. "But he didn't want to stay on a path," Naftalin said. "He wanted to retreat. And he did it again and again." They would get on a roll, Bloomfield would play beautifully, and then Bloomfield's phone calls would cease. For Jones, whom Bloomfield had instantly won over ten years earlier at their first meeting in San Francisco—as he strode into the room where Jones was rehearsing with his current group, the Tits & Ass Rhythm & Blues Band, Bloomfield had exclaimed, what am I hearing, Otis Redding singing and Al Jackson on drums?—it was the same. The last years with Bloomfield were a struggle. "He would get to the day in the week where you'd have to catch the plane to the gig, and he would be in various stages of denial," Jones said. "I would go to his house early. Whatever condition he was in, I would find his equipment and throw him in the van and off we'd go, either to the gig, if it was local, or to the airport to catch a plane." It grew even worse in 1978, Jones said, but once Bloomfield was safely onstage, he almost always hit the music hard, just as he'd always done.

Throughout his life Bloomfield had devoted a good deal of time to visiting doctors, trying to find ways to calm his insomnia, and there had also been emergency calls on the road in the 1960s and during the later years he lived on Reed Street. The local paramedics knew their way up the hill. He went to the Stanford Sleep Center in the mid-1970s and, according to Norman Dayron, used this and other opportunities to charm his doctors into giving him downers and sleep medication. "They were his fans, these doctors," Dayron said. Norman remembered Chicago days, when he took Bloomfield to the University of Chicago hospital after Michael underwent a particularly severe bout of sleepless-ness. Bloomfield had a certain relationship with medical practitioners that Dayron believed was, in some bizarre way, actually creative.

Allen Bloomfield took the view that Michael had, when all was said and done, a divided consciousness—a set of impulses that he remained unaware of. "He did not know that they were operating within him," Allen said about these motivations. Their father had suffered from long bouts of severe depression, and the family had a history of suicide. Allen had been diagnosed with manic depression when he was fourteen. In Allen's estimation, Michael saw what should have been therapeutic as a game to be played.

"He unfortunately gave credence to the fact that he was a very bright, very on-top-of-it individual, in that he felt that he knew more than the doctors did," he said. Allen thought that Michael's famed indifference to material possessions and the niceties of the music business were products of his vexed relationship with their father. If Harold Bloomfield was immersed in the world of measurability—cof-feemakers, salt shakers, ketchup dispensers, money—Michael mea-sured time by the music he played, the records he heard, and the teetering stacks of novels he had already read. Bloomfield read every-thing: novels by Saul Bellow, Philip Roth, and Bruce Jay Friedman, medical books, and the odd science-fiction paperback. Allen couldn't think of one material object Michael really cared about, except maybe some trinket B. B. King had once given him. One of Michael's friends said that all of his cars looked like they had been rolled down a hill with the doors open.

"My father would have been more disappointed that Michael didn't maximize his financial benefits," Allen said. "For one reason or another, he didn't take that to be the most serious part of it. Michael rejected, to some extent, the hard, logical business application that would have had to have been done to negotiate properly his fair share. Trying to watch somebody who was letting it run through his fingertips isn't something that my father could appreciate."

———————

Christie Svane had moved to New York, where she did some modeling for Arnie Levin, the *New Yorker* cartoonist, and she reconnected with Michael in October 1978 during his two-day stint at the Bottom Line. After one of his sets, Bloomfield took Christie to his hotel room, where she told him that she had gotten pregnant with his child when she was seventeen and had had an abortion. They realized they were in love, even though each of them was involved in another relationship at the time. Bloomfield returned to San Francisco, where he began receiving postcards from Svane that described their beautiful relationship. Bloomfield's current girlfriend read them as well, and she moved out of Michael's house. Svane spent time in 1979 at Naropa, a Buddhist college in Boulder whose instructors included Allen Ginsberg, before she made the decision to go to Mill Valley to take care of Michael.

By 1979 Bloomfield had developed an addiction to Placidyl, a powerful hypnotic that was commonly prescribed in the 1970s. It produced dizziness and other side effects when it was taken over a long time. He entered a state mental hospital for a month that fall to get off the drug. While he was recuperating, Christie visited him. After recovering from his addiction, Bloomfield started drinking, a turn of events that distressed Christie and his friends, who knew that Bloomfield had always preferred weed to alcohol. Christie moved back to New York in the winter of 1979, and Bloomfield followed her there, only to return home two months later.

———————

Woody Harris had met Bloomfield during one of Michael's Bay Area shows. Harris was a classical guitarist who recorded an album titled

American Guitar Solos for Chris Strachwitz's Arhoolie label in 1976. He and his wife, cellist Maggie Edmondson, began playing shows with Bloomfield in 1979, and Michael and Woody recorded an album of gospel music duets that year, *Bloomfield/Harris*, at Norman Dayron's house. The following year, through his New York agent, Harris booked the trio into a late-summer tour of Italy and Sweden. With Christie along to help Michael, they left for Italy in early September 1980. On the flight over, Harris noticed the way Bloomfield deftly snatched the small bottles of gin from the tray the flight attendants would wheel by at regular intervals.

"The trip to Italy was a beautiful trip," Svane told me later. The sunlight and the ruins were inspirational. She remembered that he played in top form. This was also the point at which Michael intensified his assault on her resistance to marrying him. He'd already proposed once, and she'd turned him down, since she was still involved with a man in her dance troupe. But he continued. "It was in Pisa on a Saturday night," she remembered, "and he said, 'Look, in two hours it's gonna be sunrise. We're in Italy. There are thousands of Catholic churches in every alley down there. Let's go downstairs right now and get married. Come on, don't tell anyone, just get up, get dressed, and let's go.' And all the time I was grilling him. 'What happened between you and Susan? Why didn't that work out?' And his answer was 'I wasn't a man then, I wasn't a man.'" (How two Americans, one Jewish, would have been able to figure out how to get married on a Sunday morning in Italy, though, is something Michael never considered.)

But Bloomfield also drank steadily, insisting on taking part in contests with his Italian fans to see who could drink the most grappa. The Italian fans wanted *Super Session*, and Svane remembered how they threw bottles and yelled for "Albert's Shuffle." She left the tour before it continued on to Sweden. There, Harris said, Bloomfield "drank himself absolutely wild." They were backed by pickup groups on some dates, and their repertoire included Paul Siebel's "Louise" and James Taylor's "Bartender's Blues," a song that George Jones had cut in 1978.

They returned to New York in late September, and Harris said Bloomfield simply abandoned his guitars at the airport to take a $300 cab ride to visit people he knew in Connecticut. Bloomfield, Edmondson, and Harris continued to play dates together, including a December 11 show at the Childe Harold in Washington, DC, at which

Bloomfield dedicated "Amazing Grace" to John Lennon, who had been murdered three days before.

Three weeks earlier, Bloomfield sat in at a Bob Dylan show at the Warfield Theater in San Francisco. The engagement came about after Maria Muldaur, who had known Dylan since 1962 and had also heard reports that Bloomfield wasn't doing well, invited Dylan and his band, which included bassist Tim Drummond and guitarist Fred Tackett, to her house in Mill Valley for a home-cooked meal. "Dylan was very nervously sitting aside from everybody," Muldaur said later. "He kept looking around, and finally he said, 'Bloomfield, Michael Bloomfield, lives around here in Mill Valley, doesn't he? Can we call him up? I'd love to go see him.'"

Muldaur and Dylan got into their car, and Muldaur directed the driver to Reed Street. The television was on inside the house. Maria Muldaur stood on tiptoe in front of a window to assess the situation. Bloomfield was in his bathrobe, watching an old movie. She and Dylan entered the house, actually crawling through a window to get in, and Bloomfield did a double take and turned down the television. They talked for a half hour. "Bob said, 'You've got to come down and sit in with us, man,'" Muldaur recalled. "'Maria came down, and Jerry Garcia came down.' Mike said, 'Oh, I don't know. I'm not playing much these days.'" Dylan invited him to catch Etta James that night in San Francisco, but Bloomfield begged off, said he was in for the night. He wanted to get back to watching the movie. Bloomfield promised he would go down and play, and Dylan rose to leave.

Before Dylan could get to the door, Michael handed him a gift. It was a thick, square Bible with a filigreed cover, and it had been in Bloomfield's family for generations. "On the way into the city, Bob was looking at the Bible and going, 'Wow, man, look at this book,'" Muldaur said. "He was really touched that Michael would just, out of the blue, give him his family Bible. He seemed to really appreciate it."

Bloomfield made his last major appearance at Dylan's November 15 show. Bob Johnston, who had produced *Highway 61 Revisited*, was there. According to Greil Marcus, who wrote about the event in his 2005 book *Like a Rolling Stone: Bob Dylan at the Crossroads*, Bloomfield approached Johnston. "Can you help me?" he asked Johnston.

"No one will talk to me." Bloomfield had showed up at the Warfield with Norman Dayron, who helped him find his way to the box office. "Michael was wearing tattered blue jeans," Dayron said. "You could see his knees through them. . . . And he's wearing house slippers, those old brown slippers that you just slip on."

They finally got someone's attention, and they went to the dressing room. "Dylan gave him about a five-minute introduction onstage, because he knew his audience didn't know who he was, though this was San Francisco—and they didn't," Dayron told me later. "So he gave this tremendous introduction, and here was Michael by the side of the stage, holding on to some guitar, wearing his bedroom slippers and a black leather jacket, and he shuffled on to the stage, plugged in, and just brought the house down."

That night he played "Like a Rolling Stone" and "The Groom's Still Waiting at the Altar," a song Dylan would include on his 1981 *Shot of Love* album. "When Michael started playing, the music came alive like nothing you've ever heard," Dayron recalled. "I mean, it was just like that killer slide guitar on the *Highway 61* album—only it was louder and cleaner and more mature and more thoughtful, faster and cleverer. It was really quite a job he did, and it surprised the hell out of me, because he was not in great shape that night.

"Afterwards, Dylan was so happy. He said, 'Man, I had no idea how much I've missed hearing you in my music, those notes that ring, that guitar style!' He begged Michael to come back the next night, and I think we all knew it wasn't going to happen, that Michael wasn't capable of recreating that magic, that it would spoil the occasion."

———————

While they were traveling in Italy with Woody Harris, Bloomfield had made a confession to Christie Svane: Norman Dayron had told him, he said, that the only way to win her back was to get back to work and become a performer again. "He kept saying the most frightening things to me, expressions of love like, 'Give me a reason to live,'" she said later. "'Give me an occasion to rise to. Let's have a kid. Nothing matters to me now. I've been to the top.'" After playing with Dylan on November 15, Bloomfield called her in New York. Svane was preparing to go on a three-month European teaching and performing tour, and he offered to pay her to cancel it. She declined—she would see him after she got back.

Near the end of 1980, Bloomfield asked Norman Dayron to drive him into San Francisco. As Dayron remembered it, Michael lay on the backseat, making commentary from a position where he could see nothing. Dayron had noticed that Bloomfield was recently in even more distress than usual—drinking endless bottles of gin, passing out, fouling himself. Norman found it uncomfortable to be with him. As he said later, "I couldn't stand it, and I felt very guilty about it, because I felt as his friend I should take care of him. But he wouldn't let anybody take care of him." Dayron thought that Michael was hanging around hard characters and was proud of it. "It was like playing with fire, because the guy was an armed robber and a dope dealer," Dayron said of one of Michael's new friends. "I believe he was a dope dealer who didn't use dope, which was kind of dangerous, because he never knew what he was selling."

Bloomfield played his last show, an acoustic set, at the student union at San Francisco State College on February 7, 1981. He had come full circle from his days at the University of Chicago's twist parties at Ida Noyes Hall. Six days later, Tom Yates and Kate Hayes walked through the tunnel of foliage that covered the walkway leading to the house on Reed Street and knocked on the door. Michael gave them his final interview.

At 11:00 AM on February 15, Ted Ray, a reporter who lived at 572 Dewey Street in San Francisco, saw a man slumped over in a banged-up 1971 Mercury Marquis. Ray went back to his place and called the cops and the paramedics. The car doors were locked, so the ambulance steward had to reach in through one of the windows, which was partly rolled down, to open the door. The keys were in the ignition. The corpse carried no identification. Michael Bloomfield was registered as John Doe #15 for the year, and his body was taken downtown to the medical examiner's office.

Susan Buehler identified the body. Then she made the call to Allen Bloomfield. Allen notified his mother and father, who came to the Bay Area with their current spouses. (Harold and Dorothy had divorced many years earlier.) "My mother proceeded to pass out," Allen said later. "Her new husband was understandably shocked by this. My father did not falter and navigated the situation in a detached manner."

Christie Svane received the news in Paris, where she had just seen a troupe of dancing bears be put through their routine by the Moscow circus. She said later that she finally understood what Michael had endured in Italy.

The pathologist ruled the cause of death as cocaine and methamphetamine poisoning. There was also a drug called benzoylecgonine and a slight trace of a morphine-type alkaloid found in Bloomfield's system.

What on earth had happened? Michael had never used cocaine; he didn't like the drug. Would a lifelong insomniac be intentionally taking not only that but also methamphetamine—two drugs that keep you awake? In addition, nobody knew whom he'd been visiting there in San Francisco. The place where he was found wasn't near any of his known associates. Had he been looking for heroin and mistakenly taken the wrong drug? But then, why would he have wanted heroin when he'd been off it for so long? Once he'd made the mistake, did his tired body just short-circuit, and, thinking he just needed to ride it out, did his unknown companions walk him to his car and hope he'd wake up and drive back to Mill Valley?

We'll never know the answer to these questions. All we know is that Michael Bloomfield found sleep for the last time and, perhaps, as he left this earth, heard the hellhounds' baying receding into the darkness.

18

AFTERMATH

Country Joe McDonald and Bill Graham were among the friends who attended Bloomfield's memorial service on February 18, 1981, at San Francisco's Sinai Chapel. Bloomfield was laid to rest two days later at Hillside Memorial Park in Culver City. Barry Goldberg gave the eulogy.

Kurt Loder's obituary for Michael appeared in *Rolling Stone* on April 2. "According to friends, he still had the old instrumental fire whenever he chose to flash it," Loder wrote. "Two weeks before his death, for example, he sat in with the Sir Douglas Quintet at the Catalyst, a club in Santa Cruz, California. 'We just plugged him in,' said Doug Sahm. 'He said, "Let's play some blues," and man, he got up that night and played more damn blues—I mean, he sounded like the old Michael. I couldn't believe it.'"

Bloomfield did indeed make great music in the last five years of his life, but most of it was in live performances, not on the records he made for Denny Bruce's Takoma label or the other small labels he and Norman Dayron signed with. Like many of his later records, Bloomfield's last album, the posthumously released *Cruisin' for a Bruisin'*, indicates a decline that may have had as much to do with a paucity of musical conception as with Bloomfield's technical execution or the acuity of his ear. In his later years, Bloomfield was a musician out of time—a singer, guitarist, scholar, and song junkie who would have fit perfectly into what became known as Americana music in the first decade of the twenty-first century. If he had outlived his era, he would almost certainly have matched up with another one.

Nick Gravenites gets the last word: an epigram for musicians and listeners who want to ponder the relationship between people who need to make music and the people who want them to, at any cost. "That's the way life is, and that's the way all real things are," Gravenites told Jan Mark Wolkin and Bill Keenom. "They have their ups and downs and middles. Everything else is show business."

———————

The Paul Butterfield Blues Band was inducted into the Rock and Roll Hall of Fame in April 2015. Mark Naftalin, Sam Lay, and Elvin Bishop were on hand. Gabriel Butterfield accepted the award for his father, who died in 1987. Tom Morello, Zac Brown, and Kim Wilson performed "Born in Chicago," and the ceremony included a screening of film clips of the Butterfield Band in the 1960s. J. Geils Band singer Peter Wolf remembered seeing them at Club 47 in 1966. "They played every night like it was their last night on Earth," he said. Mark Naftalin thanked Paul Butterfield for inducting him into his band, and Elvin Bishop summed it up: "That was a butt-kickin' band, and we helped blues cross over to the regular public." Michael's niece, Nicole, accepted on his behalf. Born in 1978, Nicole spent time with her uncle in 1980, when Allen Bloomfield and his family were living in Scarsdale, New York. Allen recalled how gently Michael cradled her in his arms during his visit.

Nicole ended her remarks by quoting the prescient observation Michael made to Tom Yates and Kate Hayes in 1981: "The music you listen to becomes the soundtrack of your life. It may be the first music you made love to or got high to or went through your adolescence to, went through poignant times of your life—well, that music is going to mean a lot to you. It's going to take on much more import than just the sound of the notes, because it's the background track for your existence."

EPILOGUE

Altar Songs

Susan Beuhler: "We took our first steps into adulthood together. It was fun, it was scary, and most of all, it was exciting and interesting. I couldn't have done it with a more perfect person."

Muddy Waters: "When I first heard Michael, I knew he was gonna be a great guitar player. I let him play with me all the time, sit in with my band. Every time he and Paul would come in, let 'em sit in and do a couple of numbers. That's the way kids learn, you know, sittin' in and getting the feeling and getting the smoke of it. I like to take kids tryin' to get across and give 'em a helpin' hand, you know. I didn't get so many helpin' hands, and that's why I'm so nice to people.

"Every time I went off to California, he'd come see me. Every time I went anywhere near, and he wasn't doing anything, he'd come to see me. And any time he could get around, he definitely gonna sit in!

"As a guitar player? One of the greats! Mike was a great guitar player. He learned a lot of slide from me. Plus I guess he picked up a little lick or two from me, but he learned how to play a lot of slide and pick a lot of guitar."

George Mitchell: "On March 31, 1963, I arrived in Chicago by bus from Atlanta. I had already lined up a job at the Jazz Record Mart, the original location at 7 West Grand Avenue on the Near North Side. The next day, my first day on the job, I was sitting at the cash register. Bloomfield walks in and we meet. Started talking and hit it off. We had similar interests in old-time blues, and we were the same age: nineteen years old.

"The night before, Bob Koester had held his last concert at the Fickle Pickle, a coffeehouse on Rush Street, a popular nightclub area. Mike and I got to talking about that—and right then and there, we decided the two of us would see if we could keep them going.

"We reasoned we could not do like Bob did and bring in big names, and we would need a lot more promotion. Mike, we decided, would be in charge of promotion: he knew Chicago and, I soon found out, had a good mouth for going around and talking to people. I would locate old-time solo blues singers around Chicago, because I had experience from down South doing that, and I would book the musicians.

"We would need to pay the musicians a minimum, we knew that, and we decided on twenty dollars for each of two acts, an opener and a final act—and, somehow, the two of us would have to come up with forty bucks every week, at least until we were packing the house. I was making forty a week at the Jazz Record Mart, which meant that I would really have to scrimp. Mike had just lost his job heading up a band at a small nightclub, because the owner told him to play only rock 'n' roll, no blues, but Mike and his band kept playing the blues. The main way Mike would make his share was to sit on the street wearing sunglasses, holding a cane, with a tin cup in front of him, while playing acoustic guitar. I got such a kick out of that I'd go observe sometimes, and watch folks toss change into the blind fellow's cup.

"Mike did a good job at promotion, and we were featuring some really fine bluesmen (including, eventually, Sunnyland Slim, who had a car and was nice enough to volunteer to drive me around looking for musicians: Homesick James, John Henry Barbee, St. Louis Jimmy, Washboard Sam, Jazz Gillum, Lazy Bill Lucas, Little Johnny Jones, Billy Boy Arnold, Maxwell Street Jimmy, Blind James Brewer, and, of course, Big Joe Williams, who lived in the basement of the Jazz Record Mart), and pretty soon we were making the owner so much money selling meals that he offered us Monday nights as well as Tuesday nights. We loved it! And as much time as Mike and I spent working with each other, you might think there would be at least an argument or two, but there wasn't—not one! We got along great!

"And Bloomfield did all this not to promote himself (the only person I can remember him playing onstage with was Sunnyland Slim) but to introduce young Chicagoans to the type of music he loved, and to help out the musicians.

"At nineteen years old, he was so devoted to the blues!

"And, at nineteen years old, he could play the old country blues like no one I'd ever heard—and I mean before or since! I loved asking him, 'You know any Blind Lemon, Mike?' And he'd start playing *just* like Blind Lemon. 'Okay, let's hear Blind Willie Johnson,' and he'd play *just* like Blind Willie. You name the musician, Bloomfield could play just like him! Unbelievable!

"I have such fond memories of Mike Bloomfield: working with him at the Fickle Pickle . . . hitting Maxwell Street with him just about every Sunday . . . enjoying the meals cooked by his wife . . . going to Milwaukee to hear Sonny Boy Williamson, and for Michael, very nervous, to ask to play a song with him, which he did, beautifully . . . and, of course, our famous trip to St. Louis with Big Joe . . ."

Nick Gravenites: "If it weren't for Michael, I would never have gotten out of the hole. He was a big booster of mine; he helped me with record deals, gigging. He helped me with my self-confidence, and he helped me understand things with Jewish eyes instead of goy eyes.

"He did that for a lot of people—it was just his nature. He could boost you, make you think better of yourself, make you think you were worth more than maybe what you thought you were. He put a different value on it. I always had a crazy singing style, weird, nuts, never would fit in with the popular stuff, but Michael would say, 'Hey, you sing well, you're a good blues singer, don't get down on yourself.' And I overcame it.

"It was Michael's nature to help people, reach out and give 'em a boost. That's an important part of him, a very generous guy. When we played as Michael Bloomfield and Friends, we always split the money even. He was always equitable in his dealings with people.

"He had ambivalent feelings about blues and blues music. He loved it, but at the same time he knew it was played by human beings, and they were less than perfect. Just because you were a bluesman didn't mean you were a beautiful person.

"But, Mike, he had a certain verve about his playing. A certain charisma that drew people to him for his music and his humorous wit. He epitomized music to me."

―――――――――

Paul Butterfield: "Michael never really had nothing to prove. I used to hang out in his living room, and we'd play. We were friends for years, always on good terms. But he just sort of hung out in Mill Valley, and I was out working."

―――――――――

Barry Goldberg: "I just really loved him, as a soul brother, as part of my life, musically and intellectually. He was a consummate intellectual, one of the smartest people I've ever known, if not the smartest. He'd play these little games, almost like the Magic Christian. He'd create little scenes that were hilarious, that would make it all make sense for me.

"He'd put people in the correct perspective. If he saw somebody who was a wise guy or an asshole, a mockie from New York, he'd call 'em on it. People would get real down to earth quick, and I could see what it was all about through him. He could break down all those weird pretentiousnesses. I'd feel a lot more human around him.

"His death was a tremendous shock to me. Life doesn't have the same meaning to me. At least when he was alive, I knew he was going through the same things I was, life at the same time, and it was some sort of consolation to me. And even now, when something weird goes down, I'll always say, What would Michael make of this situation? If he were here, it wouldn't be that heavy."

―――――――――

Charlie Musselwhite: "When Mike was enthusiastic about something, you couldn't help but get enthusiastic, too. Nobody ever lived that could be more enthusiastic than Mike. He would just be filled with joy . . . just bubbling over with pure joy, and it was very infectious. Like he might play some recording of a guitar solo and he'd be yelling, 'Listen to that! Just listen to that!' And jumping up and down and running around the room filled with joy. He couldn't help himself.

"He was real smart, real interesting, and he investigated every part of music, you know, that interested him, to the nth degree. He wanted to have it all down and know exactly the whole history of it, the structure of it. In those ways he was great. He shoulda been a teacher."

"It was real sad. I knew he was tormented. Not being able to sleep. Maybe due to a chemical imbalance. I felt like he was always searching for peace, but his body wouldn't let him have it. As sad as it was to hear of his passing, it was not a big surprise. I wish he could've lived a long life and enjoyed playing music and telling stories and having those big laughs."

Mark Naftalin: "I first ran across Mike when he showed up with a band at a University of Chicago dormitory-lounge 'Twist Party.' This night was a raucous free-for-all where two or even three bands might be playing simultaneously. Mike's presence was exciting, as were his extraordinarily fast rock 'n' roll licks. Afterwards, without introduction, I asked him why he played so fast. He said, 'Because I practice a lot.' This was in 1962. I was seventeen and Mike was eighteen. I did not see him again until the summer of 1965, when I joined the Butterfield Band and our friendship began.

"By the time Mike left the group in early 1967, the two of us had, through various youthful escapades and many long conversations, become pretty good friends. So I missed his company. As for the music, the band lost something irreplaceable when Mike left, and I believe that Mike lost something irreplaceable, too.

"Following Mike's departure, I stayed on the road with Paul for a little over a year, then settled in the Bay Area and, in 1969, started playing local clubs with Mike. After that, Mike and I worked together for the better part of a decade, playing concerts and club dates on the West Coast and around America and Canada. We did hundreds of shows altogether, sometimes as a duo, but usually with a rhythm section as a four-piece band.

"We played blues and rock 'n' roll, mostly, but not always. For two nights at the Other Cafe in San Francisco, for example, we played only waltzes—songs that we already knew like 'Goodnight, Irene,' and some other three-four tunes that we worked up from sheet music. I used a 12-bass accordion, a gift from Mike, on the Cajun waltz 'Drunkard's Dream.' We were billed as the Waltz Kings.

"Mike was a great friend, a hilarious companion, and an inspiring music-playing partner. The joy of the music we played together will always be part of me, as will the pain of knowing that he's gone. I miss him every day."

Mitch Ryder: "The last time I saw him was when I went to Colorado to make my retreat. I went into this little club, and this comedian named Steve Martin was opening for Michael in this club in Boulder. I went back into the dressing room to talk to him to see if I could borrow $35, which I never paid back. That's the kind of guy he was."

B. B. King: "What do you say about your son? If he favors you, you think that's a great thing, makes you happy. And it's the same with playing guitar.

"We talked many times. We had many man-to-man talks, but it always led up to music, you know. From the very first meeting we had a very good relationship with each other. And when the subject would, as I said, change to music, it would deal with something we wanted to do, musically, and he'd ask my advice on what to do. Michael was a warm person, a real good-hearted person, a friend, a dear friend. If he liked you, he'd tell the world about you, and that helped me out a whole lot. I met his mother, and she said he'd told her about me.

"Michael was very talented. I think of him as an old friend, the sky's the limit. That's the kind of guy he was. No telling what he might have accomplished if he'd lived longer, that's how talented he was. I miss him."

Toby Byron: "Michael was my door into a grown-up world. Early in 1971, Susan had moved back, and he asked me in such a tender way to move into his house while he and Jon Cramer went to Europe, ostensibly to hang out with the Rolling Stones (they didn't).

"He gave me a ringside seat at life beyond suburban America. Exposure to Nick, the sage; Susan, his best friend; Muddy's big, warm hand; Jewishness, Seders, and his mother, Dottie, whom I would see whenever I was in L.A. until nearly the day she died.

"Deep soul food (pulled pork, lox, and White Castles) and a lot of music, Sunnyland, prewar blues; Claude Jeter, Freddy Fender, and Charlie Rich. Comic geniuses like Redd Foxx and Myron Cohen. Talented hustlers like Chris McDougal, sex and earthly delights. Bukowski, *Mean Streets*, and *The Confessions of Nat Turner*. The Wailers and an unknown Bob Marley (we hung out backstage and partook!). Randy Newman, Mac Rebennack, and studio wizards Roy Segal and Tom Dowd. Michael allowed me to ride shotgun with him and his cohorts (though I nearly always drove) across North America—gigs at the Fillmore, Tahoe, Santa Cruz, L.A. to Vancouver, Halifax to Florida, and dozens of points in between. Every minute invaluable. He could be generous to a fault. Irresponsible, too (uncaringly losing my vintage lap steel). His appetites were enthusiastic, and his soul ran deep. Beyond my family he had the most profound impact on my life."

Allen Bloomfield: "My remarkable brother was a powerful presence to grow up with. He was not your typical Wally in *Leave It to Beaver*. He was highly perceptive, compassionate, and had a savage wit. To share time with Mickey was like engaging in the wholesale slaughter of ideas and values which I took naively for granted and he had already realized were just hollow platitudes. He saw too much, too soon. He was looking through his heart more often than his eyes or mind. He was not motivated by money or the things it could provide. He was not impressed by manicured lawns or opulent homes or social acceptability, in conformance to a specific clique.

"This fearless quality cuts both ways—musical savant and self-destructive. I miss and love him every day."

> *My friend, this body is His lute. He tightens the strings and*
> *plays its songs.*
> *If the strings break and the pegs work loose, this lute, made*
> *of dust, returns to dust.*
> *Kabir says: Nobody else can wake from it that heavenly music.*

ACKNOWLEDGMENTS

TO THE 1983 EDITION

Putting this book together was not nearly as difficult as it could have been, and for that I've got an army of people to thank. First, the folks in Mill Valley, especially Michael's extended family, including Christie Svane, Susan and Bonner Beuhler (for everything except the pickled brussels sprouts), Robin Pritzker and John Goddard, and Norman Dayron. Special thanks to Nick Gravenites, a great singer, a great raconteur, and a gentleman of the old school. Bob Watts and Kristi Eurich put up with two weeks of craziness and jokes about vegetarians while I stayed in their house, which is beyond the call of duty, and I was immeasurably helped by the solid contributions of Dan McClosky, Tom Yates, and Kate Hayes.

Back in Texas, I have to thank Jeff Bruce and the Austin *American-Statesman* for the leave of absence; the tape transcribers, in particular Margaret Moser, Chris Walters, Nels Jacobson, and the other proofreaders.

There were the voices over the phone: Muddy Waters, B. B. King, the ever-soulful Barry Goldberg, Mitch Ryder, John Hammond Sr., Paul Butterfield, and Toby Byron "just checking."

TO THE 2016 EDITION, BY ED WARD

Considering how short a time it was in print, this book has had quite an impact on the few folks who were able to get a copy, and so the news that Toby Byron was interested in finally doing a new edition was a relief: at last people would stop asking me where they could get a copy. This time around, a lot of things were different, but in particular I'm indebted to David Dunton of Harvey Klinger Inc. for his diligence in setting up a working agreement for an e-book, then, almost accidentally, selling it as a physical book to Yuval Taylor at A Cappella/Chicago Review Press.

As it turned out, I didn't have the time to do much of the research that remained to be done, so heartfelt thanks are due to Edd Hurt, who interviewed a lot more people and interpolated their stories into the original. On his—and my—behalf, I'd like to thank Don Allred, Carmine Appice, David Bastin, Elvin Bishop, Allen Bloomfield, Joe Boyd, Mickey Buckins, Norman Dayron, Bruce Dickinson, Ted Drozdowski, David Duncan, Robben Ford, Dan Forte, Barry Goldberg, Nick Gravenites, Kate Hayes, David Hood, Julius Lester, Nell Levin, Ronnie Lyons, George Mitchell, Mark Naftalin, Jas Obrecht, Paul Petraitis, Ed Pettersen, Caroline Peyton, Barry Tashian, Jon Tiven, Elijah Wald, Tom Wheeler, Peter Yarrow, and Tom Yates. It should be noted that opinions of Michael's work after *Super Session* included in the text are Edd's; I no longer have access to the later records, which are locked up at the University of Texas, still being catalogued after fifteen years.

After many years out of the country, I'm back in Austin, and would like to thank Roland Swenson, Bob Simmons, Rob Hamlet, Kelly McEntee, Minerva Koenig, Andrew Halbreich, and the folks at *Fresh Air* (via satellite) and at Taqueria Arandinas. Tip of the hat to Terry Byrnes for a fine author photo, too.

TO THE 2016 EDITION, BY TOBY BYRON

In addition to all those previously mentioned, special thanks go to Bonner Beuhler, Toby Beuhler, John Hammond Sr., Charlie Musselwhite, and Robin Pritzker. And I cannot thank Dottie and Allen enough, especially for their great friendship over the many years.

Thanks as well to the many who helped with the original edition and those who helped with, inspired, or supported this new edition: Pete Welding, Peter Guralnick, Jann Wenner, Marcia Gravenites, Pinkie Black, Mikey Harris, Alan Betrock, Jim Delehant, Jim O'Neal, Dick Waterman, Donna Koch Gower, Jim Marshall, Dan Kramer, Don Paulsen, Jeff Rosen, Rene Aagaard, Olof Björner, Michael Cuscuna, Ed Berger, Dick Waterman, Tom Reney, Murray Lerner, Eliot Kissileff, Scott Dirks, Jay Blakesberg, Cliff Radix, Jonathan Hyams, Michael Ochs, and Christine Shea. Thanks to Che Williams, Tom Tierney, Toby Silver, and Jennifer Goodman at Sony Music, and to Jim Braden at Duggal and Tere Tereba for their assistance in the end days of this project. And David Dunton for placing the book with Chicago Review Press. Big thanks to Mark Adams, Cathy Mitchell, Peter Tarr, Paul Petraitis, Michael's thousands of Facebook friends (Rick O'Connor!) and fans, and, especially, the Reich and Goldberg families.

Thanks to George Mitchell, an original. And Dan McClosky, Tom Wheeler, Tom Yates, and Kate Hayes for their lengthy conversations with Michael. Ceci Peterson (a gem) at the Smithsonian and Todd Harvey at the Library of Congress moved speedily when needed.

Two who gave *so* much: Edd Hurt, who came on board to do additional research for this edition, expanding and correcting chronologies, performed a gallant effort under less than ideal circumstances. Bill Levay did a tremendous job assembling the discography, building on the work of many others, eschewing existing errors, sloppiness, and false assumptions and applying his superb meticulousness.

Extra special thanks goes to Yuval Taylor for making a commitment to publish the book, putting up with everyone, not to mention his great care and patience, and to Devon Freeny for managing the production.

Above all, special gratitude to Judy, Jackson, Noah (including key technical assistance), and Jasper, too. And to Michael, Susan, and Nick, guiding lights in this long story.

THE *ROLLING STONE* INTERVIEW: MIKE BLOOMFIELD

by Jann S. Wenner

Mike Bloomfield is well known as one of the handful of the world's finest guitarists. His first substantial professional experience was with a group known as "the group" in Chicago. Shortly after that he joined the Paul Butterfield Blues Band, did several sessions for Bob Dylan, and then left Butterfield to form his own group, the Electric Flag, which has just released their first album.

Rolling Stone, April 6 and April 27, 1968

This interview was conducted by Jann Wenner at the end of February just before the Flag left for a string of appearances across the country. The taping was done at Michael's home in Mill Valley.

Wenner:
You were telling me that Eric Clapton was a perfect guitarist. What makes you think that?

Bloomfield:
His attack is flawless, that's one of the things. A perfect musician is dedicated. He has ideas, attack, touch, ability to transmit emotion and ability to transmit his ideas. His ability to transmit his ideas and his emotion logically is kineticism; he can build. Eric does all of these about as well as you can do them. It shows in the area that he plays that his attack is perfect. His tone is vocal; his ideas are superb; he plays almost exclusively blues—all the lines he plays in the Cream are blues lines. He plays nothing but blues; he's a blues guitarist and he's taken blues guitar to its ultimate thing. In that field he's B. B. King cum the Freddie King and Ernie Cahill style of guitar playing. Eric is the master in the world. That is why he is a perfect guitarist. Eric plays in bad taste when he wants to. He can play crappy. But, like, Eric plays almost exclusively perfect.

Wenner:
Does the adaptability of the guitar to the blues account for its popularity as an instrument today?

Bloomfield:
No, I don't think so. The blues is a very vocal music, most Afro-American music is very vocal. It's music that's sung. Its fullest form is vocal music more than instrumental music. The best blues is sung blues, not played blues. Like the best gospel music is sung gospel music, not a tune played on a piano. You can reach more people with the human voice so blues is extremely emotional and involved with instruments and minor scales, vibrato and all the things that the voice has. I think that Indian music, any musical form that has kineticism and involvement, that has emotionality to it, is a valid moving musical form. A guitar or orchestra to six strings is suitable for any music.

Wenner:
Most of the young blues guitarists today seem to be playing vocal lines.

Bloomfield:
It's funny you should mention that because the Procol Harum can play very vocally. They have a very beautiful guitar player, very funky, very bluesy guitar player. He plays blues and he plays minor Bach changes.

Wenner:
Then why the popularity of the guitar?

Bloomfield:
It's got the most commercial soul. Hula hoops once were the most popular thing. The public was masturbating with hula hoops; now it's guitars. Guitars are easy, they're cheap, everybody plays them. Simple, a few chords. That's why they are buying them. There's really no reason at all.

Wenner:
When, how and why did you start playing the guitar?

Bloomfield:
Well, I was left-handed and I couldn't play well. I took lessons for about a year, a year or so. I learned rhythm. I learned dance band guitar, straight rhythm chops. When I was around fifteen I was a monster rock guitar player: I played Chuck Berry, and I played stuff like "I've Had It." And I tried to play some Scotty Moore solos. I liked to play with dance bands. Some dance bands they had clarinets and things. I wasn't hip to anything. Man, all you knew about electric guitars is that they were loud . . . And they had a high tone, like I could sound like Chuck Berry and that's all I cared. High, shrill, whatever, I don't know how they did it. I thought the spade cats had some sort of magic device. There was something in rock and roll, all kinds of rock and roll that always moved me: Gene Vincent's rock and roll, hill-billy rock and roll, spade rock and roll. Little Richard moved me much more than anything else. Man, when I first got hip to real soul people singing, real spade music—I mean it was like not at all white oriented—you know, I don't mean "do wah" music because that really didn't knock me out too much, you know, like really as in Blues Jordan and Charles Gile

and over the radio "Deep Feeling" like Chuck Berry, or a B. B. King record that was so heavy and that was soulful—that was where it was at. I couldn't even believe that was music. I couldn't believe . . .

Wenner:
What guitar players got to you first, as guitar players?

Bloomfield:
The rock guitar players that got to me first: Gene Vincent's guitar player, Jimmy Burton, Scotty Moore. I dug them first. The first spade guitar player I heard was Chuck Berry. I dug him but I didn't consider him blues oriented. I started hearing blues when I was around sixteen. That was just a whole other thing. Like I was playing the same notes that they were playing but when I would take my solos they weren't the same. I wasn't playing together like them. It was like fast bullshit; it wasn't right at all. And those cats were using the same notes and it was all right. And I just couldn't figure out the difference. It takes a long time to really learn how to play the real shit, knowing where you're supposed to be you see and that's the shit you want to master.

Wenner:
Your major influence is B. B. King, of course.

Bloomfield:
Well, when I'm playing blues guitar real well—that's when I'm not fooling around but I'm really into something—it's a lot like B. B. King. But I don't know, it's my own thing when there are major notes and sweet runs. You know I like sweet blues. The English cats play very hard funky blues. Like Aretha sings is how they play guitar. I play sweet blues. I can't explain it. I want to be singing. I want to be sweet.

Wenner:
Do you hear yourself in other guitarists?

Bloomfield:
Millions of them, billions of them. I've heard young kids say "Man, you sound just like B.B." and others say "I've never heard of him, who's he?" I can pick out certain things in what the Rolling Stones play, a few things that I know are exactly the licks that I play. Then I hear

guitar players like Jerry Garcia. He sounds amazingly like he's trying to sound like me but I don't think he is. I think he came that way himself.

Wenner:
Do you play any other instruments?

Bloomfield:
Well, I dig the piano. Once I had a piano, man, and I didn't touch the guitar at all. The piano is a whole other field, a whole different shot. I don't like to sing and play a guitar but I do like to sing and play the piano. I can express myself much easier on it than with other instruments.

Wenner:
Why do you choose to play the guitar then?

Bloomfield:
Expression, pure expression. Without a guitar, I'm like a poet with no hands. Actually, I can articulate much clearer on the guitar than anything else.

Wenner:
How did you form The Electric Flag?

Bloomfield:
I was with Butter [Paul Butterfield] and I flipped out and went crazy. I didn't dig anything. Elvin [Bishop] was really dragged, he wanted to play lead. He was tired of playing second guitar. I felt it was being shitty and that was a drag. So I quit Butter, hacked around for a while and that was more of a drag. I wanted to get a band of my own. Always wanted to and so me and Barry Goldberg put a band together.

We knew this guy named Peter Strassa, that's three, and Nick the Greek [Gravenites], that's four. I knew Nick in Chicago. Harvey [Brooks] volunteered his services. I really didn't dig the way he played but I knew he was supposed to be really good. I'd heard him play folk-rock. Harvey's good. Harvey's learned a lot of how to play funky bass; he's on his way to being a master. Then we met Buddy [Miles]. Buddy's so good that no one could believe it. Best fucking drummer in the world, unbelievable. He wanted to play in the band. He asked and we said yes. We had the band and we had hired another horn player who is an amazing organ player . . . He played horn and then switched over to organ. And that's how I got the band.

We all lived here and I lost my ass—a fortune feeding and housing them. We worked and like the millions of ideas that I had never came true. The band sort of fell into the bag of a soul band because of Buddy's dominant personality. I kinda didn't dig it, but now I really dig it. The band has become an extremely good soul band. That's where it's going. There are a lot of good ideas which will come about eventually if the band gets to know each other. You've got to be thrown together a long time to get close and share knowledge. I thought the whole thing through, planning it out. I'm very influenced by producers, especially Phil Spector. I think it would be really better if the groups would produce themselves.

There's another thing. The Rolling Stones are a really good band, but, like, I consider them like a boys' band because they don't play men's music. They don't play professional music for men, they play music for young people, and even with their most intelligent material as a stimulant, they play music for the young. Then there's a whole other thing—the masters of music—the Beatles who slowly evolved to music for men with serious patterns and serious and curious ideas. There's no juvenality about it at all. They developed the pop scene. And soul music is as serious as you can get, even in its most frivolous moments.

Wenner:
Do you pay the boys in the band as sidemen or share the bread equally?

Bloomfield:
No one makes money, man. It's completely cooperative.

Wenner:
Are there a lot of hassles in a big band venture?

Bloomfield:
Millions of them. There's the ego hassles, the personality hassles. One cat is not as good as another cat.

Buddy . . . Buddy is a person who plays well, who sings well. Any band can be centered around him. He's got talent and feeling. It's very easy to get Buddy to be a star. Everybody is very familiar with R&B. It's quite easy to get Buddy over to that area.

That shit is really well ironed out now. We have had some weird changes, really weird changes. Everybody got really bizarre for a while and most of it ironed out. The problem is we're instrumentally really radioactive. Put a bunch of people in a room together and break it down and get it together and break all of that personal shit down. You gotta be able to really combine and catalyze yourself when you're playing together. You got to look at the other cat and get off right there. And the people are able to get off because the other cats are getting off behind you and your whole sound and your whole thing. There's got to be that kind of thing going very strongly. It's got to be that one thing, because if that doesn't happen it's all over. You can't make it.

You dug Albert King. You notice his band is absolutely nothing. They were dead schleps, dead schleps playing behind him and Albert was the only one who really measured up to Albert's own sound. It was like they were old tired blues players and it was a drag. But Albert was exquisite. It was weird to see this exquisitely exciting cat, Albert King, freaking out and all these kids digging him. Here, this whole vast audience of which he was unaware. He's been scuffling around the blues for all these years and his band, who weren't hip to it at all—I mean they didn't even care. It was just a bunch of white faces and that was a drag.

Everybody was willing to cooperate, but the groove has gotta be there. In other words, with Buddy it's very easy to groove. He's mixed up: sometimes it's easy to groove and sometimes it isn't. But when the groove isn't there, it's very hard. Once you establish the feeling, once everyone knows what he has to say, then it just becomes a matter of saying as best as you can say it, because you really say it right.

Wenner:
Why did you choose "Groovin' Is Easy" for your first single?

Bloomfield:
We did "Groovin'" because "Groovin'" . . . well for several reasons: One, because I had a really groovy arrangement in mind for it; number two, because groovin was the thing for a pop record, groovin all over the place. I figured well we got a pop record. In my opinion "Groovin'" is a great pop record, a really pop record from beginning to end. The horns, the guitar, the drums. I think the voice is a little old-timey, but it's a pretty groovy record and that's why we chose it. When we came out of the

studio and we heard it, we thought it was really good. I mean it blew our minds. Beautiful, big, lovely. I think it's the best thing we are ever going to do, pop-wise. But it wasn't released right which was a drag.

Wenner:
Who produced it?

Bloomfield:
We produced "Groovin'" ourselves.

Wenner:
What do you think of some of the current producers? What do you get from them?

Bloomfield:
I would like to be personally produced by Jerry Ragavoy in New York. He's one of the greatest soul producers I've ever heard. John Simon, he produced some Dylan stuff. He's very heavy. Phil Spector, George Martin, cats like that know everything. They know every line, every cue, every idea. Every bit of percussion. They can constantly come up with original ideas. They understand the idiom; they understand the history of rock and roll; they know the board like they know their hands. It's an instrument to them. They know every sound.

Wenner:
What about John Court?

Bloomfield:
No, he's not that hip to rock for all those years. The sound is not as good as it could be for all those records, not as good as a Stones' record, as good as a Beatle's record, as good as a Motown or Stax record.

Those are the standards of the trade and I don't think his records are that good. John did a lot with the Butterfield records. I don't think he's a really groovy producer. I can see other producers who are much groovier, who with those artists would be much groovier. I think Jim Stewart, if not better, would be just as good. Or perhaps Jerry Wexler would be groovier. Something along the lines of the earlier Ray Charles things.

What you need is a cat who will say "well, dig man, you're not play-ing what's hip; there's a lot groovier bass line; dig what's happening today, why don't you try to get in a funkier heavy beat instead of that old shuffle beat because that's not what's happening; you can better groove with a little more groovy horn line." And that's where a producer should be at.

Wenner:
Are the differences between Butterfield's band and the Flag as easily characterized as the difference between soul music and the blues?

Bloomfield:
Yeah, not quite that easy. With Paul's band, we always wanted to play like a real professional blues band. The Electric Flag is a real blues band and it's in that bag. You get the soul feeling of Afro-American popular music. The Flag probably handles it about as good as it can be handled . . . and that's what the Flag can do other bands couldn't do. Paul's band had a unique thing: Paul could blend certain talents to make the unique sound that is the Butterfield Band and which it has today but the sound of the Butterfield Band is really more standardized than it was when I was playing with it. I played further out riffs. Now it's a little more standardized except they freak out a bit, sort of a not-really-jazz but jazz-oriented on some things. I don't know. In my opinion, our band is sort of leaving them behind. In ours a lot of ideas—as well as personalities—have blended together.

Herbie, our organ player, is a monster on keys, really heavy. He will get to be just as good as anybody. He plays like Hendrix plays guitar.

Wenner:
Some of your best stuff is Stax material. Even though your group is larger and more complex, do you find a strong similarity in your group to the Stax house band?

Bloomfield:
No, because they have a very weird concept of exactly what they want to do in just the area where they're working. They are directed and guided by a different combination of talents, Duck Dunn, Al Jackson. They have been playing that way since they were in high school together. Seven years is a good thing. Look at the Beatles going on for years. Stax will go on; Nashville will go on. The reason is that they bothered to

find really good things. They bothered to find the best possible. When I first heard "Hold On, I'm Coming," well I heard a new type of singing. I mean Sam and Dave. I mean I hadn't heard anything like that since I heard some of those cats on Arhoolie Records or something. Those cats have voices like steel and young leather or something. Otis was so unique, so individual, you know, and like that's where Stax is at.

It's like with Motown, except that Motown is a little more shitty, like, really more and more sugary. Except that Motown is like, well there's hope. Motown is trying to be funky now like with "I Heard It Through the Grapevine." On that they are funkier than blues and playing as about as down home as you can get that's really voodoo music, man, boogaloo music. All music is extremely sophisticated. There's no primitive music made anymore, you know, in popular American music. The most primitive thing I remember hearing was like the Troggs, they were pretty primitive you know.

Wenner:
Do you do any Motown material?

Bloomfield:
I think the one we do is "Uptight." I'd like to do "Reach Out For Me." It's a very soulful song.

Wenner:
It seems like you do a lot of Stax material.

Bloomfield:
We do it, yeah. We do it once in a while. We do "Loving You Too Long." That's a Stax thing . . .

Wenner:
You do "Knock on Wood."

Bloomfield:
No, no we don't do that. I don't know. We don't do many Stax things. I sing a couple of them. We do our own things, dark blues. I want to do all kinds of things, American music. That's our thing, American music, whatever strikes our fancy, whatever there's no staying in one bag when there are way lot more things to do.

Wenner:
Are you interested in modern country music?

Bloomfield:
Yeah, of course, because Harvey and I really dig it. I know a lot about it. I played with bluegrass bands. I really love country music, I'm really into it, I adore it. I love country singing and writing, and its styles. Today it's better than ever, except that today they're stuffing it with strings and stuff. Cats in that field are beautiful, like the young Buck Owens imitators.

The cats after Buck, Merle Haggard, David Houston, Tammy Wynette, great, great singers. I definitely want the band to do that music, I really want to do American music. Have you ever dug Lonnie Mack or "Where There's a Will There's a Way," or "Why Not Tonight?" by Jimmie Hughes? That's like country music, but it's soul music too. It would be a little of each; it would be an intelligent hybrid. Like I dig the horns to play like steel guitar.

Wenner:
Have you any interest in the sitar?

Bloomfield:
No, I can't give up my life. You know I'd have to sit down and just do that. Man, it's too heavy.

Wenner:
Jerry Garcia incorporates a country picking style into his playing and the Dead do a couple of fine rocked-up country songs. Have you ever wanted to incorporate country sounds in that way?

Bloomfield:
Sure, I fucking love country music. I love it. There's really dimensional form. I like it all, I like even the most insipid period of country music, country swing. Are you hip to that? . . . Spade Cooley and Bob Willis and the Country Playboys whatever or Texas Playboys. I dig walks, chicken walks, stuff like that.

I could play almost every song, man, I know country music up the ass on the guitar. I could play about every country style guitar there is: old Flatt picking, Travis picking, Chet Atkins, right on down to chicken picking. I have played a lot of country music, I have played it for years. I could put it into my guitar playing, but I don't want to. I won't play country music. Well, one of our tunes has it in there. I'll play country music, when we play country music. I sort of prefer to remain relatively valid to the idiom unless it adds to idiom like when Ray [Charles] does country music. I would put country guitar into the same way Ray does country music. When Ray does country music man, it was good spade-oriented country music.

Wenner:
Do you see the differences between soul music and the blues?

Bloomfield:
Absolutely, the difference is quite clear. Soul is from the church; soul music's whole trend has singing like church music, no snaps, melisma, a lot of notes. Monosyllabic singing, extreme virtuosos of the voice. It's right after gospel singing . . .

Wenner:
And Aretha is the perfect representation of that.

Bloomfield:
Of course, man, she's a monster. She's like the best of that type of singer. But all the new soul singers man, all the best, like Sam and Dave, all sing like fucking preachers. They're gospel singers is what they are. Blues is secular, not religious, right? Blues is a secular music. It's a bar music. It's a simpler thing you know. Even the blues today is getting kind of soulful. I don't mean soulful, I mean gospel-oriented. It's decidedly different structure-wise, right down the line. Soul songs preach a sermon, tell the story . . . blues tell the story, but it's much more accurate, it's like a newspaper. It says "this is what happened." There's not that much velocity involved. It's more accurate reporting maybe using different words . . . while soul music is really different you know it's more of a preaching, Joe Tex, velocity. It's like "The Love You Save." Just a beautifully, superbly written music for the Negro masses. Soul music is more behind the church.

Wenner:

Has this led you into the purer forms of gospel music?

Bloomfield:

Lately, man, yeah I've gotten extremely into gospel music, just plain gospel music. That's my favorite music today in the whole world. I think that's the most happening thing in the world now. It was the best singing in all of American Music, those are the best. I mean gospel singers, real good gospel singers, they have the same voice, like Yma Sumac, or like an opera singer, except they sing in a more funky way. I find like listening to Eddie Jackson. Oh man. . . . I'll play you a record by the Swan Silvertones. Man, the voices are unearthly.

Wenner:

What singers and groups would you recommend for someone who was interested in learning about gospel forms?

Bloomfield:

I would recommend the Silvertones, Blind Boys, any of those groups, they're all top notch gospel groups. The Staple Singers are a little hokey for my taste. Now, they are very good, they have their own thing. They're real folky, too. Mavis is about as exciting a female singer as ever walked on this earth. It's just that I think there are groups that are better than that . . . like the Blind Boys, they're really groovy. The Soul Stirrers are another, they are really heavy. Little Richard is a very poor gospel singer.

Wenner:

How did you get involved with the blues? What was happening then in Chicago from which so much new blues talent has come?

Bloomfield:

Well, I'll tell you a little bit about the Chicago blues scene, the white Chicago blues scene. The whole story as best as I can remember it. Now what originally went down, the first cats I knew on the scene— there were several areas, where there were people interested in blues in Chicago—the collectors, and the record cats, the historians and the discoverers who somewhere in their life realized that they were living in a city that was fraught with the real shit—all the old cats on the records that had moved out of Pigeonfoot, Georgia—and had ended up in Chicago. And I was one of those cats, like Bob [Koester] and Pete Welding. There were a whole lot of people. And then there were cats around who were folkies, esoteric folkies, who put blues among other esoteric, ethnic folk music.

Wenner:
Was Charles Keil one of those cats?

Bloomfield:
Charlie Keil, yeah, Charles was one of those cats. And then there were a very few cats who dug blues because they were living in that neighborhood and there were nothing but spades around and they dug hanging out in the bars. And there were a few cats like that. The first cat on the scene that I picked up on—the old granddaddy of the white Chicago blues scene—was Nick the Greek. Nicholas was from the West Side man, a very tough Polak neighborhood, like they were smoking reefers. And the next cat down there on the really tough scene was Butter [Butterfield] and like Butter wanted to play harp. And he went down there when he was a young man, right down on the street which was the hardest fucking scene in the world, the baddest, filled with bad mother fuckers. He went down there. Butter went down there with his harp and sucked up to Junior Wells, and Cotton and Little Walter. After a bit Butter got better than them. At that time Butter was going to the University of Chicago, but he spent most of his time on the street and I felt that for all practical purposes, Butter was just a tough street spade—like Malcolm X—a real tough cat, man.

At that time I was hanging around the folk scene, with the ethnic folks freaking out with "Little Sandy Review," flipping out with Gary Davis and Lighting Hopkins and folk music. Oh man, everything from Woody Guthrie to the country blues. That's where I was at. But basically my heart really belonged down there, with blues singing. Because that was like rock and roll but only a million times better. That was the real thing.

When I was around eighteen years old I had been sort of messing around and Paul sort of accepted me. Well, he didn't really accept me at all, he just sort of thought of me as a folky Jew boy, because like

Paul was there and I was just sort of a white kid hanging around and not really playing the shit right, but Paul was there man. I guess that was about where the scene was at and I didn't know many people, I just knew Paul and Nick and Elvin (who was working with Paul at that time) and a few folkies. Then when I was around eighteen this cat, Charlie Musselwhite, came up from Memphis and he dug blues too. He was from an old blues scene at home in Memphis. Mostly it was like Paul's scene, in which he hung around with Furry Lewis and other old blues singers. I was also pretty much, by this time, pretty blues conscious.

I was managing this club and every Tuesday night I'd try seriously to have concerts with Muddy Waters and Sleepy John Estes, all the blues singers in Chicago that I could get hold of, that I'd ever met or I tried to get especially the rare cats.

I was around eighteen and got this band together. We played a year with Big Joe Williams. I played piano with them and Charlie played harp. Eventually Joe left and when we worked there, we played nothing but blues.

The band was Charles, and this cat from the Sopwith Camel named Norman Mayell who is from Chicago, yeah . . . and this bass player who was from a Roy Rogers band. Mike Johnson was the name of our lead guitar player. He was sort of a rock player, he sang rock and roll. When we got together we didn't play nothing but blues and we weren't real good, but we had a lot of feeling.

After that I left that club and went to another club, after playing there for a year, and gave Butter my gig there. I said, "Listen, my gig's done there, why don't you work there?" Butter had a band that had a sound all its own, an out of sight band, the best band to ever come down in that area, tight, tough, blew everybody's mind. So Butter played there. And right after that, cats started saying that the white groups were really getting down to it, because the rules had been laid down: you had to be as good as the spades in town; you had to be as good as Otis Rush, you had to be as good as Buddy Guy, as good as Freddie King, whatever instrument you played at that time, you had to be as good as they were. And who wanted to be bad on the South Side? Man, you were exposed all over I mean right in that city where you lived, in one night you could hear Muddy Waters, Howling Wolf, Buddy Guy, Otis Rush, Big Walter, Little Walter, Junior Wells, Lloyd Jones, just dozens of different blues singers, some famous, some not so famous. They were all part of the blues, and you could work with them if you were good enough. If you wanted to gig, that's where you went and that's where you worked, and like all these cats, man, these white kids in Boston, like Geoff Muldaur was playing the blues, and in New York Bob Dylan and his cats were playing their thing of the blues.

But like in Chicago they were playing the real blues because that's where they were working they were working with the cats. Corky Siegal, and Jim Schwall, who are not really good, worked a year in Pepper's Lounge, one of the funkiest clubs, for a year as a novelty act. Corky played the drums and the piano. Applejack, cats you don't know about, Chicago Slim, and Steve Miller and all the cats in Steve's band.

The thing is all the Chicago musicians played the blues and all the other cats were imitators. We were playing right along with them and an imitation just could not do. It had to be the real thing, it had to be right. They had to stand up. It was Buddy Guy playing just two doors down from you. You wanted to burn him if you could, you know, you just wanted to get up there and burn him off the stage. I think it was very healthy.

Wenner:
What professional bands did you play with or sit in with at that time?

Bloomfield:
Millions of them. It would take a day to give you all the names. I didn't play with as many as many cats did, because I got my own band. I stayed with them for two years. We were signed by John Hammond and we recorded for Columbia. And it was really weird . . . we looked like the Stones then you know . . . really long hair . . . and outlandish clothes . . . this was years before the Stones and it was never issued. They never issued a fucking track that we cut.

Wenner:
Did you play with about all the major blues men?

Bloomfield:
Millions of them, really, millions of blue cats. I played with them, I was helped by them. There are pictures of them on my wall; different cats

who are special friends. Like Big Joe Williams, he was like a father, a close friend. With cats like Muddy, man, it's like seeing your old uncle. Seeing Muddy on the road or at a gig or something, it's like giging with the whole family or something, with your older brothers and uncles or something like that. It's a very close thing. The older cats have gotten a lot of work because the younger cats have talked about them, and said "man, you think I'm good, you should hear cats like Little Walter . . . man that cat can play harp." That's what Butter said.

It's like me with B.B. They're at the Fillmore now. Man, they wouldn't be at the Fillmore if there weren't cats talking about them. The main reason you talk about them is because you love them. I know I love them. These cats who were so groovy to teach me and they were so groovy because they weren't satisfied with just the little white boy playing those licks. You had to be good in order for them to dig you. They just weren't happy, they weren't grabbed, just to see a white cat playing that music. That wasn't where it was at. It was when a white cat socked it to them. They'd yell at the right time and say that was the real shit. That's so good, man!

Wenner:
Do you get educated response from white audiences?

Bloomfield:
No, man, hell no. White people, are well, yeah I'm getting it now, so many people at the Fillmore and the Avalon have heard B. B. King at the Regal. They've heard enough live albums to know what's happening. But hell man, it's a call and response thing; you've got to know the vernacular. You gotta know what's going down. In an Indian thing you've got to know when a cat played a good way. If you were at a fuck-a-thon, you'd have to know when a good fuck went down to know what's happening. These kids don't know; they know a good show, they know when you're down on your knees because they can see, (he's down on his knees) so something is happening.

But like when Buddy sings a line man, that just wrenches your heart out, when he bends his voice about ten fucking ways, goes from falsetto to bass, oh man, it just soothes your soul. For the first five years I remember that when I listened to records I didn't listen to anything but the guitar. I wouldn't even listen to records with horns on them, and that's where a lot of kids' heads are at. They just hear certain things; but to understand the whole vernacular, the whole mystique, the whole thing, that's a whole different thing.

Wenner:
Do you get good response from black audiences?

Bloomfield:
I don't know. We've never played for strictly spade audiences. We're good. We're a good rock and sock and soul band; we get good responses from almost anybody because we cook real hard, honestly. I think people like to see extravagantly planned plays, like the Who and Jimi. Like passion plays.

Wenner:
Much like the way Buddy sings "I've Been Lovin' You Too Long"?

Bloomfield:
Yeah, a play, exactly. Very much like James Brown falling to the ground with a cape thrown around him. A revival, a play. People like spectacles. In my opinion one of the most pleasing spectacles is to see a band playing their asses off, hard as they can, you can see them grinning. You can feel it driving you nuts and all that good hard driving energy. That's why I dig the Young Rascals. And that's especially what a spade audience thinks.

Wenner:
You said that "there's no white bullshit with Butterfield." He's set apart from all the rest of the white Chicago cats—why?

Bloomfield:
It's amazing. It's a sociological thing. He did it by so adapting himself to that environment, that he turned over, that he transformed, changed and anything that's in his background, is completely dissolved, by the earnesty and the complete tough masculinity of the street. The world of the street, that dog eat dog world. He met it on its own terms and that set him apart. Very few other cats have gone through that experience and that's what set Paul apart. That's what I noticed about him immediately, he was there.

It's hard to put into words what the real blues is and what it isn't. It's when there's an absolute confidence about it and you're not studiously trying to cop something; you're not listening to a Robert Johnson record and trying to sound like it, you are merely playing the most natural music for you, the music you can play. If Paul opens his mouth to sing it would have to be blues, because that's his thing. That's the most natural thing for him to play. It's like breathing for him. He picked it up fast and just got better and better. And that's why I say there's . . . its a very entertaining sight. That's why I dig Otis, or the Vanilla Fudge, they work very hard. That's one thing white people who have seen us really dig: when we are playing good, we play our asses off. And it sounds good. We're really digging it, and digging it is a neces—no white bullshit. It's just completely natural. At one time maybe it wasn't but by completely immersing himself in the environment, and in the competition of the environment, now it is.

Wenner:
How did you come to join his band?

Bloomfield:
Oh, well, I went to Magoo's and Butter was going to make a record and he wanted someone to play slide guitar on the record and I could play slide. He brought Paul Rothchild to listen to me and I played on the record.

I didn't dig Butter, you know. I didn't like him; he was just too hard a cat for me. But I went to make the record and the record was groovy and we made a bunch more records. One thing led to another and he said "Do you want to join the band?" And it was the best band I'd ever been in. Sammy Lay was the best drummer I ever played with. But whatever I didn't like about Paul as a person, his musicianship was more than enough to make up for it. He was just so heavy, he was so much. Everything I dug in and about the blues, Paul was. There he was: a white cat as tough as he could be and it was a gas. So we went to Newport right after that and I was going to play with Dylan, you know it was a choice between Dylan and Butter and I chose Butter because that's where my head was. That kind of music.

Wenner:

Who do you think are the best blues musicians? The top two or three cats?

Bloomfield:

Ray and B.B. I mean I could name a million cats, but there's no one better than Ray Charles or B. B. King. They are the last word.

Wenner:

Do you consider yourself primarily a bluesman or a rock and roll star?

Bloomfield:

In my own head, I'm a bluesman, because that's what I play the best and that's what I dig the most and can play the most authoritatively. I think finally, at last, I've reached an understanding about and with my guitar. I just know all about it now. I finally know all about it. As a music form and as a social scene, man I just know it, it's in my heart. But yeah, I am a rock and roll star.

Wenner:

Why did you leave Butterfield?

Bloomfield:

I flipped out. And like Elvin was uptight. So I left and when I went home, it was even worse. And besides, I wanted to get a band of my own. I had a lot of ideas that are mine. I saw cats like Buddy who is so heavy I was content to do Buddy's thing. It's such a pleasure. It was a delight just to play that music. Like I really didn't know shit from soul music. I didn't know anything about it. I never even listened to it before. I just dug blues.

Wenner:

You're of course hip to Aretha. She's operating in the same area as your band.

Bloomfield:

I don't think she is really. She's more New York than she is Memphis because her records don't sound like the Memphis sound. They are a little more complex. She's very gospely. Aretha is the last word. She's the best female R&B singer. The Supremes have syrupy voices and

Martha's all right . . . but Aretha will sock it to you; she's the hardest of them all. She has the most dynamic voice, the most engaging style. She's sexy, she's a red hot mama. She's not slick or anything; She's just soul. In a way it's kinda unhealthy, it's kinda Uncle Tommy. When she sings "Dr. Feelgood," that's where she's at. While the Supremes are the other thing, you know they're the urban Negro, airline stewardesses or something like the Kim sisters. So like its a very weird sociological thing.

Wenner:
Soul music is more popular now than it ever was before. Do you think this will be the direction of rock and roll and dominate all styles?

Bloomfield:
No. Just as important are long head pieces. Soul music is heart music, it's not head music. Just as happening are Simon and Garfunkel.

Then there's the hybrid. There's the English soul, you know, Procol Harum with their soulful voices. No, I don't think it's going to be the trend; I don't think it will ever get to the white heart, the big record buyer, the white adolescent heart. He just can't amplify his movement enough. You know, he can dig it and love it and buy it, and dance to it and boogaloo to it, and shake himself, and come with his girlfriend to it. But that's not where his head is. Because when he goes to bed, when he or she goes to bed, at night, it's Herman who she wants to be fucking. Certainly not Sam and Dave or Albert King. And I think that basically that's where they identify. You know, kids can identify with wild funky shit. They much more readily identify sexually and personally with a white person than like with Otis . . .

Wenner:
What you're saying is that it comes down to a racial thing.

Bloomfield:
I think yeah, it's definitely a racial thing. I think kids are to the point . . . like kids around today are very much more enlightened, they smoke pot you know and they're enlightened to a great deal more sounds, sonority. They can be moved by many other things. It's musical value; like many kids wouldn't listen to spade groups a few years ago, "Why listen to a

spade group? Let's go listen to beautiful Frankie Avalon." Now they'll listen to a lot of things. I think it's racial, but America is racial. It's a basic problem of identification. You must identify with something you can identify with. Kids can identify with the Beatles very easily.

Wenner:
Are bands like yours, Steve's, and even Paul's headed in an electronic direction?

Bloomfield:
They are headed in the direction of the amalgamation of the personality between the bands. We've all heard the same licks; Steve, me, Paul, the English cats, we've all dug the same things, we've all dug the same records. If you question me or Steve Miller or Butter, or Eric, we probably all have the same favorite records basically and we've dug the same thing. It's the same influences that have come out.

Each cat has its own way of saying the same things. Whoever has dug more of different types of things, that's going to be where he's at. You take a little baby and put him in a white cotton box and he'll have a very limited horizon. You take someone who's dug a lot of ways and that's going to come out in his music. He's going to come on with a lot more than a cat who's only been listening to one kind of music. So it's very hard for me to predict.

There's a whole host of white soul bands that are completely unheard of. No one has ever heard of them. Like Wayne Cochran and the C.C. Riders. Millions of them, all over the south and the mid-west, who play nothing but Top-40 soul music, with horns and singing it just like the record.

Wenner:
Like Mitch Ryder?

Bloomfield:
Exactly, but heavier than Mitch, way better than Mitch. Years, man, this has been happening in America for years. Bill Haley was one of the first of those type bands, like Joe Turner sort of. Those cats play the same circuit of lounges in Vegas and Miami. I don't know, I run into them and they play fabulous. Really professional, but they play that

Top-40 shit. They stay with whatever is happening at the time because they really don't have it. I mean, like once in a while you hear a group like the Vanilla Fudge, you know just these guys from New York, who can really follow that New York Italian pattern, you know Dion and the Belmonts or Jay and the Americans, who are Jewish, but fell into that same pattern. Sort of a Four Seasons type of thing but they didn't. They took after the Rascals, they took a little of their own personalities.

Wenner:
Do you hear much of interest in jazz?

Bloomfield:
Sort of. I tried. I didn't dig it. I mean it's fantastic musicanship, very heavy, but I really don't dig it that much.

Wenner:
The thing that strikes me is that it's so "tired."

Bloomfield:
Yeah, it's over. I'm much more folk-oriented—I want someone to speak to me on clearly definable terms, that I understand with very little oblique shit.

Wenner:
Do you do much song-writing?

Bloomfield:
Yeah. I write sometimes like Stax songs. I wrote one we did on our album. It's for Steve Cropper. I do all kinds of song writing.

Wenner:
How did you end up doing the sessions on *Highway 61*?

Bloomfield:
Well, I met Dylan at this funny little club called the Bear in Chicago just after his first album came out. The liner notes described him as a real hot shot, you know, a real great guitar player. And I heard the album and it sounded just shitty. He came to Chicago and I welcomed the opportunity to go down there and cut him. So I went

to see him in the afternoon to talk to him and he was really nice. He was just so nice. I saw him at a few parties and then out of the clear blue sky, he called me on the phone to cut a record which was "Like a Rolling Stone." So I bought a Fender, a really good guitar for the first time in my life, without a case, a Telecaster. And that's how. He called me up.

Wenner:
And then?

Bloomfield:
Then I went with Butter and it was over until the next session. Dylan is very weird about loyalty you know. Like he sort of felt I belonged with him and I did too. But I didn't. He's a very weird cat. Albert manages both of us. Like when I played with Bob, I didn't know anything about that kind of music. But I think I could play with him a lot better now.

Wenner:
Why do you think you could play better with Dylan now?

Bloomfield:
When they played the songs back in the studio and the cats were listening, it was an incredible thing. Bob is a weird cat, you know: weird music, weird words, weird session. You know, "Where's the charts? Where's the papers? Chord sheets?" Very weird. But I had never been on a professional, big-time session with studio musicians. I didn't know anything. I liked the songs. If you had been there, you would have seen it was a very disorganized, weird scene. Since then I've played on millions of sessions and I realize how really weird that Dylan session was.

Wenner:
How long did the album take?

Bloomfield:
Not long, two or three days.

Wenner:
Did Dylan take a strong control of the session?

Bloomfield:

No, he's never in charge of anything. He merely sings his songs. He sings them and the musicians fit themselves around them. He sings these long, complex, meaningful songs over and over. It's a drag for him to do over. And Dylan didn't want to have a hand in the music. He's a poet. He wants to publish in a listenable, consumable form. The music was not his job. It's the musicians' job. His job is to write.

Wenner:

But it doesn't look like it will continue like that, does it?

Bloomfield:

It's going to be different on the next album. He's with a band, he plays with a band, he's a real band cat. He has lots to say about what's happening. The next album will probably be more developed as a piece of music with more emphasis on change.

Wenner:

What other dates have you played?

Bloomfield:

The Mitch Ryder Album, *What Now My Love*, a couple of Sleepy John Estes albums and John Hammond albums, and a record recorded by a Chicago group. All sorts of singles. I've done a lot of studio work.

Wenner:

What kind of material have you done on your album?

Bloomfield:

A soul tune, and there's a shuffle, a blues that shuffles like an old rock and roll number. The album is all-right. Some of it's really groovy. But some of it isn't groovy at all. It's not at all what I would dig it to be, because I didn't know what I know now.

Wenner:

I saw your band debut at Monterey. The audience seemed to love it, but the group seemed pretty poor to me. It was like a setup.

Bloomfield:

I felt we played abominably, and they loved us. I thought it was flooky. I couldn't understand man, how could a band play that shitty and have everyone dig them? I said "Well, it's festival madness." Yeah, it was a set up.

I don't know who did it. I don't know who was guilty. I think still that it's flooky from that moment on. I don't know what it was. Monterey will remain a straight, jive pop phenomenon. You now, if we'd gone on first we would have bombed. We went on last.

Wenner:

I'm glad you know, too.

Bloomfield:

Man, Barry and I looked at each other and we figured, "Wow, what a bomb." How could we have the image of a super band? We're shlebs, secret assholes. This is not a super band; the only thing super in the band is Buddy. Buddy is Super-spade. If you melted down James Brown and Arthur Conley and Otis Redding into one enormous spade, you'd have Buddy. He's about all that there is: He is the quintessence of all R&B amassed in one super talented human being. Buddy is super power; everybody else is just human.

Wenner:

You really think he's that superlative?

Bloomfield:

In that field he's the last word. A genius. His singing is just superb, his drumming is just the best. He's the superman. That's what they were digging in Monterey; everybody dug him. Dig, man, after all that white blues, they got to see the real McCoy, and that was Buddy Miles. Man, after Miller and Big Brother and Butter, and Canned Heat and all of this, finally there he was, a big blues man, socking it to you. And that's what they dug, I think we were very earnest, we played very hard. Everyone was very nervous. I was so nervous, man. I had just heard Butterfield, I had never heard anything sound better. Then I heard Miller who sounded so good I was dizzy; everyone sounded out of sight. Then we went up there and it was like cripples.

Wenner:

Do you like playing for audiences whose form of appreciation is lying around the stage, totally zonked?

Bloomfield:

I see it so much now I don't care. It's just that the Avalon looks funny when it's empty. There's just nothing but bodies laying there. And it's just funny. I've played in places where old colored women in their sixties have lifted their dresses in front of me with nothing on underneath. Man, I've seen it; I've seen gusty shit. You know, gusty shit is gusty shit. You know what really put me up tight? I played Holy Cross and there was nothing but goyim. That really put me up tight. It was wrong, I didn't see any Jews. I didn't know what it was, but I knew it was wrong. What really put me up tight was to see all those Wasps in one room.

Wenner:

You just played on the same show with Jimi Hendrix—what do you think?

Bloomfield:

Great. Monstrous. Really talented cat, super together cat. Now here is a young cat, extremely talented. For years, all the Negroes who'd make it into the white market made it through servility, like Fats Domino, a lovable, jolly, fat image, or they had been spades who had been picked up by the white market. Now here's this cat you know—"I am a super spade man, I am like black and tough. And I will fuck you and rape you and do you in, and I'm bad-assed and weird." Not only that, I mean that's his image which he sets forward about as well as anyone can. I mean there's no mistaking what's happening. He plays his ass off; he writes cool songs; he's got a good group. His few albums are some of the best albums ever recorded in the world. How often do you ever see someone really together in image and in head? In everything it's all there, out front. The music fits in with the person, the person fits in with the music and all is one.

Wenner:

What other guitar players, other than B.B., do you dig?

Bloomfield:

I'll tell you other people that I like. I like the guitar player for the Beatles, George Harrison. I like Peter Townshend, he's a good guitar player. Henry Vestine, he plays with Canned Heat. One of the best bands I have heard was the Sons of Champlin, a San Francisco group, pretty outrageous, fantastic lead, guitar player. Oh man, things are just on really high standards of musicianship. I like most everything.

Now, man, you're going to get drugged by this. I've read almost all your articles about San Francisco and you love them, because you love San Francisco and you love them, and it's got your head—man, music coming out of the parks in the sunlight—but I don't dig San Francisco groups. I love San Francisco and I love the guys in the groups, and I love the people here, I love this nice cheap house that I live in in a groovy neighborhood. I like it here. But I think San Francisco music isn't good music. Not good bands. They're amateur cats; they're the amateurs. . . . I don't dig "Good Morning, Little School Girl," by the Grateful Dead. I don't dig Pigpen trying to sing blues; it don't sound like blues. It sounds like some white kid trying to sing blues. It drags me, they're not funky. They don't have a good beat. I can't explain it. It's not the real shit, and it's not even a good imitation. It's not even like the Stones. I don't dig the Airplane. I think they're a third rate rock and roll band. I don't dig Country Joe and the Fish. I find them an abomination, a fraud perpetrated on people. I don't dig Big Brother; I dig Janis, but I think Big Brother is just a wretched, lame group of cats who she carries for no reason at all.

Wenner:

First off, the cats in Big Brother are not good at all, but Janis is just incredible . . .

Bloomfield:

I know man, they're lame. Now, I saw them when she first got with them; she had to work them into shape. But you know, it's a fraudulent scene. I don't think that many good bands have come out of San Francisco. The Quicksilver, fine band but what the hell? It's a band, you know a good band. I don't think San Francisco is the most prolific, groovy, Liverpool thing, at all. Too amateurish; not enough good musicians, no real heavies. There's no real heavies out here at all. Cassady is a pretty good bass player. Jorma is not one of the best rock guitar players, I just don't think he is . . .

Wenner:
If you think it's got my head, it's also got yours. Jorma is not a good technician, and he's not prolific, but his lines are interesting, well-suited to the material and well thought out. I'd rather listen to him than to a dozen cats imitate you or Eric.

Bloomfield:
I think Jorma, imitating me, things he's heard. I have all his works; when he plays blues, he plays it sloppy. Or he doesn't play blues, he plays different melodies. It's fairly individual. Yeah, I guess I would rather hear Jorma than someone trying to imitate Eric or unless they could imitate Eric real good. I mean I'd rather hear that because I just don't think he's really that good a guitar player. I don't know. I don't think there's emotion in San Francisco blues . . . I mean they just don't move me enough. I have to be moved in some way. The Who moves me, their madness moves me. I like to be moved be it by spectacle, be it by kineticism, be it by the same throbbing on "Papa ooh mau mau" as a chorus, a million times over. It'll get to me eventually, I have open tastes. I like most everything.

Wenner:
I don't want to argue about San Francisco. There's a lot of shit here, like Blue Cheer is a joke, but there's shit everywhere. But there are a lot of good bands and good performers.

Bloomfield:
Have you ever dug Mother Earth? That's a great band. They have a great piano player named Wayne. They sound just like a gospel group, very moving. I sort of dug Moby Grape, 'cause they were tight. But they were just too slick, too superficial.

Wenner:
I especially like the Grateful Dead, 'cause they are the essence of San Francisco, they're just where it's all at.

Bloomfield:

They're San Francisco, everything that is San Francisco. They're hip. Really, and I like them for that. Just like the Stones for those uptight, meth-y little teenagers, that's where the Stones are. Everything that's involved with that scene and I dig them for that.

Wenner:

The English have some weird ideas about the blues.

Bloomfield:

Good singing, but it's weak. The English groups are intimidated. All Europeans are intimidated by Negroes. They feel that they just can't do good. Except cats like Eric, who are so unmistakably good that they know no one can touch them. John Mayall is a good blues singer but I saw night after night, people were let down, they expected him to be tops. Have you ever seen Jimmie Cotton? Not out of the ordinary, but he works his balls off. John doesn't work hard enough really, I'd like to see him work a little harder and get himself into it a little bit.

Wenner:

What advice would you give a young guitarist who listens to your records and respects your playing?

Bloomfield:

What's that group that's trying to imitate Eric, Blue Cheer? Those are kids that just play for hours and hours and never say anything. When I heard that bullshit, I really, man . . . Well, if someone listens to me, he should listen to what I have listened to to know how I got to where I am. I just can't think of the names. I think most of all he has to remember how to transmit his emotions, how he's feeling, his attacks to other people, so other human beings can understand it, so his music says what he's feeling. Until he gets to understand what music is, he won't know that it's not all a matter of runs and hot licks. I can't explain that to a new guitar player. A young guitar player won't know anything about what I'm talking about. There's really nothing to say. They can come close, but you've got to understand.

MICHAEL BLOOMFIELD DISCOGRAPHY

by William J. Levay

This discography comprises commercially released recordings of studio sessions and live performances in which Michael Bloomfield participated as instrumentalist, vocalist, or producer. We also included recordings of interviews with Bloomfield and home video releases of films that feature Bloomfield's playing. For certain live performances where the set list is well known from bootlegs or other sources—the Butterfield Blues Band at the 1965 Newport Folk Festival, for example—we included the full set lists, though some of the recordings have not yet seen commercial release. However, bootlegs and the like are generally not included.

René Aagaard's primary Bloomfield discography served as our foundation and we consulted several other discographies including David Dann's Bloomfield performance history. Many discrepancies exist among the sources, so we consulted copies of the recordings whenever possible. Additionally, we used Olof Björner's Bob Dylan sessionography to help sort out the *Highway 61 Revisited* recording sessions. (*The Cutting Edge 1965–1966: The Bootleg Series, Vol. 12; Collector's Edition* is a limited edition eighteen-CD set that includes all recorded takes from the *Highway 61 Revisited* sessions. In the interest of concision, only those takes included on the two- and six-disc versions of this release are listed here.)

Special thanks to Steve Albin, author of BRIAN, a free discography application (www.jazzdiscography.com/Brian), Greil Marcus, Ed Berger, and Michael Cuscuna.

INSTRUMENT, ROLE, AND TRACK ABBREVIATIONS

acc	Accordion		per	Percussion
acg	Acoustic Guitar		p	Piano
alt	Alternate Take		prod	Producer
as	Alto Sax		rds	Reeds
bkv	Backing Vocals		sax	Saxophone
bj	Banjo		sit	Sitar
bar	Baritone Sax		s-g	Slide Guitar
b	Bass		ss	Soprano Sax
cga	Congas		stg	Steel Guitar
dbr	Dobro		str	Strings
d	Drums		syn	Synthesizer
org	Electric Organ		tam	Tambourine
ep	Electric Piano		ts	Tenor Sax
eng	Engineer		tpl	Tiple
g	Guitar		tb	Trombone
h	Harmonica		t	Trumpet
hns	Horns		vn	Violin
key	Keyboards		v	Vocals
man	Mandolin			

Date: 1962 or 1963
Location: Chicago, IL
Westwind Singers
Michael Bloomfield (v, h, g); Gus Fleming, Mike Horn (v); Don Wilson (v, g)

a. "San Francisco Bay Blues"
b. "Swing Down Chariot"
c. "I Can't Get 'Nuff Your Love"
d. "The Monkey and the Engineer"
All titles on: Balkan CD: CD-1007—*The Westwind Singers—1960–63*

Date: March 31, 1963
Label: Delmark
Yank Rachell's Tennessee Jug-Busters
James "Yank" Rachell (v, man); Big Joe Williams (v, g); Hammie Nixon (h, jug);
Michael Bloomfield, Sleepy John Estes (g); Bob Koester (prod)

a. "Stop Knocking on My Door"
   Delmark LP 12″: DL-606—*Mandolin Blues*
b. "Doorbell Blues"
   Delmark LP 12″: DL-606—*Mandolin Blues*
c. "Move Your Hand"
   Delmark LP 12″: DL-606—*Mandolin Blues*
d. "Get Your Morning Exercise"
   Delmark LP 12″: DL-606—*Mandolin Blues*
e. "When My Baby Comes Back Home"
f. "Up and Down the Line"
   Delmark LP 12″: DL-606—*Mandolin Blues*
g. "Bye Bye Baby"
   Delmark LP 12″: DL-606—*Mandolin Blues*
All titles on: Delmark CD: DE-606—*Mandolin Blues*
Big Joe Williams (v) on c, (g) on a–f.

Date: c. May 1963
Location: The Fickle Pickle, Chicago, IL
Little Brother Montgomery
Little Brother Montgomery (v, p); Michael Bloomfield (g); Norman Dayron (eng)

a. "Michigan Water Blues"
b. "Pleadin' Blues"
Both titles on: Takoma LP 12″: TAK 7115—*The Best of Mike Bloomfield*
                 Takoma CD: CDP 72922—*Takoma Blues*
                 Takoma CD: TAKCD-8905-2—*The Best of Mike Bloomfield*

Date: July 9, 1963
Location: Nina's Lounge, Chicago, IL
J. B. Lenoir, Sunnyland Slim & Friends
John Lee Granderson (v, g); Sunnyland Slim (v, p); Michael Bloomfield (g)

a. "Brown Skin Woman"
b. "J.L's Blues"
c. "Everything's Gonna Be Alright"
d. "That's All Right"

All titles on: Fuel 2000 CD: 302 061 300 2—*Live in '63*
John Lee Granderson (v) on b–d, (g) on b–d; Sunnyland Slim (v) on a, (p) on a.

Date: January 28, 1964
Location: Norman Dayron's apartment, Chicago, IL
Michael Bloomfield
Michael Bloomfield (v, g)

        a. "Bullet Rag"
        b. "Kingpin"
        c. "J.P. Morgan"
All titles on: Miller Freeman Books CD—*Rare Performances 1964*

Date: March 1964
Location: Columbia Studios, New York, NY
Label: Columbia
Michael Bloomfield
Michael Bloomfield (v, h, kazoo, g); Bill Lee (b); John Hammond Sr. (prod)

        a. "I'm a Country Boy"
            Columbia Legacy CD: 88765476342—*From His Head to His Heart to His Hands*
        b. "Judge, Judge"
            Columbia Legacy CD: 88765476342—*From His Head to His Heart to His Hands*
        c. "Hammond's Rag"
            Columbia Legacy CD: 88765476342—*From His Head to His Heart to His Hands*
        d. "Got the Blues (Feelin' Called the Blues)"
        e. "Got My Mojo Working"
        f. "God Don't Like Ugly"
        g. "Baby What You Want Me to Do (You Got Me Runnin')"
        h. "Don't Lay That Snake on Me"
        i. "J.P. Morgan"
Michael Bloomfield (h) on e, g, (kazoo) on f, h; Bill Lee (b) on a–d.

Date: March 3, 1964
Location: Sound Studios, Chicago, IL
Sleepy John Estes/The Tennessee Jug Busters
Sleepy John Estes (v, g); Hammie Nixon (h); Michael Bloomfield (g); James "Yank" Rachell (g, man); Bob Koester (prod)

        a. "3:00 Morning Blues"
            Delmark LP 12": DL-608—*Broke and Hungry*
        b. "Beale Street Sugar"
            Delmark LP 12": DL-608—*Broke and Hungry*
        c. "Broke and Hungry"
            Delmark LP 12": DL-608—*Broke and Hungry*

    d. "Freedom Loan"
        Delmark LP 12": DL-608—*Broke and Hungry*
    e. "Everybody Oughta Change"
    f. "Olie Blues"
        Delmark LP 12": DL-608—*Broke and Hungry*
All titles on: Delmark CD: DD-608—*Broke and Hungry*
James "Yank" Rachell (man) on c.

Date: May 16, 1964
Location: Sutherland Lounge, Chicago, IL
Eddie Boyd/Yank Rachell
Eddie Boyd (v, p); James "Yank" Rachell (v, man); Michael Bloomfield (g, p); John Lee Granderson (g)

    a. "Five Long Years"
    b. "Her Picture in the Frame"
    c. "Early Grave"
    d. "The Big Question"
    e. "Look over Yonder Wall (Nothing but Trouble)"
    f. "Going to Pack Up My Things"
    g. "Every Night and Every Day"
    h. "Rock Me Baby (My Baby Rocks Me)"
    i. "My Baby's Gone"
All titles on: Jefferson Records CD: SBACD 12653/4—*I Blueskvarter—Chicago 1964, Vol. One*

Eddie Boyd (v) on a–e, (p) on a–e; James "Yank" Rachell (v) on f–i, (man) on f–i; Michael Bloomfield (g) on a–e, (p) on f–i; John Lee Granderson (g) on f–i.
Recorded by Olle Helander and engineer Hans Westman for Swedish radio.

Date: May 19, 1964
Location: Sutherland Lounge, Chicago, IL
Sunnyland Slim/St. Louis Jimmy
St. Louis Jimmy (v); Sunnyland Slim (v, p); Michael Bloomfield (g); Washboard Sam (washboard)

    a. "Brownskin Woman"
        Jefferson Records CD: SBACD 12653/4—*I Blueskvarter—Chicago 1964, Vol. One*
    b. "It's You Baby"
        Jefferson Records CD: SBACD 12653/4—*I Blueskvarter—Chicago 1964, Vol. One*
    c. "One Room Country Shack"
        Jefferson Records CD: SBACD 12653/4—*I Blueskvarter—Chicago 1964, Vol. One*
    d. "Sunnyland's Jump"
        Jefferson Records CD: SBACD 12653/4—*I Blueskvarter—Chicago 1964, Vol. One*

   e.   "Rock Me"
        Jefferson Records CD: SBACD 12653/4—*I Blueskvarter—Chicago
        1964, Vol. One*
   f.   "The Devil Is a Busy Man"
   g.   "I Done You Wrong"
   h.   "Early One Morning"
   i.   "Can't Stand Your Evil Ways"
        Jefferson Records CD: SBACD 12655/6—*I Blueskvarter—Chicago
        1964, Vol. Two*
   j.   "Complete This Order"
        Jefferson Records CD: SBACD 12655/6—*I Blueskvarter—Chicago
        1964, Vol. Two*
   k.   "Poor Boy Blues"
        Jefferson Records CD: SBACD 12655/6—*I Blueskvarter—Chicago
        1964, Vol. Two*
   l.   "The Girl I Love"
        Jefferson Records CD: SBACD 12655/6—*I Blueskvarter—Chicago
        1964, Vol. Two*
   m.   "Monkey Faced Woman"

St. Louis Jimmy (v) on i–m; Sunnyland Slim (v) on a–h; Washboard Sam (washboard) on i–m.
Recorded by Olle Helander and engineer Hans Westman for Swedish radio.

Date: May 21, 1964
Location: Sutherland Lounge, Chicago, IL
Little Brother Montgomery
Little Brother Montgomery (v, p); Michael Bloomfield (g)
   a.   "West Texas Blues"
        Jefferson Records CD: SBACD 12655/6—*I Blueskvarter—Chi-
        cago 1964, Vol. Two*
   b.   "Up the Country Blues"
        Jefferson Records CD: SBACD 12655/6—*I Blueskvarter—Chicago
        1964, Vol. Two*
   c.   "Cow Cow Blues"
        Jefferson Records CD: SBACD 12655/6—*I Blueskvarter—Chicago
        1964, Vol. Two*
   d.   "Mama, You Don't Mean Me No Good"
        Jefferson Records CD: SBACD 12655/6—*I Blueskvarter—Chicago
        1964, Vol. Two*
   e.   "Suitcase Blues"
        Jefferson Records CD: SBACD 12655/6—*I Blueskvarter—Chicago
        1964, Vol. Two*
   f.   "The Vicksburg Blues Road"

Recorded by Olle Helander and engineer Hans Westman for Swedish radio.

Date: c. June 1964
Location: New York, NY
John Hammond

John Paul Hammond (John Hammond Jr.) (v, h, g, prod); Charlie Musselwhite (h); Robbie Robertson (g); Michael Bloomfield (p); Garth Hudson (org); Jimmy Lewis (b); Levon Helm (d)

- a. "Down in the Bottom"
  Vanguard LP 12": VSD-79178—*So Many Roads*
- b. "Long Distance Call"
  Vanguard LP 12": VSD-79178—*So Many Roads*
- c. "Who Do You Love"
  Vanguard LP 12": VSD-79178—*So Many Roads*
  Vanguard LP 12": VSD-11/12—*The Best of John Hammond*
- d. "I Want You to Love Me"
  Vanguard LP 12": VSD-79178—*So Many Roads*
- e. "Rambling Blues"
  Vanguard LP 12": VSD-79178—*So Many Roads*
- f. "You Can't Judge a Book by the Cover"
  Vanguard LP 12": VSD-79178—*So Many Roads*
- g. "Gambling Blues"
  Vanguard LP 12": VSD-79178—*So Many Roads*
- h. "Big Boss Man"
  Vanguard LP 12": VSD-79178—*So Many Roads*
  Vanguard LP 12": VSD-11/12—*The Best of John Hammond*
- i. "I Wish You Would"
  Vanguard LP 12": VSD-11/12—*The Best of John Hammond*
  Vanguard LP 12": VSD-79245—*Mirrors*
- j. "Traveling Riverside"
  Vanguard LP 12": VSD-11/12—*The Best of John Hammond*
  Vanguard LP 12": VSD-79245—*Mirrors*

All titles on: Vanguard CD: VMD 79178—*So Many Roads: The Complete Sessions*

Date: September 1964
Location: Maxwell Street Market, Chicago, IL
Robert Nighthawk

Robert Nighthawk, Johnny Young (v, g); Michael Bloomfield, John Lee Granderson (g); Jimmy Collins (d); Norman Dayron (eng)

- a. "Excerpts from Interview/Kansas City"
  Rounder LP 12": 2022—*Live on Maxwell Street 1964*
- b. "Bloomfield Interviews Night Hawk"
  Rooster CD: R2641—*And This Is Maxwell Street*
- c. "The Sun Is Shining"
  Rooster CD: R2641—*And This Is Maxwell Street*

d. "Dust My Broom"
    Rooster CD: R2641—*And This Is Maxwell Street*
e. "Peter Gunn Jam"
    Rooster CD: R2641—*And This Is Maxwell Street*
f. "All I Want for My Breakfast"
    Rooster CD: R2641—*And This Is Maxwell Street*
g. "Back Off Jam"
    Rooster CD: R2641—*And This Is Maxwell Street*
h. "Love You Tonight"
    Rooster CD: R2641—*And This Is Maxwell Street*
i. "Interview"
    Bullseye CD: 9624-2—*Live on Maxwell Street 1964*

Johnny Young (v) on c, f, (g) on c, f; Michael Bloomfield (g) on c–d; John Lee Granderson (g) on d–e, g–h; Jimmy Collins (d) on d–e, g.

Date: October 15, 1964
Location: Big John's, Chicago, IL
Michael Bloomfield/The Group
Michael Bloomfield (v, g, p); Charlie Musselwhite (h); Michael Johnson (g); Sid Warner (b); Norm Mayell (d); Norman Dayron (eng)

a. "Blues for Roy"
b. "Country Boy"
c. "Intermission Blues"
d. "Gotta Call Susie"

All titles on: Miller Freeman Books CD—*Rare Performances 1964*
Charlie Musselwhite (h) on b, d; Michael Bloomfield (g) on a–b, d, (p) on c; Michael Johnson (g) on a–b, d; Sid Warner (b) on a–b, d; Norm Mayell (d) on a–b, d.

Date: December 7, 1964
Location: Columbia Studio A, Chicago, IL
Label: Columbia
Michael Bloomfield
Michael Bloomfield (v, g); Charlie Musselwhite (h); Michael Johnson (g); Brian Friedman (p); Sid Warner (b); Norm Mayell (d); John Hammond Sr. (prod)

a. "I Feel So Good"
    Columbia Legacy CD: CK 57631—*Don't Say That I Ain't Your Man!: Essential Blues 1964–1969*
b. "I Feel So Good" (alt)
    Sundazed LP 12": 5105—*I'm Cutting Out*
c. "I Feel So Good" (alt)
    Sundazed LP 12": 5105—*I'm Cutting Out*
d. "Goin' Down Slow"
    Columbia Legacy CD: CK 57631—*Don't Say That I Ain't Your Man!: Essential Blues 1964–1969*

e. "Goin' Down Slow" (alt)
Sundazed LP 12": 5105—*I'm Cutting Out*

f. "I've Got You in the Palm of My Hand"
Columbia Legacy CD: CK 57631—*Don't Say That I Ain't Your Man!: Essential Blues 1964-1969*

g. "I've Got You in the Palm of My Hand" (alt)
Sundazed LP 12": 5105—*I'm Cutting Out*

h. "The First Year I Was Married"
Sundazed LP 12": 5105—*I'm Cutting Out*

i. "I Got My Mojo Working"
Sundazed LP 12": 5105—*I'm Cutting Out*
Columbia LP 12": C2 37578—*Bloomfield: A Retrospective* (as "I've Got My Mojo Workin'")

j. "Last Night"
Columbia Legacy CD: CK 57631—*Don't Say That I Ain't Your Man!: Essential Blues 1964-1969*

k. "Last Night" (alt)
Sundazed LP 12": 5105—*I'm Cutting Out*

Date: March 1, 1965
Location: Columbia Studios, New York, NY
Label: Columbia
Michael Bloomfield
Michael Bloomfield (v, g); Charlie Musselwhite (h); Michael Johnson (g); Brian Friedman (p); Sid Warner (b); Norm Mayell (d); Bob Morgan (prod)

a. "I Got My Mojo Working"
Columbia Legacy CD: CK 57631—*Don't Say That I Ain't Your Man!: Essential Blues 1964-1969*

b. "I'm Cutting Out"

c. "Lonesome Blues"

All titles on: Sundazed LP 12": 5105—*I'm Cutting Out*
Contrary to the credits listed by Columbia, the personnel for this demo session may actually include Bill Lee (b) and Sam Lay (d), along with other Paul Butterfield Blues Band members.

Date: March/April 1965
Location: Mastertone Recording Studios, New York, NY
Label: Elektra
Paul Butterfield Blues Band
Paul Butterfield (v, h); Elvin Bishop (g); Michael Bloomfield (g, p, org); Mark Naftalin (org); Jerome Arnold (b); Sam Lay (d); Mark Abramson, Paul A. Rothchild (prod)

a. "Good Morning Little Schoolgirl"
Elektra LP 12": EKL-4002—*What's Shakin'*
Elektra CD: R2 73505—*The Original Lost Elektra Sessions*

b. "Just to Be with You"
   Elektra CD: R2 73505—*The Original Lost Elektra Sessions*
c. "Help Me"
   Elektra CD: R2 73505—*The Original Lost Elektra Sessions*
d. "Hate to See You Go"
   Elektra CD: R2 73505—*The Original Lost Elektra Sessions*
e. "Poor Boy"
   Elektra CD: R2 73505—*The Original Lost Elektra Sessions*
f. "Nut Popper #1"
   Elektra CD: R2 73505—*The Original Lost Elektra Sessions*
g. "Everything's Gonna Be Alright"
   Elektra CD: R2 73505—*The Original Lost Elektra Sessions*
h. "Lovin' Cup"
   Elektra LP 12″: EKL-4002—*What's Shakin'*
   Elektra CD: R2 73505—*The Original Lost Elektra Sessions*
i. "Rock Me"
   Elektra CD: R2 73505—*The Original Lost Elektra Sessions*
j. "It Hurts Me Too"
   Elektra CD: R2 73505—*The Original Lost Elektra Sessions*
k. "Our Love Is Driftin'"
   Elektra CD: R2 73505—*The Original Lost Elektra Sessions*
l. "Take Me Back Baby"
   Elektra CD: R2 73505—*The Original Lost Elektra Sessions*
m. "Mellow Down Easy"
   Elektra CD: R2 73505—*The Original Lost Elektra Sessions*
n. "Ain't No Need to Go No Further"
   Elektra CD: R2 73505—*The Original Lost Elektra Sessions*
o. "Love Her with a Feeling"
   Elektra CD: R2 73505—*The Original Lost Elektra Sessions*
p. "Piney Brown Blues"
   Elektra CD: R2 73505—*The Original Lost Elektra Sessions*
q. "Spoonful"
   Elektra LP 12″: EKL-4002—*What's Shakin'*
   Elektra CD: R2 73505—*The Original Lost Elektra Sessions*
r. "That's All Right"
   Elektra CD: R2 73505—*The Original Lost Elektra Sessions*
s. "Goin' Down Slow"
   Elektra CD: R2 73505—*The Original Lost Elektra Sessions*
t. "Born in Chicago"
   Elektra LP 12″: S-78—*Folksong '65*
   Elektra CD: 62124-2—*An Anthology: The Elektra Years*
u. "One More Mile"
   Elektra LP 12″: EKL-4002—*What's Shakin'*
   Elektra CD: 62124-2—*An Anthology: The Elektra Years*

v. "Off the Wall"
    Elektra LP 12": EKL-4002—*What's Shakin'*
    Elektra CD: 62124-2—*An Anthology: The Elektra Years*
Michael Bloomfield (org) on t; Mark Naftalin (org) on o.
*Elektra dates these recordings to late 1964, but other evidence suggests a spring 1965
date; track o was likely recorded later in 1965.*

Date: c. Spring–Summer 1965
Location: Cafe au Go Go, New York, NY
Label: Elektra
Paul Butterfield Blues Band
Paul Butterfield (v, h); Elvin Bishop, Michael Bloomfield (g); Jerome Arnold (b); Sam
Lay (d)
    a. unknown titles
*The band was recorded live over four nights for Elektra by Paul Rothchild, who then
declined to release the recordings.*

Date: June 15, 1965
Location: Studio A, Columbia Recording Studios, New York, NY
Label: Columbia
Bob Dylan
Bob Dylan (v, h, g, p); Michael Bloomfield, Al Gorgoni (g); Frank Owens (p); Paul
Griffin (org); Joe Macho Jr. (b); Bobby Gregg (d); Tom Wilson (prod)
    a. "It Takes a Lot to Laugh, It Takes a Train to Cry" (take 1)
        Columbia CD: 88875124412—*The Cutting Edge 1965–1966: The
        Bootleg Series, Vol. 12*
    b. "It Takes a Lot to Laugh, It Takes a Train to Cry" (take 8)
        Columbia CD: 88875124412—*The Cutting Edge 1965–1966: The
        Bootleg Series, Vol. 12*
        Columbia CD: 88875124422—*The Best of the Cutting Edge 1965–
        1966: The Bootleg Series, Vol. 12*
    c. "It Takes a Lot to Laugh, It Takes a Train to Cry" (take 9)
        Columbia Legacy CD: C2K 93937—*No Direction Home: The
        Soundtrack (The Bootleg Series, Vol. 7)*
    d. "Sitting on a Barbed-Wire Fence" (take 2)
        Columbia CD: 88875124412—*The Cutting Edge 1965–1966: The
        Bootleg Series, Vol. 12*
        Columbia CD: 88875124422—*The Best of the Cutting Edge 1965–
        1966: The Bootleg Series, Vol. 12*
    e. "Sitting on a Barbed-Wire Fence" (take 3)
        Columbia CD: C3K 47382—*The Bootleg Series, Vols. 1–3 [Rare &
        Unreleased] 1961–1991*
    f. "It Takes a Lot to Laugh, It Takes a Train to Cry" (take 1, remake)
        Columbia CD: C3K 47382—*The Bootleg Series, Vols. 1–3 [Rare &
        Unreleased] 1961–1991*

g.　"Like a Rolling Stone" (take 1, rehearsal)
Columbia CD: 88875124412—*The Cutting Edge 1965–1966: The Bootleg Series, Vol. 12*

h.　"Like a Rolling Stone" (take 2, rehearsal)
Columbia CD: 88875124412—*The Cutting Edge 1965–1966: The Bootleg Series, Vol. 12*

i.　"Like a Rolling Stone" (take 3, rehearsal)
Columbia CD: 88875124412—*The Cutting Edge 1965–1966: The Bootleg Series, Vol. 12*

j.　"Like a Rolling Stone" (take 4, rehearsal)
Columbia CD: C3K 47382—*The Bootleg Series, Vols. 1–3 [Rare & Unreleased] 1961–1991*
Columbia CD: 88875124412—*The Cutting Edge 1965–1966: The Bootleg Series, Vol. 12*

k.　"Like a Rolling Stone" (take 5, breakdown)
Columbia CD: 88875124412—*The Cutting Edge 1965–1966: The Bootleg Series, Vol. 12*
Columbia CD: 88875124422—*The Best of the Cutting Edge 1965–1966: The Bootleg Series, Vol. 12*

All titles on:　Columbia CD: 888751240218—*The Cutting Edge 1965–1966: The Bootleg Series, Vol. 12; Collector's Edition*

Date: June 16, 1965
Location: Studio A, Columbia Recording Studios, New York, NY
Label: Columbia
Bob Dylan

Bob Dylan (v, h, g); Michael Bloomfield (g); Paul Griffin (p); Al Kooper (org); Joe Macho Jr. (b); Bobby Gregg (d); Bruce Langhorne (tam); Tom Wilson (prod)

a.　"Like a Rolling Stone" (rehearsal)
Columbia CD: 88875124412—*The Cutting Edge 1965–1966: The Bootleg Series, Vol. 12*

b.　"Like a Rolling Stone" (take 1, rehearsal)
Columbia CD: 88875124412—*The Cutting Edge 1965–1966: The Bootleg Series, Vol. 12*

c.　"Like a Rolling Stone" (take 2, false start)
Columbia CD: 88875124412—*The Cutting Edge 1965–1966: The Bootleg Series, Vol. 12*

d.　"Like a Rolling Stone" (take 3, false start)
Columbia CD: 88875124412—*The Cutting Edge 1965–1966: The Bootleg Series, Vol. 12*

e.　"Like a Rolling Stone" (take 4)
Columbia 45: 4-43346—"Like a Rolling Stone" / "Gates of Eden"
Columbia LP 12″: CL 2389—*Highway 61 Revisited*
Columbia LP 12″: CS 9189—*Highway 61 Revisited*

Columbia CD: CK 9189—*Highway 61 Revisited*
Columbia Legacy CD: 88765476342—*From His Head to His Heart to His Hands* (instrumental version)
Columbia CD: 88875124412—*The Cutting Edge 1965-1966: The Bootleg Series, Vol. 12*

f. "Like a Rolling Stone" (take 5, rehearsal)
Columbia CD: 88875124412—*The Cutting Edge 1965-1966: The Bootleg Series, Vol. 12*

g. "Like a Rolling Stone" (take 6, false start)
Columbia CD: 88875124412—*The Cutting Edge 1965-1966: The Bootleg Series, Vol. 12*

h. "Like a Rolling Stone" (take 8, breakdown)
Columbia CD: 88875124412—*The Cutting Edge 1965-1966: The Bootleg Series, Vol. 12*

i. "Like a Rolling Stone" (take 9, false start)
Columbia CD: 88875124412—*The Cutting Edge 1965-1966: The Bootleg Series, Vol. 12*

j. "Like a Rolling Stone" (take 10, false start)
Columbia CD: 88875124412—*The Cutting Edge 1965-1966: The Bootleg Series, Vol. 12*

k. "Like a Rolling Stone" (take 11)
Columbia CD: 88875124412—*The Cutting Edge 1965-1966: The Bootleg Series, Vol. 12*
Columbia CD: 88875124422—*The Best of the Cutting Edge 1965-1966: The Bootleg Series, Vol. 12*

l. "Like a Rolling Stone" (take 12, false start)
Columbia CD: 88875124412—*The Cutting Edge 1965-1966: The Bootleg Series, Vol. 12*

m. "Like a Rolling Stone" (take 13, breakdown)
Columbia CD: 88875124412—*The Cutting Edge 1965-1966: The Bootleg Series, Vol. 12*

n. "Like a Rolling Stone" (take 14, false start)
Columbia CD: 88875124412—*The Cutting Edge 1965-1966: The Bootleg Series, Vol. 12*

o. "Like a Rolling Stone" (take 15, breakdown)
Columbia CD: 88875124412—*The Cutting Edge 1965-1966: The Bootleg Series, Vol. 12*

All titles on: Columbia CD: 888751240218—*The Cutting Edge 1965-1966: The Bootleg Series, Vol. 12; Collector's Edition*

Date: July 23–25, 1965
Location: Newport Folk Festival, Freebody Park, Newport, RI
Paul Butterfield Blues Band
Paul Butterfield (v, h); Nick Gravenites (v); Elvin Bishop, Michael Bloomfield (g); Jerome Arnold (b); Sam Lay (d); Bruce Langhorne (tam)

a. "Juke"
Eagle Rock Entertainment DVD—*Festival: A Film by Murray Lerner*

b. "Blues with a Feeling"
Vanguard CD: VCD2-77005—*Blues with a Feeling*

c. "Look over Yonders Wall"
Vanguard CD: VCD2-77005—*Blues with a Feeling*

d. "Blues for Ruth"

e. "Why Don't You All Quit It"

f. "Elvin's Blues"

g. "That's Alright"

h. "It's About Time"

i. "It's True"

j. "Work Song"

k. "Born in Chicago"
Columbia LP 12″: C2 37578—*Bloomfield: A Retrospective*
Sony CD: SICP 1969–70—*Bloomfield: A Retrospective*

l. "Mellow Down Easy"
Vanguard LP 12″: VSD-79225—*Festival: The Newport Folk Festival/1965*

m. "Michael Bloomfield Introducing Lightnin' Hopkins"
Eagle Rock Entertainment DVD—*Festival: A Film by Murray Lerner*

n. "Michael Bloomfield Speaks on Son House and Butterfield"
Eagle Rock Entertainment DVD—*Festival: A Film by Murray Lerner*

o. "Michael Bloomfield Speaks on Playing the Blues"
Eagle Rock Entertainment DVD—*Festival: A Film by Murray Lerner*

Nick Gravenites (v) on g–i.

Date: July 24–25, 1965
Location: Newport Folk Festival, Freebody Park, Newport, RI
Bob Dylan
Bob Dylan (v, h, g, org); Michael Bloomfield (g); Barry Goldberg (p); Al Kooper (org); Jerome Arnold (b); Sam Lay (d)

a. "Organ Riffs" (rehearsal)
Eagle Rock Entertainment DVD—*Festival: A Film by Murray Lerner*

b. "Maggie's Farm" (rehearsal)
Eagle Rock Entertainment DVD—*Festival: A Film by Murray Lerner*

c. "Like a Rolling Stone" (rehearsal)
Eagle Rock Entertainment DVD—*Festival: A Film by Murray Lerner*

d. "Maggie's Farm"
Eagle Rock Entertainment DVD—*Festival: A Film by Murray Lerner*

e. "Like a Rolling Stone"

f. "Phantom Engineer" ("It Takes a Lot to Laugh, It Takes a Train to Cry")
Bob Dylan (org) on a.

Date: July 29, 1965
Location: Studio A, Columbia Recording Studios, New York, NY
Label: Columbia
Bob Dylan

Bob Dylan (v, h, g, p); Michael Bloomfield (g); Paul Griffin, Frank Owens (p); Al Kooper (org, g); Harvey Brooks, Joe Macho Jr., Russ Savakus (b); Bobby Gregg (d); Bob Johnston (prod)

a. "It Takes a Lot to Laugh, It Takes a Train to Cry" (take 3, incomplete)
Columbia CD: 88875124412—*The Cutting Edge 1965–1966: The Bootleg Series, Vol. 12*

b. "Tombstone Blues" (take 1)
Columbia CD: 88875124412—*The Cutting Edge 1965–1966: The Bootleg Series, Vol. 12*
Columbia CD: 88875124422—*The Best of the Cutting Edge 1965–1966: The Bootleg Series, Vol. 12*

c. "Tombstone Blues" (take 9)
Columbia Legacy CD: C2K 93937—*No Direction Home: The Soundtrack (The Bootleg Series, Vol. 7)*
Columbia CD: 88875124412—*The Cutting Edge 1965–1966: The Bootleg Series, Vol. 12*

d. "Tombstone Blues" (take 12)
Columbia LP 12": CL 2389—*Highway 61 Revisited*
Columbia LP 12": CS 9189—*Highway 61 Revisited*
Columbia CD: CK 9189—*Highway 61 Revisited*
Columbia Legacy CD: 88765476342—*From His Head to His Heart to His Hands* (with Chambers Brothers vocal overdub)

e. "It Takes a Lot to Laugh, It Takes a Train to Cry" (take 3, remake)
Columbia CD: 88875124412—*The Cutting Edge 1965–1966: The Bootleg Series, Vol. 12*

f. "It Takes a Lot to Laugh, It Takes a Train to Cry" (take 4)
Columbia LP 12": CL 2389—*Highway 61 Revisited*
Columbia LP 12": CS 9189—*Highway 61 Revisited*
Columbia CD: CK 9189—*Highway 61 Revisited*

g. "Positively 4th Street" (take 1, false start)
Columbia CD: 88875124412—*The Cutting Edge 1965–1966: The Bootleg Series, Vol. 12*

h. "Positively 4th Street" (take 2, false start)
Columbia CD: 88875124412—*The Cutting Edge 1965–1966: The Bootleg Series, Vol. 12*

i. "Positively 4th Street" (take 3, false start)
Columbia CD: 88875124412—*The Cutting Edge 1965–1966: The Bootleg Series, Vol. 12*

j. "Positively 4th Street" (take 4)
Columbia CD: 88875124412—*The Cutting Edge 1965–1966: The Bootleg Series, Vol. 12*

k. "Positively 4th Street" (take 5)
Columbia CD: 88875124412—*The Cutting Edge 1965–1966: The Bootleg Series, Vol. 12*
Columbia CD: 88875124422—*The Best of the Cutting Edge 1965–1966: The Bootleg Series, Vol. 12*

l. "Positively 4th Street" (take 12)
Columbia 45: 4-43389—"Positively 4th Street" / "From a Buick 6"

m. "Desolation Row" (take 1)
Columbia Legacy CD: C2K 93937—*No Direction Home: The Soundtrack (The Bootleg Series, Vol. 7)*

All titles on: Columbia CD: 888751240218—*The Cutting Edge 1965–1966: The Bootleg Series, Vol. 12; Collector's Edition*

Date: July 30, 1965
Location: Studio A, Columbia Recording Studios, New York, NY
Label: Columbia
Bob Dylan

Bob Dylan (v, h, g, p); Michael Bloomfield (g); Paul Griffin (p); Al Kooper (org, celeste); Harvey Brooks (b); Bobby Gregg (d); Bob Johnston (prod)

a. "From a Buick 6" (take 1)
Columbia CD: 88875124412—*The Cutting Edge 1965–1966: The Bootleg Series, Vol. 12*

b. "From a Buick 6" (take 4)
Columbia CD: 88875124412—*The Cutting Edge 1965–1966: The Bootleg Series, Vol. 12*

c. "From a Buick 6" (take 5)
Columbia 45: 4-43389—"Positively 4th Street" / "From a Buick 6"
Columbia LP 12": CL 2389—*Highway 61 Revisited*
Columbia LP 12": CS 9189—*Highway 61 Revisited*
Columbia CD: CK 9189—*Highway 61 Revisited*

d. "Can You Please Crawl out Your Window" (take 1)
Columbia CD: 88875124412—*The Cutting Edge 1965–1966: The Bootleg Series, Vol. 12*
Columbia CD: 88875124422—*The Best of the Cutting Edge 1965–1966: The Bootleg Series, Vol. 12*

e. "Can You Please Crawl out Your Window" (take 17)
Columbia CD: 88875124412—*The Cutting Edge 1965–1966: The Bootleg Series, Vol. 12*

All titles on: Columbia CD: 888751240218—*The Cutting Edge 1965–1966: The Bootleg Series, Vol. 12; Collector's Edition*

Track b was mistakenly released on the first pressing of Highway 61 Revisited; *e was mistakenly released as the A-side of the first pressing of the "Positively 4th Street" / "From a Buick 6" single.*

Date: August 2, 1965
Location: Studio A, Columbia Recording Studios, New York, NY
Label: Columbia
Bob Dylan
Bob Dylan (v, h, g, p); Michael Bloomfield (g); Paul Griffin, Frank Owens (p); Al Kooper (org, ep, celeste); Harvey Brooks (b); Bobby Gregg, Sam Lay (d); Bob Johnston (prod)

a. "Highway 61 Revisited" (take 3)
   Columbia CD: 88875124412—*The Cutting Edge 1965–1966: The Bootleg Series, Vol. 12*
   Columbia CD: 88875124422—*The Best of the Cutting Edge 1965–1966: The Bootleg Series, Vol. 12*

b. "Highway 61 Revisited" (take 5)
   Columbia CD: 88875124412—*The Cutting Edge 1965–1966: The Bootleg Series, Vol. 12*

c. "Highway 61 Revisited" (take 6)
   Columbia Legacy CD: C2K 93937—*No Direction Home: The Soundtrack (The Bootleg Series, Vol. 7)*

d. "Highway 61 Revisited" (take 7, false start)
   Columbia CD: 88875124412—*The Cutting Edge 1965–1966: The Bootleg Series, Vol. 12*
   Columbia CD: 88875124422—*The Best of the Cutting Edge 1965–1966: The Bootleg Series, Vol. 12*

e. "Highway 61 Revisited" (take 9)
   Columbia LP 12″: CL 2389—*Highway 61 Revisited*
   Columbia LP 12″: CS 9189—*Highway 61 Revisited*
   Columbia CD: CK 9189—*Highway 61 Revisited*

f. "Just Like Tom Thumb's Blues" (take 1, breakdown)
   Columbia CD: 88875124412—*The Cutting Edge 1965–1966: The Bootleg Series, Vol. 12*

g. "Just Like Tom Thumb's Blues" (take 3)
   Columbia CD: 88875124412—*The Cutting Edge 1965–1966: The Bootleg Series, Vol. 12*
   Columbia CD: 88875124422—*The Best of the Cutting Edge 1965–1966: The Bootleg Series, Vol. 12*

h. "Just Like Tom Thumb's Blues" (take 5)
   Columbia Legacy CD: C2K 93937—*No Direction Home: The Soundtrack (The Bootleg Series, Vol. 7)*

i. "Just Like Tom Thumb's Blues" (take 13)
   Columbia CD: 88875124412—*The Cutting Edge 1965–1966: The Bootleg Series, Vol. 12*

j. "Just Like Tom Thumb's Blues" (take 16)
   Columbia LP 12″: CL 2389—*Highway 61 Revisited*

Columbia LP 12″: CS 9189—*Highway 61 Revisited*
Columbia CD: CK 9189—*Highway 61 Revisited*

k. "Queen Jane Approximately" (take 2)
Columbia CD: 88875124412—*The Cutting Edge 1965-1966: The Bootleg Series, Vol. 12*

l. "Queen Jane Approximately" (take 5)
Columbia CD: 88875124412—*The Cutting Edge 1965-1966: The Bootleg Series, Vol. 12*
Columbia CD: 88875124422—*The Best of the Cutting Edge 1965-1966: The Bootleg Series, Vol. 12*

m. "Queen Jane Approximately" (take 7)
Columbia LP 12″: CL 2389—*Highway 61 Revisited*
Columbia LP 12″: CS 9189—*Highway 61 Revisited*
Columbia CD: CK 9189—*Highway 61 Revisited*

n. "Ballad of a Thin Man" (take 2, breakdown)
Columbia CD: 88875124412—*The Cutting Edge 1965-1966: The Bootleg Series, Vol. 12*

o. "Ballad of a Thin Man" (take 3)
Columbia LP 12″: CL 2389—*Highway 61 Revisited*
Columbia LP 12″: CS 9189—*Highway 61 Revisited*
Columbia CD: CK 9189—*Highway 61 Revisited*

p. "Desolation Row" (take 5)
Columbia CD: 88875124412—*The Cutting Edge 1965-1966: The Bootleg Series, Vol. 12*
Columbia CD: 88875124422—*The Best of the Cutting Edge 1965-1966: The Bootleg Series, Vol. 12*

All titles on: Columbia CD: 888751240218—*The Cutting Edge 1965-1966: The Bootleg Series, Vol. 12; Collector's Edition*

Date: 1965
Location: New York, NY
Peter, Paul and Mary
Paul Stookey, Peter Yarrow (v, g); Mary Travers (v); Paul Butterfield (h); Michael Bloomfield (g); Mark Naftalin (org); Bill Lee (b); Buddy Saltzman (d); Albert Grossman (prod)

a. "The King of Names"
Warner Bros. LP 12″: WS 1648—*Album*

Date: Late 1965
Location: New York, NY
Judy Collins
Judy Collins (v, g); Michael Bloomfield (g); Al Kooper (org)

a. "I'll Keep It with Mine"
Elektra 45: EK-45601—"I'll Keep It with Mine" / "Thirsty Boots"

Date: September 1965
Location: Mastertone Recording Studios, New York, NY
Paul Butterfield Blues Band
Paul Butterfield (v, h); Sam Lay (v, d); Elvin Bishop, Michael Bloomfield (g); Mark Naftalin (org); Jerome Arnold (b); Mark Abramson, Paul A. Rothchild (prod)
  a. "Born in Chicago"
  b. "Shake Your Money-Maker"
  c. "Blues with a Feeling"
  d. "Thank You Mr. Poobah"
  e. "I Got My Mojo Working"
      Elektra 45: EKSN 45.016—"I Got My Mojo Working" / "Mellow Down Easy"
  f. "Mellow Down Easy"
      Elektra 45: EKSN 45.016—"I Got My Mojo Working" / "Mellow Down Easy"
  g. "Screamin'"
  h. "Our Love Is Drifting"
  i. "Mystery Train"
  j. "Last Night"
  k. "Look over Yonders Wall"
All titles on: Elektra LP 12": EKS 7294—*The Paul Butterfield Blues Band*
Sam Lay (v) on e; Elvin Bishop (g) on a, c, e–g, i–k; Mark Naftalin (org) on a–e, g–i.

Date: September 1–2, 1965
Location: Ter-Mar Studios, Chicago, IL
Label: Chess
Chuck Berry
Chuck Berry (v, g); Peter Hogan (h); Michael Bloomfield (g); Johnnie Johnson (p); Chuck Bernard (b); Jasper Thomas (d)
  a. "It Wasn't Me"
      Chess 45: 1943—"It Wasn't Me" / "Welcome Back Pretty Baby"
  b. "Ain't That Just Like a Woman"
Both titles on: Chess LP 12": LPS-1498—*Fresh Berry's*
                BGO Records CD: BGOCD395—*Chuck Berry in London / Fresh Berry's*
Bloomfield and Butterfield may have been overdubbed later.

Date: October 1965
Location: Universal Recording Studios, Chicago, IL
Label: Mercury
Dick Campbell
Dick Campbell (v, g); Artie Sullivan (v, tam); Paul Butterfield (h); Michael Bloomfield, Jimmy Vincent (g); Marty Grebb (p, tam, per); Mark Naftalin (org); Peter Cetera (b); Billy Herman, Sam Lay, Larry "Wild" Wrice (d); Eddie Mascari, Lou Reizner (prod)
  a. "The Blues Peddlers"

    b.   "You've Got to Be Kidding"

    c.   "Sandi"

    d.   "The People Planners"

    e.   "Aphrodite's Child"

    f.   "Despairs Cafeteria"

    g.   "Approximately Four Minutes of Feeling Sorry for D.C."

    h.   "Object of Derision"

    i.   "Where Were You"

    j.   "Girls Named Misery"

    k.   "Ask Me If I Care"

    l.   "Don Juan of the Western World"

All titles on: Mercury LP 12": SR 61060—*Dick Campbell Sings Where It's At*

Date: 1966

The Chicago Loop

Judy Novy (v, per); Bob Slawson (v, g); Michael Bloomfield (g); Barry Goldberg (p, org); Carmine Riale (b); John Siomos (d); Bob Crewe, Al Kasha (prod)

    a.   "(When She Wants Good Lovin') My Baby Comes to Me"

        DynoVoice 45: 226—"(When She Wants Good Lovin') My Baby Comes to Me" / "This Must Be the Place"

        US Army LP 12"—*The "IN" Sound: For Broadcast Week of November 14, 1966* (as "She Comes to Me")

        US Army LP 12"—*The "IN" Sound: For Broadcast Week of November 21, 1966* (as "She Comes to Me")

        US Army LP 12"—*The "IN" Sound: For Broadcast Week of December 12, 1966* (as "She Comes to Me")

        Sequel Records CD: NEM CD 669—*Love Power: Hard to Find US Hot 100 Hits of the 60's* (as "(When She Needs Good Lovin') She Comes to Me")

        Eric Records CD: 11521—*Teen Time: The Young Years of Rock 'n' Roll, Volume 2: I Got Rhythm* (as "(When She Needs Good Lovin') She Comes to Me")

    b.   Macleans toothpaste spot

All titles on: Macleans LP 12": MR-6555—*Macleans Is What's Happening!*

Date: February 1966

Location: Whisky a Go Go, Los Angeles, CA

Paul Butterfield Blues Band

Paul Butterfield (h, maracas); Elvin Bishop, Michael Bloomfield (g); Mark Naftalin (key); Jerome Arnold (b); Billy Davenport (d)

    a.   "Just to Be with You"

        Winner CD: 446—*Strawberry Jam*

    b.   "East-West #1"

        Winner CD: 447—*East-West Live*

Date: May 1966
Location: Poor Richard's, Chicago, IL
Paul Butterfield Blues Band
Paul Butterfield (h); Elvin Bishop, Michael Bloomfield (g); Mark Naftalin (key); Jerome Arnold (b); Billy Davenport (d)

    a.   "East-West #2"
        Winner CD: 447—*East-West Live*

Date: May 1966
Location: Unicorn Coffee House, Boston, MA
Paul Butterfield Blues Band
Paul Butterfield (v, h); Elvin Bishop (v, g); Michael Bloomfield (g); Mark Naftalin (org); Jerome Arnold (b); Billy Davenport (d)

    a.   "Instrumental Intro"
    b.   "Look over Yonders Wall"
    c.   "Born in Chicago"
    d.   "Love Her with a Feeling"
    e.   "Get Out of My Life, Woman"
    f.   "Never Say No"
    g.   "One More Heartache"
    h.   "Work Song"
    i.   "Coming Home Baby"
    j.   "Memory Pain"
    k.   "I Got a Mind to Give Up Living"
    l.   "Walking by Myself"
    m.   "Got My Mojo Working"
All titles on: Real Gone Music CD: RGM-0456—*Got a Mind to Give Up Living: Live 1966*

Date: Summer 1966
Location: Chess Studios, Chicago, IL
Label: Elektra
Paul Butterfield Blues Band
Paul Butterfield (v, h); Elvin Bishop (v, g); Michael Bloomfield (g); Mark Naftalin (p, org); Jerome Arnold (b); Billy Davenport (d); Mark Abramson, Paul A. Rothchild (prod); Ron Malo (eng)

    a.   "Walkin' Blues"
    b.   "Get Out of My Life, Woman"
    c.   "I Got a Mind to Give Up Living"
        Elektra 45: EK-45609—"Come On In" / "I Got a Mind to Give Up Living"
    d.   "All These Blues"
    e.   "Work Song"

    f. "Two Trains Running"

    g. "Never Say No"

    h. "East-West"

All titles on: Elektra LP 12": EKS-7315—*East-West*

              Elektra CD: 7315-2—*East-West*

Elvin Bishop (v) on g.

Date: Summer 1966
Location: Los Angeles, CA
Label: Elektra
Paul Butterfield Blues Band

Paul Butterfield (v, h); Elvin Bishop, Michael Bloomfield (g); Mark Naftalin (p, org); Jerome Arnold (b); Billy Davenport (d); Barry Friedman (prod)

    a. "Mary, Mary"

        Elektra LP 12": EKS-7315—*East-West*

        Elektra CD: 7315-2—*East-West*

Date: September 1966
Location: Chicago, IL
Label: Elektra
Paul Butterfield Blues Band

Paul Butterfield (v, h); Elvin Bishop, Michael Bloomfield (g); Mark Naftalin (p, org); Jerome Arnold (b); Billy Davenport (d); John Court, Albert Grossman (prod)

    a. "Come On In"

        Elektra 45: EK-45609—"Come On In" / "I Got a Mind to Give Up Living"

Date: December 1966
Location: New York, NY
Barry Goldberg

Barry Goldberg (v, key); Michael Bloomfield, Frank Zappa (g); Tom Wilson (prod)

    a. "Carry On"

        Verve Folkways 45: KF 5045—"Carry On" / "Ronnie Siegel from Avenue L"

Date: January or February 1967
Location: The Golden Bear, Huntington Beach, CA
Paul Butterfield Blues Band

Paul Butterfield (h); Elvin Bishop, Michael Bloomfield (g); Mark Naftalin (key); Jerome Arnold (b); Billy Davenport (d)

    a. "Tollin' Bells"

        Winner CD: 446—*Strawberry Jam*

    b. "Come On in This House"

        Winner CD: 446—*Strawberry Jam*

   c.   "Born in Chicago"
        Winner CD: 446—*Strawberry Jam*
   d.   "East-West #3"
        Winner CD: 447—*East-West Live*

Date: March 24, 1967
Location: New York, NY
Label: Verve
James Cotton

James Cotton (v, h); Robert Anderson (v, b); Luther Tucker (g); Alberto Gianquinto (p); Sam Lay (d); James F. Barge (ts); McKinley Easton, Delbert Hill (bar); Paul Serrano (t); Louis E. Satterfield, John M. Watson (tb); Michael Bloomfield, Norman Dayron, Barry Goldberg (prod)

        a.   "Sweet Sixteen"
        b.   "Oh Why"
        c.   "Blues in My Sleep"
All titles on: Verve/Forecast LP 12": FTS 3023—*The James Cotton Blues Band*
                Verve CD: 314 527 371-2—*Best of the Verve Years*

Date: March 1967
Location: New York, NY
Eddie "Cleanhead" Vinson

Eddie "Cleanhead" Vinson (v, as); Buddy Lucas (h, ts); Michael Bloomfield (g); Patti Bown (p, org); Bob Thiele (prod)

        a.   "Juice Head Baby"
            Flying Dutchman 45: BT 45004—"Alimony Blues" / "Juice Head Baby"
        b.   "Alimony Blues"
            Flying Dutchman 45: BT 45004—"Alimony Blues" / "Juice Head Baby"
        c.   "Flat Broke Blues"
        d.   "Workin' Blues"
        e.   "Goodnight Baby Blues"
All titles on: Bluesway LP 12": BL-6007—*Cherry Red*
                One Way Records CD: MCAD 22169—*Cherry Red*
Buddy Lucas (h) on b; Patti Bown (org) on a, e.

Date: March 1967
Location: Mira Sound Studios; Sound Center; Bell Sound, New York, NY
Mitch Ryder

Mitch Ryder (v); Michael Bloomfield, Hugh McCracken (g); Barry Goldberg (p, org); Carmine Riale (b); John Siomos (d); Bob Crewe (prod)

        a.   "Whole Lotta Shakin' Goin' On"
        b.   "Sally Go 'Round the Roses"

  c. "Brown-Eyed Handsome Man"
  d. "I Need Lovin' You"
  e. "That's It, I Quit"
All titles on: DynoVoice LP 12″: DY-31901—*What Now My Love*
      Westside CD: WESD 202—*Detroit Breakout! : An Ultimate Anthology*

Date: April/May 1967
Location: Los Angeles, CA
The Electric Flag
Nick Gravenites (v, g); Michael Bloomfield (g); Barry Goldberg (key); Paul Beaver (syn); Harvey Brooks (b); Buddy Miles (d, per); Peter Strazza (ts); Marcus Doubleday (t, flügelhorn); Bob Notkoff (vn); John Court (prod)

  a. "Peter's Trip"
    Sidewalk 45: 929—"Peter's Trip" / "Green and Gold"
    Curb Records CD: D2-77863—*The Trip: Original Motion Picture Soundtrack*
  b. "Joint Passing"
  c. "Psyche Soap"
    Curb Records CD: D2-77863—*The Trip: Original Motion Picture Soundtrack*
  d. "M-23"
    Curb Records CD: D2-77863—*The Trip: Original Motion Picture Soundtrack*
  e. "Synesthesia"
    Curb Records CD: D2-77863—*The Trip: Original Motion Picture Soundtrack*
  f. "A Little Head"
  g. "Hobbit"
    Curb Records CD: D2-77863—*The Trip: Original Motion Picture Soundtrack*
  h. "Inner Pocket"
  i. "Fewghh"
    Curb Records CD: D2-77863—*The Trip: Original Motion Picture Soundtrack*
  j. "Green and Gold"
    Sidewalk 45: 929—"Peter's Trip" / "Green and Gold"
    Curb Records CD: D2-77863—*The Trip: Original Motion Picture Soundtrack*
  k. "The Other Ed Norton"
  l. "Flash, Bam, Pow"
    Curb Records CD: D2-77863—*The Trip: Original Motion Picture Soundtrack*

m. "Home Room"
   Curb Records CD: D2-77863—*The Trip: Original Motion Picture Soundtrack*

n. "Peter Gets Off"

o. "Practice Music"
   Curb Records CD: D2-77863—*The Trip: Original Motion Picture Soundtrack*

p. "Fine Jung Thing"
   Curb Records CD: D2-77863—*The Trip: Original Motion Picture Soundtrack*

q. "Senior Citizen"
   Curb Records CD: D2-77863—*The Trip: Original Motion Picture Soundtrack*

r. "Gettin' Hard"

All titles on: Sidewalk LP 12″: ST 5908—*The Trip: Original Motion Picture Soundtrack*

Date: June 17, 1967
Location: Monterey International Pop Festival, Monterey, CA
The Electric Flag
Michael Bloomfield (v, g); Nick Gravenites (v); Buddy Miles (v, d, per); Barry Goldberg (org); Harvey Brooks (b); Peter Strazza (ts); Marcus Doubleday (t)

a. "Groovin' Is Easy"
   Rhino CD: R2 70596—*The Monterey International Pop Festival*

b. "(Drinkin') Wine"
   Rhino CD: R2 70596—*The Monterey International Pop Festival*

c. "The Night Time Is the Right Time"
   Columbia CD: CK 57629—*Old Glory: The Best of Electric Flag*

d. "Over-Lovin' You"

Date: July 1967, September 1967, and January 1968
Location: San Francisco, CA
Label: Columbia
The Electric Flag
Michael Bloomfield (g, per, bkv); Nick Gravenites (v); Buddy Miles (v, d, per); Harvey Brooks (g, b, per); Sivuca (g, per); Richie Havens (sit, per); Mike Fonfara, Barry Goldberg (key); Herbie Rich (key, ts, bar); Paul Beaver (syn); Joe Church (per); Marcus Doubleday (per, t); Peter Strazza (ts); George Brown, Leo Daruczek, Julius Held, Charles McCracken, Bob Notkoff (str); Mama Cass Elliot (bkv); John Court (per, bkv, prod)

a. "Groovin' Is Easy"
   Columbia 45: 4-44307—"Groovin' Is Easy" / "Over-Lovin' You"
   Columbia LP 12″: CS 9597—*A Long Time Comin'*
   Columbia CD: CK 9597—*A Long Time Comin'*

b. "Over-Lovin' You"
    Columbia 45: 4-44307—"Groovin' Is Easy" / "Over-Lovin' You"
    Columbia LP 12": CS 9597—*A Long Time Comin'*
    Columbia CD: CK 9597—*A Long Time Comin'*
c. "She Should Have Just"
    Columbia LP 12": CS 9597—*A Long Time Comin'*
    Columbia CD: CK 9597—*A Long Time Comin'*
d. "Sittin' in Circles"
    Columbia LP 12": CS 9597—*A Long Time Comin'*
    Columbia CD: CK 9597—*A Long Time Comin'*
e. "You Don't Realize"
    Columbia LP 12": CS 9597—*A Long Time Comin'*
    Columbia CD: CK 9597—*A Long Time Comin'*
f. "Sittin' in Circles" (alt)
    Columbia CD: CK 57629—*Old Glory: The Best of Electric Flag*
g. "Goin' Down Slow"
    Columbia CD: CK 9597—*A Long Time Comin'*
h. "Killing Floor"
    Columbia LP 12": CS 9597—*A Long Time Comin'*
    Columbia CD: CK 9597—*A Long Time Comin'*
i. "Texas"
    Columbia LP 12": CS 9597—*A Long Time Comin'*
    Columbia CD: CK 9597—*A Long Time Comin'*
j. "Another Country"
    Columbia LP 12": CS 9597—*A Long Time Comin'*
    Columbia CD: CK 9597—*A Long Time Comin'*
    Columbia CD: CK 57629—*Old Glory: The Best of Electric Flag*
k. "Wine"
    Columbia LP 12": CS 9597—*A Long Time Comin'*
    Columbia CD: CK 9597—*A Long Time Comin'*
l. "Easy Rider"
    Columbia LP 12": CS 9597—*A Long Time Comin'*
    Columbia CD: CK 9597—*A Long Time Comin'*
    Columbia CD: CK 57629—*Old Glory: The Best of Electric Flag*

Mama Cass Elliot (bkv) on a.

Date: December 1967
The Electric Flag
Nick Gravenites (v, per); Michael Bloomfield (g); Barry Goldberg (org); John Simon (syn); Harvey Brooks (b); Buddy Miles (d); Herbie Rich (as); Marcus Doubleday (t)

a. "Freakout"
    Columbia Master Works LP 12": OS 3240—*You Are What You Eat (Original Soundtrack Recording)*
    Columbia CD: CK 3240—*You Are What You Eat (Original Soundtrack Recording)*

b.   "Movie Music—Improvisation"
Columbia CD: CK 57629—*Old Glory: The Best of Electric Flag*
"Freakout" may have been recorded during the April/May 1967 sessions for The Trip.

Date: c. Early February 1968
Location: New York, NY
Label: Columbia
Moby Grape
Jerry Miller (g); Michael Bloomfield (p); Bob Mosley (b); Don Stevenson (d)
a.   "Marmalade"
Columbia LP 12″: MGS 1—*Grape Jam*

Date: February 20, 1968
Location: New York, NY
Label: Verve
James Cotton Blues Band
James Cotton (v, h); Alberto Gianquinto (v, p); Michael Bloomfield (g, org); Luther
Tucker (g); Robert Anderson (b); Francis Clay (d); John Court (tam, prod)
a.   "Worried Life Blues"
b.   "Fallin' Rain"
c.   "The Creeper"
All titles on: Verve Folkways LP 12″: FTS-3038—*Pure Cotton*
Michael Bloomfield (g) on a, c, (org) on b.

Date: Spring 1968
Location: Paramount Studios, Los Angeles, CA; Quinvy Recording Studio, Shef-
field, AL
Barry Goldberg
Barry Goldberg (v, p, org, prod); Charlie Musselwhite (h); Michael Bloomfield (g); David
Hood (b); Eddie Hoh (d); Soulville Horns (hns); unknown (bkv); Lewis Merenstein (prod)
a.   "That's Alright Mama"
b.   "Maxwell Street Shuffle"
c.   "Blues for Barry and . . ."
d.   "Jimi the Fox"
All titles on: Buddah LP 12″: BDS 5029—*Two Jews Blues*
Charlie Musselwhite (h) on b; Soulville Horns (hns) on a–b.
Bloomfield credited as "Great"; his guitar parts were recorded in Los Angeles.

Date: May 28, 1968
Location: Columbia Records, Los Angeles, CA
Label: Columbia
Super Session
Al Kooper (v, g, p, org, ondioline); Michael Bloomfield (g); Barry Goldberg (ep);
Harvey Brooks (b); Eddie Hoh (d)

a. "Albert's Shuffle"
Columbia LP 12": CS 9710—*Super Session*
Columbia Legacy CD: CK 64611—*Super Session*
Columbia Legacy CD: CK 63406—*Super Session*

b. "Stop"
Columbia LP 12": CS 9710—*Super Session*
Columbia Legacy CD: CK 64611—*Super Session*
Columbia Legacy CD: CK 63406—*Super Session*

c. "Man's Temptation"
Columbia LP 12": CS 9710—*Super Session*
Columbia Legacy CD: CK 64611—*Super Session*
Columbia Legacy CD: CK 63406—*Super Session*

d. "His Holy Modal Majesty"
Columbia LP 12": CS 9710—*Super Session*
Columbia Legacy CD: CK 64611—*Super Session*
Columbia Legacy CD: CK 63406—*Super Session*

e. "Really"
Columbia LP 12": CS 9710—*Super Session*
Columbia Legacy CD: CK 64611—*Super Session*
Columbia Legacy CD: CK 63406—*Super Session*

f. "Blues for Nothing"
Columbia Legacy CD: CK 64611—*Super Session*
Columbia Legacy CD: CK 63406—*Super Session*

g. "His Holy Modal Majesty" (alt)
Columbia Legacy CD: 88765476342—*From His Head to His Heart to His Hands*

Barry Goldberg (ep) on a–b.

Date: Summer 1968
Wayne Talbert & the Melting Pot
Wayne Talbert (v, p); Michael Bloomfield, Curley Cooke (g); Martin Fierro (d); Dr. John (prod)

a. "Funky Ellis Farm"
Pulsar LP 12": AR-10603—*Dues to Pay*

Date: 1968
Label: Mercury
Mother Earth
Tracy Nelson (v); John Andrews, Michael Bloomfield (g); Mark Naftalin (p, prod); Barry Goldberg (org, prod); Bob Arthur (b); George Rains (d); The Earthettes (bkv); Dan Healy (prod)

a. "Mother Earth"
Mercury LP 12": SR 61194—*Living with the Animals*

Bloomfield credited as "Makal Blumfeld."

Date: September 26–28, 1968
Location: Fillmore West, San Francisco, CA
Label: Columbia
Mike Bloomfield and Al Kooper
Michael Bloomfield (v, g); Al Kooper (v, p, key, prod); Paul Simon (v); John Kahn (b); Skip Prokop (d)

- a. "Opening Speech"
  Columbia LP 12″: KGP 6—*The Live Adventures of Mike Bloomfield and Al Kooper*

- b. "The 59th Street Bridge Song (Feelin' Groovy)"
  Columbia LP 12″: KGP 6—*The Live Adventures of Mike Bloomfield and Al Kooper*

- c. "I Wonder Who"
  Columbia LP 12″: KGP 6—*The Live Adventures of Mike Bloomfield and Al Kooper*

- d. "Her Holy Modal Highness"
  Columbia LP 12″: KGP 6—*The Live Adventures of Mike Bloomfield and Al Kooper*

- e. "The Weight"
  Columbia LP 12″: KGP 6—*The Live Adventures of Mike Bloomfield and Al Kooper*

- f. "Mary Ann"
  Columbia LP 12″: KGP 6—*The Live Adventures of Mike Bloomfield and Al Kooper*

- g. "Together 'Til the End of Time"
  Columbia LP 12″: KGP 6—*The Live Adventures of Mike Bloomfield and Al Kooper*

- h. "That's All Right"
  Columbia LP 12″: KGP 6—*The Live Adventures of Mike Bloomfield and Al Kooper*

- i. "Green Onions"
  Columbia LP 12″: KGP 6—*The Live Adventures of Mike Bloomfield and Al Kooper*

- j. "Dear Mr. Fantasy"
  Columbia LP 12″: KGP 6—*The Live Adventures of Mike Bloomfield and Al Kooper*

- k. "Don't Throw Your Love on Me So Strong"
  Columbia LP 12″: KGP 6—*The Live Adventures of Mike Bloomfield and Al Kooper*

- l. "Finale—Refugee"
  Columbia LP 12″: KGP 6—*The Live Adventures of Mike Bloomfield and Al Kooper*

- m. "Fat Grey Cloud"
  Columbia Legacy CD: CK 63406—*Super Session*

Michael Bloomfield (v) on a, c, f, h, k; Al Kooper (v) on b, g, j, (p) on g (as Roosevelt Gook); Paul Simon (v) on b.

Date: October 1968
Location: New York, NY
Label: Verve/Forecast
James Cotton Blues Band
James Cotton (v, h); Luther Tucker (v, g); Mark Naftalin (p); Robert Anderson (b); Barry Smith (d); Bill Nugent (ts); Joe Newman (t); Garnett Brown (tb); Michael Bloomfield, Elliot Mazer (prod)

a. "Back to St. Louis"
   Verve CD: 314 527 371-2—*Best of the Verve Years*
b. "Motorized Blues"
c. "The Mule"
d. "With You on My Mind"
e. "I Can't Live Without It"
f. "(Please) Tell Me Partner"
g. "Duke Patrol"
h. "Take Me by the Hand"
i. "The Coach's Better Days"
   Verve CD: 314 527 371-2—*Best of the Verve Years*
j. "Take Your Hands off Her"

All titles on: Verve/Forecast LP 12": FTS-3060—*Cotton in Your Ears*

Date: December 13–14, 1968
Location: Fillmore East, New York, NY
Michael Bloomfield / Al Kooper
Michael Bloomfield, Johnny Winter (v, g); Al Kooper (v, org); Paul Harris (p); Jerry Jemmott (b); John Cresci (d)

a. "Introductions"
   Columbia Legacy CD: CK 825278—*Fillmore East: The Lost Concert Tapes 12/13/68*
b. "One Way Out"
   Columbia Legacy CD: CK 825278—*Fillmore East: The Lost Concert Tapes 12/13/68*
c. "Mike Bloomfield's Introduction of Johnny Winter"
   Columbia Legacy CD: CK 825278—*Fillmore East: The Lost Concert Tapes 12/13/68*
d. "It's My Own Fault"
   Columbia Legacy CD: CK 825278—*Fillmore East: The Lost Concert Tapes 12/13/68*
e. "59th Street Bridge Song (Feelin' Groovy)"
   Columbia Legacy CD: CK 825278—*Fillmore East: The Lost Concert Tapes 12/13/68*

f. "(Please) Tell Me Partner"
    Columbia Legacy CD: CK 825278—*Fillmore East: The Lost Concert Tapes 12/13/68*

g. "That's All Right Mama"
    Columbia Legacy CD: CK 825278—*Fillmore East: The Lost Concert Tapes 12/13/68*

h. "Together Till the End of Time"
    Columbia Legacy CD: CK 825278—*Fillmore East: The Lost Concert Tapes 12/13/68*

i. "Don't Throw Your Love on Me So Strong"
    Columbia Legacy CD: CK 825278—*Fillmore East: The Lost Concert Tapes 12/13/68*

j. "Season of the Witch"
    Columbia Legacy CD: CK 825278—*Fillmore East: The Lost Concert Tapes 12/13/68*

k. "Santana Clause"
    Columbia Legacy CD: 88765476342—*From His Head to His Heart to His Hands*

Michael Bloomfield (v) on a–c, f–g, i, (g) on b, d–k; Al Kooper (v) on e, h, j–k, (org) on b, d–k; Johnny Winter (v) on d, (g) on d; Paul Harris (p) on b, d–k; Jerry Jemmott (b) on b, d–k; John Cresci (d) on b, d–k.

Date: January 30–February 2, 1969
Location: Fillmore West, San Francisco, CA
Michael Bloomfield and Friends
Michael Bloomfield (v, g); Nick Gravenites (v); Bob Jones (v, d); Taj Mahal (v, h); Jesse Ed Davis (g); Mark Naftalin (p); Ira Kamin (org); John Kahn (b); Reinol Andino (cga); Noel Jewkes (ts); Snooky Flowers, Gerald Oshita (bar); John Wilmeth (t); Elliot Mazer (prod)

a. "It Takes Time"
    Columbia LP 12": CS 9893—*Live at Bill Graham's Fillmore West*

b. "Oh Mama"
    Columbia LP 12": CS 9893—*Live at Bill Graham's Fillmore West*

c. "Love Got Me"
    Columbia LP 12": CS 9893—*Live at Bill Graham's Fillmore West*

d. "Blues on a Westside"
    Columbia LP 12": CS 9893—*Live at Bill Graham's Fillmore West*

e. "One More Mile to Go"
    Columbia LP 12": CS 9893—*Live at Bill Graham's Fillmore West*

f. "It's About Time"
    Columbia LP 12": CS 9893—*Live at Bill Graham's Fillmore West*

g. "Carmelita Skiffle"
    Columbia LP 12": CS 9893—*Live at Bill Graham's Fillmore West*

h. "If I Ever Get Lucky"
    Raven CD: RVCD-351—*Blues at the Fillmore 1968-1969*

i.   "Stronger Than Dirt"
     Raven CD: RVCD-351—*Blues at the Fillmore 1968–1969*
j.   "Born in Chicago"
     Raven CD: RVCD-351—*Blues at the Fillmore 1968–1969*
k.   "Work Me Lord"
     Raven CD: RVCD-351—*Blues at the Fillmore 1968–1969*
l.   "(You're) Killing My Love"
     Columbia LP 12″: CS 9899—Nick Gravenites, *My Labors*
m.   "Gypsy Good Time"
     Columbia LP 12″: CS 9899—Nick Gravenites, *My Labors*
n.   "Holy Moly"
     Columbia LP 12″: CS 9899—Nick Gravenites, *My Labors*
o.   "Moon Tune"
     Columbia LP 12″: CS 9899—Nick Gravenites, *My Labors*
p.   "Wintry Country Side"
     Columbia LP 12″: CS 9899—Nick Gravenites, *My Labors*

Michael Bloomfield (v) on b; Nick Gravenites (v) on a, d, f, j–p; Bob Jones (v) on c; Taj Mahal (v) on e, h; (h) on e; Jesse Ed Davis (g) on e.

Date: February 1969
Location: FAME Studios, Muscle Shoals, AL
Label: Cotillion
Otis Rush

Otis Rush (v, g); Duane Allman, Jimmy Johnson (g); Barry Beckett, Mark Naftalin (key); Jerry Jemmott (b); Roger Hawkins (d); Joe Arnold, Aaron Varnell (ts); Ronald Eades (bar); Gene "Bowlegs" Miller (t); Michael Bloomfield, Nick Gravenites (prod); Mickey Buckins (eng)

a.   "Me"
b.   "Working Man"
c.   "You're Killing My Love"
d.   "Feel So Bad"
e.   "Gambler's Blues"
f.   "Baby, I Love You"
g.   "My Old Lady"
h.   "My Love Will Never Die"
i.   "Reap What You Sow"
j.   "It Takes Time"
k.   "Can't Wait No Longer"

All titles on: Cotillion LP 12″: SD 9006—*Mourning in the Morning*

Date: February 1969
Wayne Talbert

Wayne Talbert (v, p); Michael Bloomfield, Mike Deasy, Ernest McLean (g); Harold L. Battiste (p); Bob West (b); Paul Humphrey (d); Curtis Amy, Plas Johnson, Herman Riley (rds); Melvin Lastie, Ike Williams (t)

    a. "Crankiola Narcissis Buds"
        Pulsar LP 12″: AR-10607—*Lord Have Mercy on My Funky Soul*

Date: Spring 1969
Soundtrack for *Medium Cool*, a film by Haskell Wexler
Paul Butterfield (h); Michael Bloomfield, Fred Olson (g); Ira Kamin (key); John Kahn (b); Bob Jones (d); Noel Jewkes (ts); Gerald Oshita (bar); Marcus Doubleday (t)
    a. Unknown titles
        Paramount VHS: 6907—*Medium Cool*
        Paramount DVD: 06907—*Medium Cool*
        Criterion Collection DVD: 658—*Medium Cool*
        Criterion Collection Blu-ray Disc: 658—*Medium Cool*

Date: April 21, 1969
Location: Ter-Mar Studios, Chicago, IL
Label: Chess
Muddy Waters
Muddy Waters (v, g); Paul Butterfield (h); Paul Asbell, Michael Bloomfield (g); Otis Spann (p); Donald "Duck" Dunn (b); Sam Lay (d); Norman Dayron (prod)
    a. "Sad Letter"
    b. "Walkin Thru the Park"
        Chess LP 12″: LPS-127—*Fathers and Sons*
        MCA/Chess CD: 088 112 648-2—*Fathers and Sons*
    c. "Standin 'Round Cryin'"
        Chess LP 12″: LPS-127—*Fathers and Sons*
        MCA/Chess CD: 088 112 648-2—*Fathers and Sons*
    d. "Live the Life I Love"
Paul Asbell (g) on b.

Date: April 22, 1969
Location: Ter-Mar Studios, Chicago, IL
Label: Chess
Muddy Waters
Muddy Waters (v, g); Paul Butterfield, Jeff Carp (h); Paul Asbell, Michael Bloomfield (g); Otis Spann (p); Donald "Duck" Dunn, Phil Upchurch (b); Sam Lay (d); Norman Dayron (prod)
    a. "Twenty Four Hours"
        Chess LP 12″: LPS-127—*Fathers and Sons*
        MCA/Chess CD: 088 112 648-2—*Fathers and Sons*
    b. "Country Boy"
        MCA/Chess CD: 088 112 648-2—*Fathers and Sons*
    c. "Sugar Sweet"
        Chess LP 12″: LPS-127—*Fathers and Sons*
        MCA/Chess CD: 088 112 648-2—*Fathers and Sons*

     d.   "Sugar Sweet" (alt)

         Chess LP 12": CH6-80002—*Muddy Waters: The Chess Box*

         Chess CD: CHD3-80002—*Muddy Waters: The Chess Box*

     e.   "Forty Days and Forty Nights"

         Chess LP 12": LPS-127—*Fathers and Sons*

         MCA/Chess CD: 088 112 648-2—*Fathers and Sons*

     f.   "All Aboard"

         Chess LP 12": LPS-127—*Fathers and Sons*

         MCA/Chess CD: 088 112 648-2—*Fathers and Sons*

     g.   "All Aboard" (alt)

         Chess LP 12": CH6-80002—*Muddy Waters: The Chess Box*

         Chess CD: CHD3-80002—*Muddy Waters: The Chess Box*

     h.   "Can't Lose What You Ain't Never Had"

         Chess LP 12": LPS-127—*Fathers and Sons*

         MCA/Chess CD: 088 112 648-2—*Fathers and Sons*

     i.   "Goin' Home (I Wanna Go Home)"

Jeff Carp (h) on f–g; Paul Asbell (g) on c–e; Donald "Duck" Dunn (b) on a–e, h–i; Phil Upchurch (b) on f–g.

Date: April 23, 1969

Location: Ter-Mar Studios, Chicago, IL

Label: Chess

Muddy Waters

Muddy Waters (v, g); Paul Butterfield (h); Michael Bloomfield (g); Otis Spann (p); Donald "Duck" Dunn (b); Sam Lay (d); Norman Dayron (prod)

     a.   "Oh Yeah!"

         MCA/Chess CD: 088 112 648-2—*Fathers and Sons*

     b.   "Mean Disposition"

         Chess LP 12": LPS-127—*Fathers and Sons*

         MCA/Chess CD: 088 112 648-2—*Fathers and Sons*

     c.   "Blow Wind Blow"

         Chess LP 12": LPS-127—*Fathers and Sons*

         MCA/Chess CD: 088 112 648-2—*Fathers and Sons*

     d.   "I'm Ready"

         Chess LP 12": LPS-127—*Fathers and Sons*

         MCA/Chess CD: 088 112 648-2—*Fathers and Sons*

     e.   "I Feel So Good"

         MCA/Chess CD: 088 112 648-2—*Fathers and Sons*

     f.   "Someday Baby"

Date: April 24, 1969
Location: Civic Auditorium, Chicago, IL
Label: Chess
Muddy Waters
Muddy Waters (v, g); Paul Butterfield (h); Michael Bloomfield (g); Otis Spann (p); Donald "Duck" Dunn (b); Sam Lay, Buddy Miles (d)

  a. "Long Distance Call"
  b. "Baby Please Don't Go"
  c. "The Same Thing"
  d. "Honey Bee"
  e. "Got My Mojo Working" (part 1)
  f. "Got My Mojo Working" (part 2)

All titles on: Chess LP 12": LPS-127—*Fathers and Sons*
                 MCA/Chess CD: 088 112 648-2—*Fathers and Sons*
Sam Lay (d) on a–e; Buddy Miles (d) on f.

Date: May 19 and other dates, 1969
Location: Los Angeles and San Francisco, CA
Label: Columbia
Michael Bloomfield
Michael Bloomfield (v, g, p); Nick Gravenites (v, prod); Bob Jones (v, d); Michael Melford (v, g, man, prod); The Ace of Cups, Diane Tribuno (v); Fred Olson (g); Orville "Red" Rhodes (stg); Ira Kamin (bj, p, org); Mark Naftalin (p, org); Roy Ruby (org); Richard Santi (acc); John Kahn (b); Noel Jewkes (ss, ts); Gerald Oshita (ts, bar); Ron Stallings (ts); Mark Teel (bar); Marcus Doubleday, John Wilmeth (t)

  a. "If You See My Baby"
  b. "For Anyone You Meet"
  c. "Good Old Guy"
  d. "Far Too Many Nights"
  e. "It's Not Killing Me"
  f. "Next Time You See Me"
  g. "Michael's Lament"
  h. "Why Must My Baby"
  i. "The Ones I Loved Are Gone"
  j. "Don't Think About It Baby"
  k. "Goofers"

All titles on: Columbia LP 12": CS 9883—*It's Not Killing Me*
                 Sony CD: SICP 8015—*It's Not Killing Me*

Date: June 15–25, 1969
Label: Columbia
Janis Joplin
Janis Joplin (v); Sam Andrew (g, bkv); Michael Bloomfield (g); Richard Kermode (org); Gabriel Mekler (org, prod); Brad Campbell (b); Maury Baker, Lonnie Castille (d); Terry Clements (ts); Snooky Flowers (bar, bkv); Luis Gasca (t)

     a. "Maybe"

     b. "One Good Man"

     c. "To Love Somebody"

     d. "Work Me, Lord"

All titles on: Columbia LP 12": KCS 9913—*I Got Dem Ol' Kozmic Blues Again Mama!*

              Columbia CD: C5K 65937—*Box of Pearls: The Janis Joplin Collection*

Date: July 1969

Location: Shrine Auditorium, Los Angeles, CA

Barry Goldberg and Friends

Michael Bloomfield (v, g); Bob Greenspan (v); Harvey Mandel (g); Barry Goldberg (org); Roy Ruby (b); Eddie Hoh (d); Morey Alexander (prod)

     a. "Sweet Home Chicago"

         Record Man LP 12": CR-5105—*Barry Goldberg and Friends*

     b. "Long Hard Journey (One More Mile)"

         Record Man LP 12": CR-5105—*Barry Goldberg and Friends*

     c. "That's Alright Mama"

         Buddah LP 12": BDS 5684—*Recorded Live*

Date: August 11–13, 1969

Location: San Francisco, CA

Sam Lay

Sam Lay (v, d); Jack Walroth (h); Michael Bloomfield (g, prod); Fred Olson (g); Mark Naftalin (p); Ira Kamin (org); John Kahn (b); Nick Gravenites (prod)

     a. "Maggie's Farm"

     b. "Mean Mistreater"

     c. "Sam Lay & Mississippi John"

     d. "Cryin' for My Baby"

     e. "Sloppy Drunk"

     f. "My Fault"

     g. "Roll Over Beethoven"

     h. "Asked Her for Water"

     i. "I Got My Mojo Working"

All titles on: Blue Thumb LP 12": BTS-14—*Sam Lay in Bluesland*

Date: November/December 1969

Location: Los Angeles, CA; Chicago, IL

Label: Chess

The Zeet Band

Michael Bloomfield, Phil Upchurch (g); Erwin Helfer, Mark Naftalin (p); Donny Hathaway (key, syn); Ira Kamin (key); Paul Beaver (syn); Joe Osborn, Ray Pohlman (b);

Richard A. Berk, John Guerin, Morris Jennings (d); Lawrence Brown, T. John Conrad (hns); Norman Dayron (prod)

         a.   "Fireball Boogie!"
         b.   "Angel's Dust Boogie"

Both titles on: Chess LP 12″: LPS-1545—*Moogie Woogie*

Date: Late 1969
Location: Golden State Recorders, San Francisco, CA; Crystal Studios, Los Angeles, CA
Label: Kama Sutra
Brewer and Shipley

Michael Brewer (v, acg, per); Tom Shipley (v, g, acg, 12-string guitar); Apple Jack (h); Michael Bloomfield, Fred Olson (g); Orville "Red" Rhodes (stg); Nicky Hopkins (p); Ira Kamin, Mark Naftalin (p, org); Robert Huberman, John Kahn (b); Bob Jones (d); Phil Ford (tabla); Reinol Andino (cga); Richard Greene (vn); Nick Gravenites (prod)

         a.   "Lady Like You"
         b.   "Rise Up (Easy Rider)"
         c.   "Boomerang"
         d.   "Indian Summer"
         e.   "All Along the Watchtower"
         f.   "People Love Each Other"
         g.   "Pigs Head"
         h.   "Oh, Sweet Lady"
         i.   "Too Soon Tomorrow"
         j.   "Witchi-tai-to"

All titles on: Kama Sutra LP 12″: KSBS 2016—*Weeds*
Nick Gravenites credited as "Nicky Gravy."

Date: March 28, 1970
Location: Columbia Studio D, Los Angeles, CA
Label: Columbia
Janis Joplin / Paul Butterfield Blues Band

Janis Joplin (v); Paul Butterfield (h); Michael Bloomfield (g); Mark Naftalin (org); Rod Hicks (b); George Davidson (d); Gene Dinwiddie (ts); Trevor Lawrence (bar); Steve Madaio (t)

         a.   "One Night Stand"
            Columbia CD: 484458 2—*Farewell Song*

Date: 1970
Location: I.D. Sound Studio, Los Angeles, CA
Label: Capitol
James Cotton Blues Band

James Cotton (v, h); Tom Cosgrove (v); Mark Klingman (v, p, org, prod); Todd Rundgren (v, g, per, prod); N.D. Smart II (v, per); Stu Woods (v, b); Michael

Bloomfield, Johnny Winter (g); Ralph Schuckett (p, acc); Joel "Bishop" O'Brien (d); Matt Murphy (per)

a. "Long Distance Operator"
b. "Nose Open"
c. "Georgia Swing"

All titles on: Capitol LP 12": SM 814—*Taking Care of Business*

Tom Cosgrove (v) on c; Mark Klingman (v) on c, (p) on a, c, (org) on b; Todd Rundgren (v) on c, (g) on a, (per) on c; N.D. Smart II (v) on c, (per) on c; Stu Woods (v) on c, (b) on a, c; Johnny Winter (g) on c; Ralph Schuckett (p) on b, (acc) on c; Matt Murphy (per) on c.

Date: January/February 1971
Location: Los Angeles, CA
Beaver & Krause

Michael Bloomfield, Rik Elswit, Ronnie Montrose (g); Paul Beaver (org, prod); Bernard Krause (syn, prod); Rod Ellicott (b); Lee Charlton, George Marsh (d)

a. "Saga of the Blue Beaver"
   Warner Bros. LP 12": WS 1909—*Gandharva*
   Warner Archives CD: 9 45663-2—*In a Wild Sanctuary / Gandharva*

Date: c. January 1971
Location: Fantasy Studios, Berkeley, CA
Label: Fantasy
Merl Saunders & Friends

Michael Bloomfield (g); Merl Saunders (key, prod); John Kahn (b); Bill Witt (d); Kenneth Nash (per); Ron Stallings (sax); John Wilmeth (t)

a. "Iron Horse"
b. "Little Bit of Righteousness"

Both titles on: Fantasy CD: FCD 7712-2—*Keepers*

Date: March 1971
Location: Wally Heider Studios, San Francisco, CA
Woody Herman

Woody Herman (v, clarinet, prod); Michael Bloomfield (g); Alan Broadbent (p, ep); Alan Read (b); Ed Soph (d); Steve Lederer, Sal Nistico, Frank Tiberi (ts); Gene Smookler (bar); Forrest Buchtel, Bill Byrne, Tom Harrell, Tony Klatka, Buddy Powers (t); Bob Burgess, Ira Nepus, Don Switzer (tb); Ray Shanklin (prod)

a. "Sidewalk Stanley"
b. "Proud Mary"
c. "Hitch Hike on the Possum Trot Line"
d. "Since I Fell for You"

All titles on: Fantasy LP 12": 8414—*Brand New*
                 Original Jazz Classics CD: 1044—*Brand New*

Date: May 17, 1971
Location: Bloomfield's home, Reed Street, Mill Valley, CA
Michael Bloomfield
Michael Bloomfield (v, g, p), Dan McClosky (interviewer)

      a. "Relaxin' Blues: Blues for Jimmy Yancey, Sunnyland Slim and Otis Spann"

      b. "Interview"

Both titles on: Columbia LP 12": C2 37578—*Bloomfield: A Retrospective*

      Sony CD: SICP 1969–70—*Bloomfield: A Retrospective*

Date: June 1971
Location: Sound Factory, Los Angeles, CA
Teda Bracci
Teda Bracci (v); Michael Bloomfield (g); Lowell George (s-g); Chris Darrow (dbr); Mark Naftalin (key); John Kahn (b); Richie Hayward (d); Denny Bruce (prod)

      a. "Jim Dandy"

      b. "Jim Dandy" (alt)

      c. "Sweet Thing"

      d. "Wang Dang Doodle"

Date: June 1971
Location: Sound Factory, Los Angeles, CA
Ann-Margret
Ann-Margret (v); Michael Bloomfield (g); Lowell George (s-g); Chris Darrow (dbr); Mark Naftalin (key); John Kahn (b); Richie Hayward (d); Denny Bruce (prod)

      a. "Shine, My Friend"

      b. "Obion Bottom Land"

Date: c. January 1972
Tim Davis
Tim Davis (v); Michael Bloomfield (g, s-g); Curley Cooke (g); Ken Adamany, Ben Sidran (p); Steve Miller (org); John Kahn, Doug Killmer (b); Rick Jaeger (d); Coke Escovedo, Pete Escovedo (per); Mel Martin (flute); Georgie Ente, Jamie Ente, Reggie Ente (bkv); Glyn Johns (prod)

      a. "Only Yesterday"

      b. "On the Other Hand Baby"

      c. "Take Me as I Am"

All titles on: Metromedia LP 12": BML1-0175—*Take Me as I Am (Without Silver Without Gold)*

Curley Cooke (g) on b–c; Michael Bloomfield (s-g) on a; Ken Adamany (p) on b; Ben Sidran (p) on a, c; Steve Miller (org) on b; John Kahn (b) on b; Doug Killmer (b) on a, c; Rick Jaeger (d) on a–b; Coke Escovedo (per) on c; Pete Escovedo (per) on c; Mel Martin (flute) on c; Georgie Ente (bkv) on c; Jamie Ente (bkv) on c; Reggie Ente (bkv) on c.

Date: 1972
Location: Golden State Recorders, San Francisco, CA
Millie Foster
Millie Foster (v); Michael Bloomfield, Eddie Duran (g); Mark Naftalin (p); Ed Wetteland (org, arranger); Mario Suraci (b); Bill Nawrocki (d); Leo de Gar Kulka (prod)

<ol type="a">
<li>"This Train"</li>
<li>"Every Time I Feel the Spirit"</li>
<li>"Didn't It Rain"</li>
<li>"Rock A My Soul"</li>
<li>"He's Got the Whole World in His Hands"</li>
<li>"Wade in the Water"</li>
<li>"Joshua Fit the Battle of Jericho"</li>
<li>"Nobody Knows the Trouble I've Seen"</li>
<li>"Swing Low, Sweet Chariot"</li>
<li>"When the Saints Go Marching In"</li>
</ol>

All titles on: MGM LP 12": SE 4897—*Millie Foster Feels the Spirit*

Date: February 1972
Location: San Francisco, CA; Los Angeles, CA
Label: Columbia
Melton, Levy, and the Dey Brothers
Rick Dey (v, b); Tony Dey (v, d); Jay Levy (v, key); Barry Melton (v, g, tb); Michael Bloomfield (g, s-g, prod); Bruce Brymer (d, bkv); Rick Jaeger (d); King Errisson (per); Carol Davis (hns); Ginette Melton, The Friends of the Band Chorus (bkv); Norman Dayron (prod)

<ol type="a">
<li>"Ooh, Ooh, Ooh"</li>
<li>"She Dances Through"</li>
<li>"Closer"</li>
<li>"Been So Fine"</li>
<li>"Sweeter the Peaches"</li>
<li>"S.O.S."</li>
<li>"Highway 1"</li>
<li>"Hold On to the Good Times"</li>
<li>"Play Little Children"</li>
<li>"Be with the One"</li>
<li>"Newsboy"</li>
<li>"Taxpayer's Lament"</li>
<li>"Bye Bye Sequence"</li>
</ol>

All titles on: Columbia LP 12": KC 31279—*Melton, Levy & the Dey Bros.*
                 Acadia CD: ACA 8020—*Melton, Levy & the Dey Bros.*

Michael Bloomfield (g) on a, c, j–l, (s-g) on a, c, j–l.

Date: June 26, July 26, 1972
Location: Los Angeles, CA
Soundtrack for *Steelyard Blues*, a film by Alan Myerson
Michael Bloomfield (v, g, bj, prod); Paul Butterfield (v, h); Nick Gravenites (v, g, prod); Maria Muldaur (v, g); Annie Sampson (v); Merl Saunders (p, org); John Kahn (b); Christopher Parker (d)

    a.   "Swing With It"
    b.   "Brand New Family"
    c.   "Woman's Love"
    d.   "Make the Headlines"
    e.   "Georgia Blues"
    f.   "My Bag (The Oysters)"
    g.   "Common Ground"
    h.   "Being Different"
    i.   "I've Been Searching"
    j.   "Do I Care"
    k.   "Lonesome Star Blues"
    l.   "Here I Come (There She Goes)"
    m.   "If You Cared"
    n.   "Theme from *Steelyard Blues* (Drive Again)"

All titles on: Warner Bros. LP 12": BS 2662—*Steelyard Blues: Original Sound Track from the Motion Picture*
Warner Music Japan CD: WPCD-10716—*Steelyard Blues: Original Sound Track from the Motion Picture*

Michael Bloomfield (v) on b, (bj) on n; Nick Gravenites (v) on a–i, l, n; Maria Muldaur (v) on c, e, j–k; Annie Sampson (v) on g, m; Paul Butterfield (h) on a–c, g–i, k–l, n.

Date: September 1972
Location: Roy Chen Studios, San Francisco, CA
King Koop
Lotti Golden (v); Michael Bloomfield (g); King Koop (g, prod); George Michalski (p); Jerome Arnold (b); Bob Jones (d)

    a.   "Slider"
    b.   "Blues w/Mike"

Both titles on: Stella CD: SR003—*The Early Years*

Date: January 1973
Location: Columbia Studios, San Francisco, CA
Label: Columbia
Mike Bloomfield / John Paul Hammond / Dr. John
John Paul Hammond (John Hammond Jr.) (v, h, g); Thomas Jefferson Kaye (v, g, prod); Michael Bloomfield (g); Dr. John (g, bj, p, org, per); Chris Ethridge (b); Fred Staehle (d); John Boudreaux, Bennie Parks (per); Jerome Jumonville (as, ts); James

Gordon (bar); Blue Mitchell (t); George Bohanon (tb); Robbie Montgomery, Lorraine
Rebennack, Jessie Smith (bkv)

- a. "Cha-Dooky-Doo"
  Columbia LP 12": KC 32172—*Triumvirate*
  Columbia CD: CK 32172—*Triumvirate*
- b. "Last Night"
  Columbia LP 12": KC 32172—*Triumvirate*
  Columbia CD: CK 32172—*Triumvirate*
- c. "I Yi Yi"
  Columbia LP 12": KC 32172—*Triumvirate*
  Columbia CD: CK 32172—*Triumvirate*
- d. "Just to Be with You"
  Columbia LP 12": KC 32172—*Triumvirate*
  Columbia CD: CK 32172—*Triumvirate*
- e. "Baby Let Me Kiss You"
  Columbia LP 12": KC 32172—*Triumvirate*
  Columbia CD: CK 32172—*Triumvirate*
- f. "Sho Bout to Drive Me Wild"
  Columbia LP 12": KC 32172—*Triumvirate*
  Columbia CD: CK 32172—*Triumvirate*
- g. "It Hurts Me Too"
  Columbia LP 12": KC 32172—*Triumvirate*
  Columbia CD: CK 32172—*Triumvirate*
- h. "Rock Me Baby"
  Columbia LP 12": KC 32172—*Triumvirate*
  Columbia CD: CK 32172—*Triumvirate*
- i. "Ground Hog Blues"
  Columbia LP 12": KC 32172—*Triumvirate*
  Columbia CD: CK 32172—*Triumvirate*
- j. "Pretty Thing"
  Columbia LP 12": KC 32172—*Triumvirate*
  Columbia CD: CK 32172—*Triumvirate*
- k. "The Trip"
  Playback EP 7": AS51 ZSM 158374

Date: April 18, 1973, and other dates
Location: Golden State Recorders, San Francisco, CA, and other locations
Label: Verve
Mill Valley Bunch
Michael Bloomfield (v, g, p, b, prod); Russell DaShiell (v, g); Rick Dey (v, b, prod);
Nick Gravenites (v, g, prod); Denise Jewkes, Jeanette Jones, Ron Stallings, The Ace
of Cups, The Pointer Sisters (v); Ron Cimille, Fred Olson, Tom Richards, Craig
Tarwater, Chicken Billy Thornton (g); Ira Kamin, Mark Naftalin (key); John Kahn,
Mark Ryan (b); Tony Dey, Rick Jaeger, Jeffrey James, Michael Shrieve, Bill Vitt (d);

Spencer Dryden (d, per); Reinol Andino (per); Freeman Lockwood (vn); Leo de Gar Kulka (prod)

 a. "I've Had It"
   Verve LP 12": V6 8825—*Casting Pearls*
   Magical CD: MMCD 00003—*Casting Pearls*

 b. "Young Girl Blues (Janis Blues)"
   Verve LP 12": V6 8825—*Casting Pearls*
   Magical CD: MMCD 00003—*Casting Pearls*

 c. "What Would I Do Without My Baby"
   Verve LP 12": V6 8825—*Casting Pearls*
   Magical CD: MMCD 00003—*Casting Pearls*

 d. "Settle It in the Bedroom, Baby (Bedroom Blues)"
   Verve LP 12": V6 8825—*Casting Pearls*
   Magical CD: MMCD 00003—*Casting Pearls*

 e. "Jimmy's Blues"
   Verve LP 12": V6 8825—*Casting Pearls*
   Magical CD: MMCD 00003—*Casting Pearls*

 f. "Let Me Down Easy"
   Verve LP 12": V6 8825—*Casting Pearls*
   Magical CD: MMCD 00003—*Casting Pearls*

 g. "Your Hollywood Blues"
   Verve LP 12": V6 8825—*Casting Pearls*
   Magical CD: MMCD 00003—*Casting Pearls*

 h. "Lettin' Go Ain't Easy"
   Verve LP 12": V6 8825—*Casting Pearls*

 i. "Last Call Blues"
   Verve LP 12": V6 8825—*Casting Pearls*
   Magical CD: MMCD 00003—*Casting Pearls*

 j. "Honky-Tonk Blues"
   Magical CD: MMCD 00003—*Casting Pearls*

 k. "Betty & Dupree"
   Magical CD: MMCD 00003—*Casting Pearls*

 l. "La Ooh-Ooh-Ooh, La, La"
   Magical CD: MMCD 00003—*Casting Pearls*

 m. "Run for Cover"
   Magical CD: MMCD 00003—*Casting Pearls*

 n. "Mellow Mountain Wine"
   Magical CD: MMCD 00003—*Casting Pearls*

 o. "Bye, Bye, I'm Goin'"
   Magical CD: MMCD 00003—*Casting Pearls*

 p. "Bells Are Gonna Ring"
   Magical CD: MMCD 00003—*Casting Pearls*

All titles on: Universe CD: UV 087—*Casting Pearls*

Date: 1973
Location: San Francisco, CA
Kingfish
John Lee Hooker (v); Matt Kelly (h, g, prod); Michael Bloomfield, Robbie Hoddinott
(g); Bob Weir (acg); Barry Flast (p); Dave Torbert (b)

      a. "Put Your Hand on Me"
         Relix LP 12": RRLP 2005—*Kingfish*
         Relix CD: RRCD 2035—*Double Dose*

Date: 1973
Location: Record Plant, Sausalito, CA
Matt Kelly
Patti Cathcart (v); Matt Kelly (v, h, prod); Michael Bloomfield, Mel Brown, Robbie
Hoddinott, Jerry Miller, Scotty Quick (g); Michael O'Neill (s-g); Mark Naftalin,
Dave Vogel (p); Bob Wright (org); Dave Torbert (b); Jerry Martini (hns); Rahni
Raines (bkv)

      a. "It Ain't Easy"
      b. "Next Time You See Me"
Both titles on: Relix LP 12": RRLP 2010—*A Wing and a Prayer*
         Relix CD: RRCD 2010—*A Wing and a Prayer*

*Patti Cathcart (v) on a; Matt Kelly (v) on b, (h) on a; Mel Brown (g) on b; Robbie Hod-
dinott (g) on b; Jerry Miller (g) on a; Scotty Quick (g) on a; Michael O'Neill (s-g) on
b; Mark Naftalin (p) on b; Dave Vogel (p) on a; Bob Wright (org) on a; Rahni Raines
(bkv) on a.*

Date: 1973
Location: Columbia Studios, San Francisco, CA
Michael Bloomfield
Michael Bloomfield (v, g, org, tam); Nick Gravenites (v); Ron Stallings (v, ts); Roger
"Jellyroll" Troy (v, b); Mark Naftalin (vibraphone, marimba, p, acc); Jimmy Vincent
(g); Barry Goldberg (org); Howard Wales (key); George Rains (d); Harry Mann (as);
Mel Graves (ts); Hart McNee (bar); John Wilmeth (t); Chuck Bennett (tb); Joe Bullock,
Ollie Griffin, Singers of the Church of God in Christ, Tommy Tony (bkv); Michael
Fusaro (prod)

      a. "Been Treated Wrong"
         CBS Special Products CD: A 21262—*Try It Before You Buy It*
      b. "When It All Comes Down"
         CBS Special Products CD: A 21262—*Try It Before You Buy It*
      c. "Lights Out"
         Takoma LP 12": TAK 7070—*Between the Hard Place & the
         Ground*
         CBS Special Products CD: A 21262—*Try It Before You Buy It*
      d. "Baby Come On"
         CBS Special Products CD: A 21262—*Try It Before You Buy It*

    e. "Shine On Love"

       Waterhouse LP 12": Waterhouse 11—*Living in the Fast Lane*

       CBS Special Products CD: A 21262—*Try It Before You Buy It*

       Era CD: 5006-2—*Living in the Fast Lane*

    f. "When I Get Home"

       Waterhouse LP 12": Waterhouse 11—*Living in the Fast Lane*

       CBS Special Products CD: A 21262—*Try It Before You Buy It*

       Era CD: 5006-2—*Living in the Fast Lane*

    g. "Try It Before You Buy It"

       CBS Special Products CD: A 21262—*Try It Before You Buy It*

    h. "Midnight on the Radio"

       CBS Special Products CD: A 21262—*Try It Before You Buy It*

    i. "Your Friends"

       Takoma LP 12": TAK 7070—*Between the Hard Place & the Ground*

       CBS Special Products CD: A 21262—*Try It Before You Buy It*

    j. "Tomorrow Night"

       CBS Special Products CD: A 21262—*Try It Before You Buy It*

    k. "Let Them Talk"

       Waterhouse LP 12": Waterhouse 11—*Living in the Fast Lane*

       CBS Special Products CD: A 21262—*Try It Before You Buy It*

       Era CD: 5006-2—*Living in the Fast Lane*

    l. "Woodyard Street"

       Columbia LP 12": C2 37578—*Bloomfield: A Retrospective*

Michael Bloomfield (v) on a, c–d, j, (org) on e–f, k, (tam) on e; Nick Gravenites (v) on b, h–i; Ron Stallings (v) on g; Roger "Jellyroll" Troy (v) on e–f, k; Mark Naftalin (marimba) on b, (acc) on j; Singers of the Church of God in Christ (bkv) on f.

Date: 1974
Location: San Francisco, CA
Soundtrack for *Sodom and Gomorrah: The Last Seven Days*, a film by James and Artie Mitchell
Michael Bloomfield (musical director); Barry Goldberg (key); Carmine Appice (d); Bert Wilson (sax); Freeman Lockwood (vn); Thomas Edge, Ken Heller (unknown); Bill Bramblett, Bruce Brymer, Doris Chapman, Bill Graig, Richi Harris, Nick Reid, Lisa Tucker (bkv)

    a. Film music

Date: c. January 1974
Location: San Francisco, CA
Michael d'Abo
Michael d'Abo (v, p); Michael Bloomfield (g); Mark Naftalin (key); Elliot Mazer (b); Denny Seiwell (d)

    a. "Broken Rainbows"

       A&M LP 12": SP 3634—*Broken Rainbows*

       Universal Japan CD—*Broken Rainbows*

Date: June or July 1974
Location: Criteria Studios, Miami, FL
The Electric Flag
Nick Gravenites (v, g); Buddy Miles (v, d); Roger "Jellyroll" Troy (v, b); King Biscuit Boy (h); Michael Bloomfield, George Terry (g); Barry Beckett, Albhy Galuten, Barry Goldberg, Richard Tee (key); Nicky Marrero (per); The Bonnaroo Horns, The Muscle Shoals Horns (hns); Jerry Wexler (prod); Tom Dowd (eng)

- a. "Sweet Soul Music"
  Atlantic LP 12": SD 18112—*The Band Kept Playing*
  Wounded Bird CD: WOU 8112—*The Band Kept Playing*
- b. "Every Now and Then"
  Atlantic 45: 45-3222—"Every Now and Then"
  Atlantic LP 12": SD 18112—*The Band Kept Playing*
  Wounded Bird CD: WOU 8112—*The Band Kept Playing*
- c. "Sudden Change"
  Atlantic LP 12": SD 18112—*The Band Kept Playing*
  Wounded Bird CD: WOU 8112—*The Band Kept Playing*
- d. "Earthquake Country"
  Atlantic LP 12": SD 18112—*The Band Kept Playing*
  Wounded Bird CD: WOU 8112—*The Band Kept Playing*
- e. "Doctor Oh Doctor (Massive Infusion)"
  Atlantic LP 12": SD 18112—*The Band Kept Playing*
  Wounded Bird CD: WOU 8112—*The Band Kept Playing*
- f. "Lonely Song"
  Atlantic LP 12": SD 18112—*The Band Kept Playing*
  Wounded Bird CD: WOU 8112—*The Band Kept Playing*
- g. "Make Your Move"
  Atlantic LP 12": SD 18112—*The Band Kept Playing*
  Wounded Bird CD: WOU 8112—*The Band Kept Playing*
- h. "Inside Information"
  Atlantic LP 12": SD 18112—*The Band Kept Playing*
  Wounded Bird CD: WOU 8112—*The Band Kept Playing*
- i. "Talkin' Won't Get It"
  Atlantic LP 12": SD 18112—*The Band Kept Playing*
  Wounded Bird CD: WOU 8112—*The Band Kept Playing*
- j. "The Band Kept Playing"
  Atlantic LP 12": SD 18112—*The Band Kept Playing*
  Wounded Bird CD: WOU 8112—*The Band Kept Playing*
- k. "I Was Robbed Last Night"

Nick Gravenites (v) on d–e, j–k; Buddy Miles (v) on a–c, f–g, i; Roger "Jellyroll" Troy (v) on a, c, h.

Date: July 18, 1974
Location: WTTW Studios, Chicago, IL
Muddy Waters and Friends
Muddy Waters (v, g); Willie Dixon, Nick Gravenites, Koko Taylor (v); Jerry Portnoy, Junior Wells (h); Michael Bloomfield, Phil Guy, Luther "Guitar Junior" Johnson, Bob Margolin, Johnny Winter (g); Dr. John, Pinetop Perkins (p); Calvin "Fuzz" Jones, Rollo Radford (b); Willie "Big Eyes" Smith, Buddy Miles (d); Ken Ehrlich (prod)

    a.   "Blow Wind Blow"
    b.   "Five Long Years" (excerpt) / Conversation
    c.   "Long Distance Call"
    d.   "Messin' with the Kid"
    e.   "Stop Breaking Down"
    f.   "Mannish Boy"
    g.   "Wang Dang Doodle"
    h.   "Walking Through the Park"
    i.   "Hoochie Kootchie Man"
    j.   "Sugar Sweet"
    k.   "Got My Mojo Working"
All titles on: Rhino VHS—*Soundstage: Blues Summit in Chicago*
               Sony Legacy DVD—*Soundstage: Blues Summit in Chicago*

Date: 1974
Location: San Francisco, CA
Michael Bloomfield
Ray Kennedy (v); Michael Bloomfield (g, prod); John McFee (stg); Mark Naftalin (p); Roger "Jellyroll" Troy (b); George Rains (d); unknown (bkv)

    a.   "Why Lord, Oh Why"
          Columbia LP 12": C2 37578—*Bloomfield: A Retrospective*
          Sony CD: SICP 1969–70—*Bloomfield: A Retrospective*

Date: November 10, 1974
Location: KSAN broadcast, Record Plant, Sausalito, CA
Michael Bloomfield and Friends
Michael Bloomfield, Nick Gravenites, Mike Henderson (v, g); Jonathan Cramer (v); Roger "Jellyroll" Troy (v, b); Mark Adams (h); Mark Naftalin (p); Barry Goldberg (org); George Rains (d)

    a.   "Orphan's Blues"
          Takoma LP 12": TAK 7070—*Between the Hard Place & the Ground*
    b.   "Six Weeks in Reno"
    c.   "Love Me or I'll Kill You Baby"
    d.   "What Time Is It"
    e.   "Tell Me You Care"
    f.   "Buy Me Some Time"
    g.   "Shadows Told Me All"

h. "Blues Medley: 'Sweet Little Angel' / 'Jelly Jelly'"
    Columbia Legacy CD: CK 65688—*Live at the Old Waldorf*
i. "Don't You Lie to Me"
    Demon CD: FIEND 92—*I'm with You Always*
j. "Shine On Love"
k. "Let Them Talk"

Michael Bloomfield (v) on a, i; Jonathan Cramer (v) on f; Nick Gravenites (v) on b–d, (g) on a–g, i–k; Mike Henderson (v) on i, (g) on i; Roger "Jellyroll" Troy (v) on e, g–h, j–k.

Date: 1975
Location: Gold Star Studios, Los Angeles, CA
Charlie Musselwhite
Charlie Musselwhite (v, h); Michael Bloomfield (g, p); Tim Kaihatsu (g); Barry Goldberg (p, org); Karl Sevareid (b); Larry Martin (d); Ray Arvizu (rds); Lynn Carey "Momma Lion" (bkv)

a. "Stranger"
b. "Business Man"
c. "Skinny Woman"
d. "Keys to the Highway"
e. "Candy Kitchen"
f. "Long as I Have You"
g. "Just Take Your Time"
h. "Early in the Mornin'"

All titles on: Capitol LP 12": ST-11450—*Leave the Blues to Us*

Date: June 1975
Location: Village Recorders, Los Angeles, CA
KGB
Michael Bloomfield (v, g); Ray Kennedy (v); Barry Goldberg (key); Rick Grech (b); Carmine Appice (d); Jim Price (prod)

a. "Let Me Love You"
b. "Midnight Traveler"
c. "I've Got a Feeling"
d. "High Roller"
e. "Sail On Sailor"
f. "Workin' for the Children"
g. "You Got the Notion"
h. "Baby Should I Stay or Go"
i. "It's Gonna Be a Hard Night"
j. "Magic in Your Touch"

All titles on: MCA LP 12": MCA-2166—*KGB*

At least some of Bloomfield's parts may have been recorded elsewhere, perhaps in the San Francisco Bay Area.

Date: 1976
Location: Blossom Studios, San Francisco, CA
Michael Bloomfield

Michael Bloomfield (v, g, bj, p, org, b, d, prod); Nick Gravenites (v, g); Ira Kamin (p, org); Eric Kriss (p, prod); Doug Killmer, Roger "Jellyroll" Troy (b); Tom Donlinger, Dave Neditch (d); Ron Stallings (ts), Hart McNee (bar)

    a.   "If You Love These Blues"
    b.   "Hey, Foreman"
    c.   "WDIA"
    d.   "Death Cell Rounder Blues"
    e.   "City Girl"
    f.   "Kansas City"
    g.   "Mama Lion"
    h.   "Thrift Shop Rag"
    i.   "Death in My Family"
    j.   "East Colorado Blues"
    k.   "Blue Ghost Blues"
    l.   "The Train Is Gone"
    m.   "The Altar Song"

All titles on: Guitar Player LP 12": 3002—*If You Love These Blues, Play'em as You Please*

                Kicking Mule CD: KMCD-9801-2—*If You Love These Blues, Play'em as You Please*

Michael Bloomfield (v) on b, d–f, i–m, (bj) on k, (p) on i, m, (org) on m, (b) on b, m, (d) on m; Nick Gravenites (v) on g, (g) on g; Ira Kamin (p) on c, e, g, k–l, (org) on a, c, i; Eric Kriss (p) on b, d; Doug Killmer (b) on a, c, e, i, k–l; Roger "Jellyroll" Troy (b) on g; Tom Donlinger (d) on a–c, e, g; Dave Neditch (d) on i, k–l; Ron Stallings (ts) on e, i; Hart McNee (bar) on e, i.

Date: 1976 or 1977
Location: Blossom Studios, San Francisco, CA
Soundtrack for the film *Andy Warhol's Bad*, a film by Jed Johnson

Michael Bloomfield (composer), Jeff Tornberg (prod), Andy Warhol (executive prod)

    a.   "Andy's Bad"
    b.   Other titles

Date: July 12, 1976
Location: Blossom Studios, San Francisco, CA
Jemima James

Jemima James (v, g); Gary Vogensen (g); Michael Bloomfield (dbr, p, b); Barry Lowenthal (d)

    a.   "Book Me Back in Your Dreams"
    b.   "Takes a Man Like You"
    c.   "Havana Cigar"

All titles on: Labor CD: LAB 7062—*Book Me Back in Your Dreams*

Michael Bloomfield (dbr) on a, (p) on a–b; Barry Lowenthal (d) on c.

Date: August 7 or 8, 1976
Location: Fourth Annual San Francisco Blues Festival, McLaren Park Amphitheater, San Francisco, CA
Michael Bloomfield
Michael Bloomfield (v, g); Ira Kamin (p); Doug Killmer (b); Bob Jones (d)

    a. "Women Loving Each Other"
       Jefferson Records LP 12″: BL-602—*San Francisco Blues Festival*
    b. "Big City Woman"
    c. "KC Shuffle"

Date: December 19, 1976
Location: The Old Waldorf, San Francisco, CA
Michael Bloomfield
Nick Gravenites (v, g); Roger "Jellyroll" Troy (v, b); Michael Bloomfield (g); Mark Naftalin (p); Bob Jones (d)

    a. "Buried Alive in the Blues"
    b. "Your Friends"
  Both titles on: Columbia Legacy CD: CK 65688—*Live at the Old Waldorf*
Nick Gravenites (v) on a, (g) on a; Roger "Jellyroll" Troy (v) on b.

Date: c. 1977
Location: McCabe's Guitar Shop, Santa Monica, CA
Michael Bloomfield and Friends
Michael Bloomfield (v, g); Mark Naftalin (p); Buell Neidlinger (b); Buddy Helm (d); Denny Bruce (prod)

    a. "Eyesight to the Blind"
       TKO Magnum CD: MM 041—*Between a Hard Place and the Ground*
       Demon CD: FIEND 92—*I'm with You Always*
    b. "Women Loving Each Other"
    c. "Linda Lu"
       TKO Magnum CD: MM 041—*Between a Hard Place and the Ground*
    d. "Kansas City Blues"
       TKO Magnum CD: MM 041—*Between a Hard Place and the Ground*
    e. "Men's Room"
       Demon CD: FIEND 92—*I'm with You Always*
    f. "Frankie and Johnnie"
       Demon CD: FIEND 92—*I'm with You Always*
    g. "Lord, Though I Am with Thee (I'm with You Always)"
       TKO Magnum CD: MM 041—*Between a Hard Place and the Ground*

    h. "Jockey Blues (My Father Was a Jockey)"
        TKO Magnum CD: MM 041—*Between a Hard Place and the Ground*
        Demon CD: FIEND 92—*I'm with You Always*

    i. "Blues in B-flat"

    j. "Darktown Strutters Ball" / "Mop Mop"/ "Call Me a Dog"
        TKO Magnum CD: MM 041—*Between a Hard Place and the Ground*
        Demon CD: FIEND 92—*I'm with You Always*

    k. "Stagger Lee"
        Demon CD: FIEND 92—*I'm with You Always*

    l. "I'm Glad I'm Jewish"
        TKO Magnum CD: MM 041—*Between a Hard Place and the Ground*
        Demon CD: FIEND 92—*I'm with You Always*

    m. "Greatest Gifts from Heaven"
        TKO Magnum CD: MM 041—*Between a Hard Place and the Ground*

    n. "Between a Hard Place and the Ground"
        TKO Magnum CD: MM 041—*Between a Hard Place and the Ground*

    o. "Don't You Lie to Me"

    p. "Cherry Red"

    q. "We Love You"

    r. "Wee Wee Hours"
        TKO Magnum CD: MM 041—*Between a Hard Place and the Ground*

    s. "Vamp in C"
        TKO Magnum CD: MM 041—*Between a Hard Place and the Ground*

    t. "Some of These Days"
        Demon CD: FIEND 92—*I'm with You Always*

    u. "Uncle Bob's Barrelhouse Blues"
        TKO Magnum CD: MM 041—*Between a Hard Place and the Ground*

    v. "One of These Days"

    w. "Hymn Tune"
        Demon CD: FIEND 92—*I'm with You Always*

    x. "A-flat Boogaloo"
        Demon CD: FIEND 92—*I'm with You Always*

Date: c. 1977
Location: McCabe's Guitar Shop, Santa Monica, CA
Michael Bloomfield
Michael Bloomfield (v, g, p)

    a. "Hully Gully"

    b. "Wings of an Angel"

    c. "Walkin' the Floor"

    d. "Don't You Lie to Me"

    e. "Junko Partner"

    f. "Knockin' Myself Out"

    g. "Cherry Red"

     h. "Rx for the Blues"

     i. "You Must Have Jesus"

All titles on: Intermedia LP 12": 5068—*Junko Partner*

             Intermedia CD: CQS 5068—*Junko Partner*

Michael Bloomfield (g) on d–g, i, (p) on a–c, h.

Date: February 27, 1977

Location: The Old Waldorf, San Francisco, CA

Michael Bloomfield

Nick Gravenites (v, g); Michael Bloomfield (g); Mark Naftalin (p); Roger "Jellyroll" Troy (b); Bob Jones (d)

     a. "Dancin' Fool"

         Columbia Legacy CD: CK 65688—*Live at the Old Waldorf*

Date: c. March 1977

Location: Beggs/American Zoetrope, San Francisco, CA

Michael Bloomfield

Michael Bloomfield (v, g, bj, tpl, ukelele, p, org, b, d); Nick Gravenites (v, g); Bob Jones (v, d); Anna Rizzo, Marcia Ann Taylor (v); Mark Naftalin (p, acc); Roger "Jellyroll" Troy (b); Richard Beggs (eng)

     a. "Peepin' an a-Moanin' Blues"

     b. "Mr. Johnson and Mr. Dunn"

     c. "Frankie and Johnnie"

     d. "At the Cross"

     e. "Big 'C' Blues"

     f. "Hilo Waltz"

     g. "Effinonna Rag"

     h. "Mood Indigo"

     i. "Analine"

All titles on: Takoma LP 12": B-1059—*Analine*

             Takoma CD: CDTAK 7059—*Analine/Michael Bloomfield*

Michael Bloomfield (v) on a, c, e, (bj) on a, (tpl) on f, (ukelele) on f, (p) on a, d–e, (org) on d–e, I, (b) on a, d–f, h, (d) on a, h; Nick Gravenites (v) on I, (g) on i; Bob Jones (v) on i, (d) on d, i; Anna Rizzo (v) on i; Marcia Ann Taylor (v) on i; Mark Naftalin (acc) on i; Roger "Jellyroll" Troy (b) on i.

Date: Several dates in 1977

Location: Palms Cafe, San Francisco, CA

Big Joe Turner

Big Joe Turner (v); Michael Bloomfield (g); Mark Naftalin (p); Pat Campbell (b); Bob Scott (d)

     a. "Every Day I Have the Blues"

         Intermedia/Quicksilver LP 12": QS 5036—*Every Day I Have the Blues*

         Cleo LP 12": CL 0018983—*Every Day I Have the Blues*

b. "Early One Morning"
   Intermedia/Quicksilver LP 12": QS 5036—*Every Day I Have the Blues*
   Cleo LP 12": CL 0018983—*Every Day I Have the Blues*

c. "I've Got a Pocket Full of Pencils"/ "I Want My Baby to Write Me"
   Intermedia/Quicksilver LP 12": QS 5036—*Every Day I Have the Blues*
   Cleo LP 12": CL 0018983—*Every Day I Have the Blues*

d. "Flip, Flop, and Fly"
   Cleo LP 12": CL 0018983—*Every Day I Have the Blues*

e. "Honey Hush"
   Cleo LP 12": CL 0018983—*Every Day I Have the Blues*

f. "T.V. Mama"
   Cleo LP 12": CL 0018983—*Every Day I Have the Blues*

g. "Chicken and the Hawk"
   Cleo LP 12": CL 0018983—*Every Day I Have the Blues*

h. "Write Me a Letter"
   Intermedia/Quicksilver LP 12": QS 5036—*Every Day I Have the Blues*
   Cleo LP 12": CL 0018983—*Every Day I Have the Blues*

i. "Chains of Love"
   Intermedia/Quicksilver LP 12": QS 5026—*The Very Best of Joe Turner*

j. "Corrine Corrina"
   Intermedia/Quicksilver LP 12": QS 5026—*The Very Best of Joe Turner*

k. "Shake, Rattle and Roll"
   Intermedia/Quicksilver LP 12": QS 5026—*The Very Best of Joe Turner*

l. "I Hear You Knockin'"
   Intermedia/Quicksilver LP 12": QS 5026—*The Very Best of Joe Turner*

m. "Give Me an Hour in Your Garden"
   Intermedia/Quicksilver LP 12": QS 5026—*The Very Best of Joe Turner*

n. "Roll Me Baby"
   Cleo LP 12": CL 0019983—*Rock This Joint*

o. "Ain't Gonna Be Your Lowdown Dog"
   Cleo LP 12": CL 0019983—*Rock This Joint*

p. "Stormy Monday Blues"
   Cleo LP 12": CL 0019983—*Rock This Joint*

q. "Roll 'em Pete"
   Cleo LP 12": CL 0019983—*Rock This Joint*

r. "Shake, Rattle and Roll" (alt)
   Cleo LP 12": CL 0019983—*Rock This Joint*

s. "When the Sun Goes Down"
   Cleo LP 12": CL 0019983—*Rock This Joint*

    t. "Morning, Noon and Night"
        Cleo LP 12": CL 0019983—*Rock This Joint*
    u. "Hide and Go Seek"
        Cleo LP 12": CL 0019983—*Rock This Joint*
    v. "How Long Blues"
        Cleo LP 12": CL 0019983—*Rock This Joint*
    w. "The Night Time Is the Right Time"
        Intermedia/Quicksilver LP 12": QS 5030—*Boss Blues*
    x. "The Things I Used to Do"
        Intermedia/Quicksilver LP 12": QS 5030—*Boss Blues*
    y. "Shoo Shoo Boogie Boo"
        Intermedia/Quicksilver LP 12": QS 5030—*Boss Blues*
    z. "On My Way to Denver Blues"
        Intermedia/Quicksilver LP 12": QS 5030—*Boss Blues*
    aa. "Jump for Joy"

Date: March 13–14, 1977
Location: The Old Waldorf, San Francisco, CA
Michael Bloomfield
Nick Gravenites (v, g); Bob Jones (v, d); Roger "Jellyroll" Troy (v, b); Michael Bloomfield (g); Mark Naftalin (p)
    a. "Bye, Bye"
    b. "Feel So Bad"
    c. "Farther up the Road"
  All titles on: Columbia Legacy CD: CK 65688—*Live at the Old Waldorf*
Nick Gravenites (v) on a, (g) on a; Bob Jones (v) on b; Roger "Jellyroll" Troy (v) on c.

Date: May 16, 1977
Location: The Old Waldorf, San Francisco, CA
Michael Bloomfield
Nick Gravenites (v, g); Bob Jones (v, d); Michael Bloomfield (g); Mark Naftalin, unknown (p); Roger "Jellyroll" Troy (b)
    a. "Bad Luck Baby"
    b. "The Sky Is Cryin'"
  Both titles on: Columbia Legacy CD: CK 65688—*Live at the Old Waldorf*
Nick Gravenites (v) on a, (g) on a; Bob Jones (v) on b; Mark Naftalin (p) on a; unknown (p) on b.

Date: 1976–1977
Location: Blossom Studios; American Zoetrope, San Francisco, CA
Michael Bloomfield
Frank Biner, Anna Rizzo, Sons of Kings (v); Michael Bloomfield (v, g, p, org, b, tam, per); Bob Jones (v, b, d); Mark Adams (h); Mark Naftalin (p, ep, syn); Clay Cotton (key); Karl Sevareid, Roger "Jellyroll" Troy (b); Dwight Dailey, George Rains (d);

Mr. Robot (per); Toots Suite (hns); Duke Tito & the Marin County Playboys (bkv); Norman Dayron (prod)

a. "Maudie"
    Waterhouse LP 12": Waterhouse 11—*Living in the Fast Lane*

b. "Roots"
    Waterhouse LP 12": Waterhouse 11—*Living in the Fast Lane*
    Era CD: 5006-2—*Living in the Fast Lane*

c. "Watkin's Rag"
    Waterhouse LP 12": Waterhouse 11—*Living in the Fast Lane*
    Era CD: 5006-2—*Living in the Fast Lane*

d. "Andy's Bad"
    Waterhouse LP 12": Waterhouse 11—*Living in the Fast Lane*
    Era CD: 5006-2—*Living in the Fast Lane*

e. "Used to It"
    Waterhouse LP 12": Waterhouse 11—*Living in the Fast Lane*
    Era CD: 5006-2—*Living in the Fast Lane*

f. "Big C Blues"
    Waterhouse LP 12": Waterhouse 11—*Living in the Fast Lane*
    Era CD: 5006-2—*Living in the Fast Lane*

g. "The Dizz Rag"
    Waterhouse LP 12": Waterhouse 11—*Living in the Fast Lane*
    Era CD: 5006-2—*Living in the Fast Lane*

h. "Sammy Knows How to Party"
    Era CD: 5006-2—*Living in the Fast Lane*

Frank Biner (v) on a; Michael Bloomfield (v) on e–f, h, (p) on f–g, (org) on a, (b) on g, (tam) on a, (per) on c; Bob Jones (v) on d, (b) on d; (d) on d, g; Anna Rizzo (v) on d; Sons of Kings (v) on b; Mark Adams (h) on e; Mark Naftalin (p) on a, (ep) on e, h, (syn) on f; Clay Cotton (key) on b; Karl Severeid (b) on b; Roger "Jellyroll" Troy (b) on a, e, h; Dwight Dailey (d) on b; Mr. Robot (per) on d; Toots Suite (hns) on b; Duke Tito & The Marin County Playboys (bkv) on e, h.

Date: c. 1976–1979
Michael Bloomfield

Michael Bloomfield (g); Norman Dayron (eng)

a. "Memphis Radio Blues (WDIA)"
b. "Blake's Rag"
c. "Hawaiian Guitar Waltz"
d. "Blues for Norman"
e. "Wheelchair Rag"

All titles on: Shanachie CD: SHCD 99007—*Blues, Gospel and Ragtime Guitar Instrumentals*

Date: 1978
Location: Tres Virgos/Tamarin, Mill Valley, CA; The Old Waldorf, San Francisco, CA, or other live venue
Michael Bloomfield
Michael Bloomfield (v, g, tpl, p, acc, syn, b); Ira Kamin (p); Doug Killmer (b); David Shorey (b, bkv); Bob Jones (d, tam, bkv); Kraig Kilby (tb); Norman Dayron (prod)

    a.   "Knockin' Myself Out"
          Takoma LP 12": TAK 7063—*Michael Bloomfield*
          Takoma CD: CDTAK 7059—*Analine/Michael Bloomfield*
    b.   "My Children, My Children"
          Takoma LP 12": TAK 7063—*Michael Bloomfield*
          Takoma CD: CDTAK 7059—*Analine/Michael Bloomfield*
    c.   "Women Loving Each Other"
          Takoma LP 12": TAK 7063—*Michael Bloomfield*
          Takoma CD: CDTAK 7059—*Analine/Michael Bloomfield*
    d.   "Sloppy Drunk"
          Takoma LP 12": TAK 7063—*Michael Bloomfield*
          Takoma CD: CDTAK 7059—*Analine/Michael Bloomfield*
    e.   "You Took My Money"
          Takoma LP 12": TAK 7063—*Michael Bloomfield*
          Takoma CD: CDTAK 7059—*Analine/Michael Bloomfield*
    f.   "See That My Grave Is Kept Clean"
          Takoma LP 12": TAK 7063—*Michael Bloomfield*
          Takoma CD: CDTAK 7059—*Analine/Michael Bloomfield*
    g.   "The Gospel Truth"
          Takoma LP 12": TAK 7063—*Michael Bloomfield*
          Takoma CD: CDTAK 7059—*Analine/Michael Bloomfield*
    h.   "Guitar King"
          Takoma LP 12": TAK 7063—*Michael Bloomfield*
          Takoma CD: CDTAK 7059—*Analine/Michael Bloomfield*
    i.   "Crisco Kid"
          Fuel 2000 CD: 302 061 256 2—*Knockin' Myself Out*

All recorded at Tres Virgos/Tamarin except d-e, which were recorded live, perhaps at the Old Waldorf.

Date: c. 1978
Location: Xandu Recording Co., San Francisco, CA
Count Talent and the Originals
Michael Bloomfield (v, g, bj, p, ep, org, b, per, bkv); Nick Gravenites, Roger "Jellyroll" Troy (v); Bob Jones (v, d, per, bkv); Anna Rizzo, Marcia Ann Taylor (v, bkv); David Shorey (v, b, bkv); Mark Naftalin (p, acc, syn); Ted Ashford (org, key); Clay Cotton (clavinet); Jack Blades, Soma Marshall, Thaddeus Reese (b); Ray Loeckle, Dennis Marcellino, Jerry Martini (sax); Max Haskett, Cal Lewiston (t); Chuck Bennett, Andrew Goldstein (tb); Norman Dayron (prod)

a. "Love Walk"
b. "You Was Wrong"
c. "Peach Tree Man"
d. "When I Need You"
e. "Sammy Knows How to Party"
f. "I Need Your Loving"
g. "Bad Man"
h. "Saturday Night"
i. "You're Changin'"
j. "Let the People Dance"

All titles on: Clouds LP 12": 8805—*Count Talent and the Originals*
Michael Bloomfield (v) on c, h, (bj) on c, (p) on c–d, g–h, (ep) on g, (org) on b, g, (b) on c, h, (per) on g, i, (bkv) on i; Nick Gravenites (v) on g; Bob Jones (v) on a, j, (per) on a, i; Anna Rizzo (v) on e–f; David Shorey (v) on i, (b) on g, i; Marcia Ann Taylor (v) on i; Roger "Jellyroll" Troy (v) on b, f; Mark Naftalin (p) on a, c, e–f, i–j, (acc) on b, (syn) on d; Ted Ashford (org) on e, (key) on j; Clay Cotton (clavinet) on a; Jack Blades (b) on e, j; Soma Marshall (b) on a, d, f; Thaddeus Reese (b) on b; Ray Loeckle (sax) on a–c, f, i; Dennis Marcellino (sax) on e, j; Jerry Martini (sax) on e, j; Max Haskett (t) on e, j; Cal Lewiston (t) on a–c, f, i; Chuck Bennett (tb) on a–c, f, i; Andrew Goldstein (tb) on e, j.

Date: 1979
Location: The Old Waldorf, San Francisco, CA
Michael Bloomfield
Michael Bloomfield (v, g); Ira Kamin, Mark Naftalin (p); Barry Goldberg (org); Doug Killmer, Roger "Jellyroll" Troy (b); Bob Jones (d); The Originals (sax); Sophie Kamin, Bill McEuen, Betsy Rice, Anna Rizzo, David Shorey, Mary Stripling (bkv); Norman Dayron (prod)

a. "Between the Hard Place and the Ground"
b. "Big Chief from New Orleans"
c. "Kid Man Blues"
d. "Juke Joint"

All titles on: Takoma LP 12": TAK 7070—*Between the Hard Place & the Ground*
Ira Kamin (p) on b–c; Mark Naftalin (p) on a, d; Barry Goldberg (org) on a; Doug Killmer (b) on b–c; Roger "Jellyroll" Troy (b) on a, d.

Date: July 9–13, 1979
Location: Norman Dayron's house, Mill Valley, CA
Michael Bloomfield & Woody Harris
Michael Bloomfield, Woody Harris (g); Norman Dayron (prod)

a. "I'll Overcome"
b. "I Must See Jesus"
c. "Great Dreams from Heaven"
d. "Gonna Need Somebody on My Bond"
e. "I Am a Pilgrim"

f. "Farther Along"
g. "Have Thine Own Way"
h. "Just a Closer Walk with Thee"
i. "Peace in the Valley"

All titles on: Kicking Mule LP 12″: KM 164—*Bloomfield/Harris*
Kicking Mule CD: KMCD-9801-2—*If You Love These Blues, Play 'Em as You Please*

Date: October 27–November 29, 1980
Location: Hyde Street Studios, San Francisco, CA
Michael Bloomfield
Michael Bloomfield (v, g, p, org); Hart McNee (v, bar); Derrick Walker (h, ts); Jonathan Cramer (p); Henry Oden (b); Tom Rizzo (d); King Perkoff (ts); Norman Dayron (prod)

a. "Cruisin' for a Bruisin'"
b. "Linda Lu"
c. "Papa-Mama-Rompah-Stompah"
d. "Junker's Blues"
e. "Midnight"
f. "It'll Be Me"
g. "Motorized Blues"
h. "Mathilda"
i. "Winter Moon"
j. "Snowblind"

All titles on: Takoma LP 12″: TAK 7091—*Cruisin' for a Bruisin'*
Magnum America CD: MACD 74—*Gospel Truth*

Michael Bloomfield (v) on a–b, d, f–g, j, (p) on a, f–j, (org) on h; Hart McNee (v) on h, (bar) on a, c–e, h; Derrick Walker (h) on g, (ts) on a, c–e, h; Jonathan Cramer (p) on b, d–e, j; King Perkoff (ts) on a, c–e, h.

Date: November 15, 1980
Location: Fox Warfield Theatre, San Francisco, CA
Bob Dylan
Bob Dylan (v, h, g); Michael Bloomfield (g); Fred Tackett (g, man); Willie Smith (key); Tim Drummond (b); Jim Keltner (d); Carolyn Dennis, Clydie King, Regina McCrary (bkv)

a. "Introduction by Bob Dylan" / "Like a Rolling Stone"
b. "The Groom's Still Waiting at the Altar"
Columbia Legacy CD: 88765476342—*From His Head to His Heart to His Hands*

Date: Late 1980
Location: Parvin Studio, Pacifica, CA
The Usual Suspects
Taj Mahal (v); Michael Bloomfield (g); Tom Stern (g, bkv); Joe Goldmark (stg); Markie Sanders (b); Doug Carrigan (d); Darol Anger (vn); Nancy Hall (bkv); Lee Parvin (bkv, eng)

    a.   "Blue Sea Blues"
        Tomistoma LP 12″: G8R—*The Usual Suspects*

Date: February 13, 1981
Location: Bloomfield's home, Reed Street, Mill Valley, CA
Michael Bloomfield
Michael Bloomfield (interviewee); Tom Yates, Kate Hayes (interviewer)
    a.   "Interview"
        Columbia LP 12″: C2 37578—*Bloomfield: A Retrospective*

BIBLIOGRAPHY

Bane, Michael. *White Boy Singin' the Blues: The Black Roots of White Rock*. New York: Da Capo, 1992.

Barley, Simon. "Butterfield Band Talks to Simon Barley." *International Times*, November 28–December 11, 1966.

Bloomfield, Michael, with S. Summerville. *Me and Big Joe*. San Francisco: RE/SEARCH, 1980.

Booth, Stanley. *Rythm Oil: A Journey Through the Music of the American South*. New York: Pantheon, 1991.

Boyd, Joe. *White Bicycles: Making Music in the 1960s*. London: Serpent's Tail/ Profile, 2006.

Dann, David. Mike Bloomfield: An American Guitarist. www.mikebloomfield americanmusic.com.

Delehant, Jim. "Mike Bloomfield (Guitarist with Paul Butterfield Blues Band) Puts Down Everything." *Hit Parader*, January 1967.

———. "Mike Bloomfield: Leader of the Band." *Hit Parader*, April 1968.

DeMichael, Don. "The Rolling Stone Interview: Miles Davis." *Rolling Stone*, December 13, 1969.

Festival. Directed by Murray Lerner. 1967; London: Eagle Rock Entertainment, 2005. DVD.

Forte, Dan. "Otis Rush: Chicago's Progressive Blues Genius." *Guitar Player*, October 1987.

Gancher, David. Review of Michael Bloomfield's *It's Not Killing Me*, Nick Gravenites's *My Labors*, and Michael Bloomfield and Friends' *Live at Bill Graham's Fillmore West*. *Rolling Stone*, November 15, 1969.

Glatt, John. *Live at the Fillmore East and West: Getting Backstage and Personal with Rock's Greatest Legends*. Guilford, CT: Lyons Press, 2014.

Gleason, Ralph J. "Perspectives: Stop This Shuck, Mike Bloomfield." *Rolling Stone*, May 11, 1968.

Gravenites, Nick. Bad Talkin' Bluesman. *Blues Revue* 18–26 (1995–1996).

———. "Stop This Shuck, Ralph Gleason!" *Rolling Stone*, May 25, 1968.

Harris, Sheldon. *Blues Who's Who: A Biographical Dictionary of Blues Singers*. New York: Da Capo, 1991.

Lester, Julius. "The Paul Butterfield Blues Band." *Sounds & Fury*, June 1966.

Loder, Kurt. "Final Days and Past Glories." *Rolling Stone*, April 2, 1981.

Marcus, Greil. *Like a Rolling Stone: Bob Dylan at the Crossroads*. New York: PublicAffairs, 2005.

Marshall, Terry. "I Wanna Be the Best." *BAM*, June 1976.

McClosky, Dan. KPFA radio interview with Michael Bloomfield, Roy Ruby, and Fred Glaser, May 17, 1971.

Medium Cool. Directed by Haskell Wexler. 1969; New York: Criterion Collection, 2013. DVD.

Mike Bloomfield official website. Accessed spring/summer 2015. www.mikebloomfield.com. Site discontinued.

Poe, Randy. *Skydog: The Duane Allman Story*. Milwaukee, WI: Backbeat, 2006.

Rooney, Jim. *In It for the Long Run: A Musical Odyssey*. Urbana: University of Illinois Press, 2014.

Rowe, Mike. *Chicago Blues: The City & the Music*. New York: Da Capo, 1981.

Ryan, Deborah Osment. "Fame Isn't Worth the Work." *Colorado Daily*, August 10, 1973.

Scaduto, Anthony. *Bob Dylan: An Intimate Biography*. New York: Grosset & Dunlap, 1971.

Wald, Elijah. *Dylan Goes Electric!: Newport, Seeger, Dylan and the Night That Split the Sixties*. New York: Dey Street, 2015.

Welding, Pete. "Caught in the Act." *DownBeat*, December 1964.

———. Liner notes for *The Paul Butterfield Blues Band*. Elektra Records K-294, 1965.

Wenner, Jann. "Booker T. and the M.G.'s." *Rolling Stone*, October 12, 1968.

———. "The Rolling Stone Interview: Mike Bloomfield, pt. 1." *Rolling Stone*, April 6, 1968.

———. "The Rolling Stone Interview: Mike Bloomfield, pt. 2." *Rolling Stone*, April 27, 1968.

———. "The Rolling Stone Interview: Phil Spector." *Rolling Stone*, November 1, 1969.

Wexler, Jerry, and David Ritz. *Rhythm and the Blues: A Life in American Music*. New York: Alfred A. Knopf, 1993.

Wheeler, Tom. "Barroom Scholar of the Blues: Michael Bloomfield." *Guitar Player*, April 1979.

Williams, Paul. "Blues '66." *Crawdaddy*, August 1966.

Wolkin, Jan Mark, and Bill Keenom. *Michael Bloomfield: If You Love These Blues*. San Francisco: Miller Freeman, 2000.

Wolkin, Jan Mark, and Neal McGarity. *Bloomfield Notes* 1–6 (1994–1996): www.bluespower.com/arbn01.htm.

Yates, Tom, and Kate Hayes. Interview with Michael Bloomfield, February 13, 1981.

INTERVIEWS

Carmine Appice
Bonner Beuhler
Elvin Bishop
Allen Bloomfield
Michael Bloomfield
Joe Boyd
Mickey Buckins
Paul Butterfield
Toby Byron
Norman Dayron
Bruce Dickinson
Barry Goldberg
Nick Gravenites
John Hammond
Kate Hayes

David Hood
B. B. King
Dorothy Klein Shinderman
Al Kooper
Ronnie Lyons
George Mitchell
Charlie Musselwhite
Mark Naftalin
Mitch Ryder
Susan Smith Beuhler
Christie Svane
Barry Tashian
Muddy Waters
Peter Yarrow
Tom Yates

PHOTO CREDITS

MAIN TEXT

ii   Photographer: George Mitchell (Michael on Maxwell Street)

157   Photographer: Baron Wolman, Iconic Images, London

187   Photographer: Peter Amft

PHOTO INSERT

1   Photographer: Daniel Kramer

2   Michael Bloomfield Legacy, LLC (all images)

3   Michael Bloomfield Legacy, LLC (top); Photographer: Amy van Singel (bottom)

4   Photographer: George Mitchell (both images)

5   Photographer: Raeburn Flerlage (both images)

6   Donna Koch Gower collection (top left and right); Photographer: Raeburn Flerlage (bottom)

7   Photographer: Mike Shea, courtesy Christine Shea (both images)

8   Photographer: Don Hunstein, courtesy Sony Music Entertainment

9   Toby Byron collection (top left); Photographer: Diana Davies, Smithsonian Institution, Center for Folklife and Cultural Heritage (top right); Photographer: John Rudoff (center); Photographer: Diana Davies, Smithsonian Institution, Center for Folklife and Cultural Heritage (bottom left and right)

10   Photographer: Diana Davies, Smithsonian Institution, Center for Folklife and Cultural Heritage (all images)

11   From the Newport film *Festival!* produced and directed by Murray Lerner (top); Photographer: David Gahr/Getty Images (bottom)

12   Alice Ochs/Getty Images (top); Diana Davies, Smithsonian Institution, Center for Folklife and Cultural Heritage (center and bottom)

13   Toby Byron collection (top left); Artwork by Wes Wilson. © 1966, 1984, 1995, Rhino Entertainment Company. Used with permission.

14   Sony Music Entertainment (top left); Toby Byron collection (top right); Artist: Rick Shubb (bottom left); Artist: John van Hamersveld (bottom right)

15   Photographer: Jim Marshall, Jim Marshall Photography, LLC

16   Photographer: Murray Neitlich, Sony Music Entertainment (top left); Tony Esparza, Sony Music Entertainment (top right and bottom)

17   Photographer: Steve Fitch (top); Photographer: Ed Caraeff (bottom)

18   Photographer: Ron Karr (top); Toby Byron collection (bottom)

19   Photographer: Jim Marshall, Jim Marshall Photography, LLC (top); Sony Music Entertainment (center); Toby Byron collection (bottom)

20   Photographer: Robert Corwin (top); Photographer: Don Paulsen (bottom)

21   Photographer: Robert Corwin (top); Photographer: Chesher Cat (bottom)

22   Toby Byron collection (all images)

23   Photographer: Peter Amft (top left); Courtesy Susan Beuhler (top right); Photographer: Jonathan Perry, Toby Byron collection (bottom)

24   Photographer: Norman Seeff (top); Photographer: Ira Kamin, Mark Naftalin Archives (bottom)

INDEX